Alexander H. Japp

Master-missionaries

Chapters in Pioneer Effort throughout the World

Alexander H. Japp

Master-missionaries
Chapters in Pioneer Effort throughout the World

ISBN/EAN: 9783744757324

Printed in Europe, USA, Canada, Australia, Japan

Cover: Foto ©ninafisch / pixelio.de

More available books at **www.hansebooks.com**

JAMES OGLETHORPE.
FRONTISPIECE.

Master Missionaries.

MASTER-MISSIONARIES.

Chapters in Pioneer Effort throughout the World.

BY

ALEXANDER HAY JAPP, LL.D.,

F.R.S.L., F.R.S.E., F.R.G.S., F.S.A.

"YE ARE THE SALT OF THE EARTH."
Matt. v. 13.

NEW YORK:
ROBERT CARTER AND BROTHERS,
530 BROADWAY.
1881.

Dedication

TO

DONALD MACLEOD, D.D.,

EDITOR OF "GOOD WORDS."

———o———

RUNNING my eye over certain letters of yours—letters that at the time made *Red-letter* days to me, and in a sense do so still—I find that in one of them, dated on a certain 14th of October, you wrote thus:—"I am so glad to hear of certain movements in the firm in so far as you are concerned. I am sure nothing will tend more to strengthen its influence; for, while no man is perfect, except such 'as dwell at home at ease,' yet some are both efficient and to be loved by all decent fellows like yours ever, D. MACLEOD." And again, later, on a certain 19th June:—"The very possibility of your parting company fills me with anxiety. No fellow could take your place and be to me as you have been. Simply, *it must not be.*" With such sentences and such assurances as these before me—so fragrant of hope and promise—what better can I do than dedicate to you this book, containing some sketches which received from you in their briefer form,—and more especially the opening one,—the warmest and most appreciative practical welcome?

ALEX. H. JAPP.

LONDON, *September* 30, 1880.

as well as war. She has on board one hundred and twenty passengers, a chaplain, two men as industrial teachers, and the leader of the expedition, who, by dint of indefatigable labour and resource, has carried his great philanthropic idea thus far towards realisation and success—an anticipatory impersonation of the idea of the "Captain of Industry," for whom a great English historian has more recently sighed through many elaborate pages. His name is James Oglethorpe, and he is a man of culture, refinement, and great practical benevolence. He has already served his country well in the field and in Parliament, where even now he has a seat; and it might seem indeed as though all his previous life—even in its minor details—had been providential preparation for the great work he has now taken in hand. He is tall, stately, soldierlike in aspect, neatly arrayed in the accepted fashion of that time; he looks in every point one accustomed to command, yet his features, somewhat sharp and stern, can soften into a smile of the sweetest paternal attractiveness. Honesty of purpose, great decision, and generous concern for others are written on every movement and expression. As the result of a careful study of old newspapers, Government reports, and pamphlets, as well as of his more systematic memoirs—English and American—by Mr. Wright and Dr. Harris, we here purpose briefly to tell the story of Oglethorpe's long and remarkable life: how his earlier years and the interests that engaged his mind prepared him for his great enterprise of founding the colony of Georgia, which was more a benevolent and missionary enterprise than anything else; of his work there and the spirit in which he did it; and lastly, the tenor and the fine influence of his declining years.

I.

James Oglethorpe was the son of Sir Theophilus Oglethorpe, of Godalming, in Surrey. His mother was the daughter of an Irish gentleman. There has been some difference of opinion about the exact date of his birth, which even registers do not wholly set at rest; but the first of June 1689 may be taken as approximate, since he was baptized on the 2d of that month. To his mother, it is evident, he owed not a little. His father was precise, methodic, a shrewd and practical country gentleman; she imparted something of elevated ideal and of poetry to the household. She was a woman of rare intellect, as well as of refinement. "Lady Oglethorpe," says Mr. Wright, "seems to have had considerable influence in the court of Queen Anne, and was on intimate terms with Swift. She was a thorough Jacobite, and appears to have been a match for the time-serving parson, who in allusion to some party intrigue, with his usual coarseness, represents her as 'so cunning a devil' that he believed she could find a remedy if they would take her advice."

By the aid of imagination, we can in some measure realise the childish days of Oglethorpe; the prim and, it may be, over-methodic instruction, the lectures, the drill of trivial etiquette, book in hand, pursued with too little regard for instincts that craved contact with things as well as with words. Luckily the associations of the beautiful scenery and the daily round of out-door observance would do much to compensate. His youth was spent amid the deep domestic peace and prosperity of the reign of William and Mary, and there was then little at home to excite the military ambition of a boy's heart. But news from abroad supplied that which was lacking, and which home history in the earlier portions of the century had abundantly presented. Marlborough's victories were the theme of talk everywhere, and doubtless Oglethorpe, as a lad, listened attentive, open-eyed, and admiring, while his elders discussed the details of Blenheim and Oudenarde and Malplaquet. We know, at all events, that from early years his liking lay towards a military life, notwithstanding a fine taste for literature which was early developed. We are therefore hardly surprised to learn that, although in 1709 he was admitted a member of Corpus Christi College, Oxford, he did not find a life of study to his taste, any more than two of his brothers had done; and that in 1710 he joined the army, as a gentleman volunteer, not very long afterwards assuming the rank of ensign, which he held till the Peace of Utrecht in 1713. Shortly after this he became attached to the suite of the

Earl of Peterborough, then Ambassador of Sicily and other Italian States, and is believed to have travelled southward in the company of the famous philosopher, Berkeley, whose views on colonisation and philanthropic reforms already developed, were of a kind to have met with response from such a mind and heart as that of Oglethorpe even then. But we have no definite accounts of their intercourse.

In 1714 he was transferred to the Queen's Guards, holding the post of Captain-lieutenant to the first troop; and we learn that, by his fine bearing and grace of manner, he soon made so favourable an impression on the Duke of Marlborough that he was recommended to the Prince Eugène, to whom he became secretary and aide-de-camp. This position enabled him to establish his character for military knowledge and resource. He speedily gained the highest praise of his general for his conduct in the campaign against the Turks. It will be remembered that, though they had already suffered severely, the Turks determined to renew the war. The forces of Prince Eugène were again in motion, and a blow was struck at the very heart of their power by the siege of Belgrade. The Turks came to its relief, and besieged the Prince in his camp; but while he was almost given over he made a sally, fell suddenly on the enemy, defeated them with great slaughter, and took their cannon, baggage, and military stores, after which Belgrade at once surrendered. On the 16th of August 1717 the capitulation was signed; the Imperialists took possession of the gate and outworks, and on the 22d the Turks quitted the city. This was the closing scene of that bloody and disastrous war. Oglethorpe was in active command at the siege and the battle, and conducted himself in such a manner as to have been reported in the most flattering way. When peace was declared he was offered rank and station in the German service, but he declined it. There were no very definite prospects of active duty, and a soldier's life in barracks had lost all its attractions for him. He returned to England.

In 1722 he succeeded his brother in the estate at Godalming, and was fortunate in being able very shortly after to secure a seat in Parliament as member for Hazlemere—a place which he held by successive elections for the long period of thirty-two years. It could never have been said of Oglethorpe what was said of Burke, that "he gave up to party what was meant for mankind." From the first we can easily detect, in going over the very slim and wholly inadequate reports of his earlier speeches which have been preserved, that he felt the irksomeness of party-ties, and was often in great difficulty on account of what they implied. He was always on the side of liberty and progress; and a fresh and vigorous philanthropic tone makes itself felt more and more. His first speech was against the banishment of Atterbury, and was worthy in many respects of a great cause. Smollett says of another speech on the King's Speech in 1731—

"Mr. Oglethorpe, a gentleman of unblemished character, brave, generous, and humane, affirmed that many other things related more immediately to the interest and honour of the nation than did the guarantee of the Pragmatic Sanction. He said he wished to have heard that the new works at Dunkirk had been entirely razed and destroyed; that the nation had received full and complete satisfaction for the depredations committed by Spain; that more care was taken to discipline the militia, on whose valour the nation chiefly depend in case of invasion; and that some regard had been shown to the oppressed Protestants in Germany. He expressed his satisfaction, however, to find that the English were not so closely united to the French as formerly, for he had observed that when two dogs were in a leash together the stronger generally ran away with the other; and this, he feared, had been the case between France and Great Britain."

The cause of the persecuted Protestants of Germany lay very near his heart; and he brought the case of the distressed Moravians several times before Parliament with effect. These poor people, whose only offence was that they wished to reform society by beginning very deep down with the individual soul and heart, and were, by their creed, indifferent to many points of form, and opposed to certain requirements of warlike states, enjoyed no rest in their native country. They looked wistfully to America, but the new colonies were more or less martial in their character; in this only too like the political constitutions of the Old World, though they had the excuse that they needed them to defend themselves against the wild Indians by whom they were surrounded. The conscience of the Moravians revolted at the thought of that military service. When a petition was presented to Parliament to relieve them from such service it was warmly supported by Oglethorpe, who explained to the House of Commons the social system, the Church, and the great missionary efforts of the Moravian community, showing how important it was to encourage the emigration of persons of such pure conscience and high character, because of the influence for good which they could not but exercise, more especially upon the members of a society as yet only half formed, and tempted by the inevitable primitiveness of the life they led into unconscious relapse in many points into a semblance of half savagery and indifference.

Every humane and noble cause exercised his heart and head, and received from him more than mere sympathy. He was essentially practical. He investigated every question for himself, taking no fact at second hand. Whether it was the question of the Porteous Mob, or the relief of persecuted religionists, he spoke with the spirit of a man ahead of his time. Social improvement, he clearly saw, lay in appealing to the higher self-interest of the people; and this is well proved by the part he took in one particular work.

In the year 1707 a company had been started in

London for the purpose of lending money to the poor on small pledges, and to prosperous men on good security, with the general aim of affording aid to the deserving. After an apparently successful career of several years, the cashier and two of the chief officers were guilty of defalcation, and absconded. Out of the vast sums of money which had been entrusted to their charge, only some £30,000 remained; but it was found that those who had connived at their villany and had profited by it, were moving about safely at home. Oglethorpe exerted himself powerfully in Parliament to have the matter thoroughly investigated, and to have those men brought to justice. Speaking in support of the motion, he said—

"For my own part, sir, I have always been for encouraging the design upon which this corporation was first established, and looked upon it as a provident act of charity to let necessitous persons have the opportunity of borrowing money upon easier terms than they could have it elsewhere. Money, like other things, is but a commodity, and, in the way of dealing, the use of it is looked upon to be worth as much as people can get for it. If this corporation let persons in limited circumstances have the use of money at a cheaper rate than individuals, brokers, or moneylenders would be willing to do, it certainly was a beneficent act. If they had demanded more than was elsewhere given, they would not have had applicants, and the design would not have proved good and useful. But the utility of it was most evident; and the better the design, and the more excellent the benefit, the more those persons deserve to be punished, who, by their frauds, have curtailed, if not wholly cut off, these sources of furnishing assistance to the industrious and enterprising, and disappointed the public reaping of the benefit which might have accrued by an honest and faithful execution of so good an undertaking."

It has been well said that a man's character is best ascertained from knowing the sources in which he finds his pleasures. Oglethorpe's pleasures were all in benevolent enterprises; and accident or providence, all through his life, as through the lives of many others, was constantly giving indications of new paths of activity. His great practical forecast, and his determination, enabled him to connect together what, in the hands of a less capable man, might have been only dissipating to his powers. The next spur to his energies was of a very decided kind. A gentleman named Robert Castell, who had showed much ingenuity in mechanics and skill in architecture, had been subject to losses, and was at last cast into the debtors' prison of the Fleet. He was by and by carried to a sponging-house in connection with the prison, kept by a man named Corbett, an underling of Bambridge, the warder. After a time, and so long as any fragment of his means remained, or friends were inclined to come thus far to his aid, he enjoyed the liberty of the rules; but, all resources failing wherewith to bribe Bambridge further, he was ordered to be recommitted to Corbett's, where at the time the small-pox raged with great intensity. In vain poor Castell urged that he had never had the small-pox, and was sure to become infected. He was removed, and in a very short time died in Corbett's house. Oglethorpe, who knew Castell and had visited him, heard the story and was greatly moved by it. He resolved, in his usual way, quietly to see things for himself; and finding that one with whom he had had some acquaintance was now in confinement there, he resolved to make a visit to this gentleman a pretext for seeing the prison and of so far examining how matters stood. It was indeed a revelation to him. Numbers of men who had formerly been in good positions were now to be seen here in most miserable plight, ragged, filthy, half-starved, and often in heavy chains. In some instances their reason had gone or was beginning to fail. The only channel of escape from such treatment was through bribes, by which Bambridge and his minions were rapidly enriching themselves.

The wardenship of the Fleet, as it was afterwards proved, had been regularly put up for sale. It had been bought from the great Lord Clarendon by John Higgins for £5000, and it had been sold by Higgins to this Bambridge for the same sum in 1728; and these men were accustomed, in addition to the large emoluments of their office, to exact heavy fees from the prisoners, and to avenge themselves upon those who were unable or unwilling to pay them by the utmost excesses of brutality.

The condition of Sir William Rich, whom Oglethorpe had ostensibly gone to see, was as bad as any. He was loaded with chains, deprived, not only of ordinary comforts and decencies, but even of the necessaries of life, and treated in everything as a common malefactor, and worse—far worse—than the worst malefactor would be treated in our time. Oglethorpe determined to make a movement for reform, to demand investigation, and the dismissal and the punishment of those who were guilty of such abuses, cruelties, and base breaches of trust. He brought the matter before Parliament in speeches that displayed not only tact but eloquence, "many of his sentences going straight to the heart." His motion prevailed; a commission was appointed to inquire into the condition of the prisons. Oglethorpe was named its chairman, and right well did he do his work.

Sir William Rich was one of those summoned before the commission to give evidence; and the daring of Bambridge was afterwards shown in an extraordinary manner. Rich had appeared in chains, put on because of some difference with Bambridge; and these the commission ordered to be taken off. No sooner, however, did the commission withdraw, than Bambridge, in defiance of their order, put them on again. For this, on Oglethorpe's representation, he was committed to the charge of the serjeant-at-arms.

The sufferings undergone in these prisons were literally

beyond description. Women were left without beds, without attendance or nourishment, till they died of neglect; men were tortured by thumbscrews and other engines of torment. One poor Portuguese had been for two months under irons so heavy that he could not rise. Another prisoner had lost all memory and the use of his limbs. One brave soldier had been falsely accused of theft, and though he was acquitted by the jury, he was seized and imprisoned as a debtor because he could not discharge the jail-fees claimed on account of his detention. It was calculated that at this date there were over 24,000 debtors languishing in prison, and that one man out of every four men died annually.

Oglethorpe was indefatigable, continually engaged in visiting prisons, examining and receiving reports. The corrupt practices and the base treatment of prisoners which had been so common were traced home to many of the guilty parties, who were prosecuted with the utmost rigour. But Oglethorpe felt that the work was not finished. He knew that in all such cases the tendency to relapse was great, and he took care to provide against this by such effective means as only an energetic practical mind such as his was likely to devise. Progress in this, as in all such matters, was slow; and in the meantime jail-fever was sending its own reports from the provinces. So late as the year 1730, jail-fever broke out. In that year Chief Baron Pengelly, Serjeant Shippen, and many others were killed by it, when attending the Dorsetshire

Assizes, and the High Sheriff of Somerset perished through the same cause.

One result of Oglethorpe's efforts was that numbers of those who had suffered especially in the debtors' prison were set free, and it was a difficult matter to reinstate them in society or to find suitable work for them. While Oglethorpe was earnestly engaged in this work, he became Deputy Governor of the Royal African Company, of which he had been for a short time a director. The knowledge which he gained through this office excited in him a keen interest in the native races with which, through our passion for colonising, we were then, as now, brought continually into contact, and also suggested that in some points the ordinary methods of dealing with them were neither the wisest nor the most profitable.

One incident seems to have had a powerful effect later in determining Oglethorpe's energy in certain directions. He became the friend of a man—once a prince in his own country—who had been carried into slavery, and escaped and was cast into prison. His demeanour there attracted the notice of the officials. He was observed to write on scraps of paper, and through the kindness of the prison officials he was enabled to gratify his desire to write to his father to "tell what condition he had fallen into." One of these strips of paper was sent home to the Governor of the Royal African Company, who gave it to Oglethorpe. He sent it to the University of Oxford to be translated, and was so struck by the piteous tone of it, that he at once wrote out instructing the agent for the African Company to free Job—for that was the man's name—and to pay the expenses of his voyage and accommodation to England. Job was gifted and intelligent, and grateful for the care and kindness extended to him. His knowledge of Arabic rendered him of service to Sir Hans Sloane, who employed him in translating Arabic manuscripts, inscriptions on coins, &c. His native place was Bunda, a city of Galumbo, in the kingdom of Futa in Central Africa, opposite to Tombuto. Ibrahim, Job's grandfather, was founder of the city, and to his dignity Job succeeded on returning home after these romantic wanderings. The lessons that he had learned—more especially the kindnesses and the counsels of Oglethorpe—were not forgotten; and certainly the lessons of Job's story were not lost on Oglethorpe, but bore fruit in the additional interest he was led to take in native races, and his desire to improve their condition, as well as in his hatred of slavery, which was so pronounced that he might well be named a precursor of Clarkson and Wilberforce.

These were the questions which were pressing themselves on Oglethorpe's mind, when there happily arose upon him the idea of founding a colony in America which should especially afford a refuge for distressed debtors and for persecuted German Protestants, and which should also, in effect, present the conditions for a more systematic effort than had yet been made to convert and to civilise the Indians. He had also resolved that it should prove the possibility of carrying on profitably the work proper to it without the aid of slave-labour. Oglethorpe's efforts to get the proper patronage and support for his scheme were unremitting. He worked night and day; he waited by the doors of influential Members of Parliament and Ministers of the Crown; he petitioned the Bank of England and powerful Corporations; he sought interviews with wealthy philanthropic men and with the heads of distinguished societies. But earnest as were his appeals, and feasible as he had proved his project to be, objectors were not wanting. To answer them in pamphlets and otherwise he stirred up his friends; his own inclinations lying towards work in other directions, though neither was his pen wholly idle. Mr. Benjamin Martin, who was a kind of secretary to Oglethorpe, and afterwards Secretary to the Trustees of Georgia at home, in this respect did good service in his "Reasons for Establishing the Colony of Georgia." An argument which has often been heard in recent years was then raised even with reference to imprisoned debtors. By such emigration schemes you take away, it was said, from their own country those whose labour is wanted at home, and thus the price of labour must be unnaturally raised. To this Mr. Martin aptly replied—

"Those at all events who are shut up in prison are certainly doing no service either to their country or to themselves. They are thrown among associations whose vile influence would mortally deprave them, while poverty and despair were the only portion they could give to their wives and children."

Mr. Martin agreed with Dr. Samuel Johnson, in estimating that the number of men thus lost to their country and to their families was no fewer than four thousand a year.

Oglethorpe had urged a more philanthropic aspect of the proposal—

"They who are oppressed with poverty and misfortune are unable to be at the charge of removing from their miseries. Those are the people intended to be relieved. Let us cast our eyes on the multitude of unfortunate people in the kingdom, of reputable families, and of liberal, or at least, easy education; some undone by guardians, some by lawsuits, some by accidents in commerce, some by stocks and bubbles, and some by suretiship. But all agree in this circumstance, that they must either be burdensome to their relatives, or betake themselves to little shifts for sustenance, which, it is ten to one, do not answer their purpose, and to which a well-educated mind descends with the utmost constraint. What various misfortunes may reduce the rich, the industrious, to the dangers of a prison, to a moral certainty of starving! Those are the people that may relieve themselves, and strengthen Georgia, by resorting thither, and Great Britain by their departure.

"I appeal to the recollection of the reader—though he be opulent, though he be noble: does not his own sphere of acquaintances furnish him with some instances of such persons as have been here described? Must they starve? What honest heart can bear to think of it? Must they be fed by the contributions of others? Certainly they must, rather than be suffered to perish. I have heard it said, and it is easy to say so, 'Let them learn to work; let them subdue their pride, and descend to mean employments; keep ale-houses or coffee-houses, even sell fruit or clean shoes, for an honest livelihood.' But, alas! these occupations and many others like them are overstocked already by people who know better how to follow them than do they whom we have been talking of. As for labouring, I could almost wish that the gentleman or merchant who thinks that another gentleman or merchant in want can thrash or dig to the value of subsistence for his family, or even for himself; I say I could wish the person who thinks so were obliged to make trial of it for a week, or—not to be too severe—for only a day. He would then find himself to be less than the fourth part of a labourer, and that the fourth part of a labourer's wage would not maintain him. I have heard a man may learn to labour by practice; 'tis admitted. But it must also be admitted that before he can learn he may starve. Men whose wants are importunate must try such expedients as will give immediate relief 'Tis too late for them to begin to learn a trade when their pressing necessities call for the exercise of it."

A general interest was awakened, and twenty-one associations petitioned for an Act of Incorporation, which was granted by letters-patent on the 9th of June 1732, for the reason that many of his Majesty's subjects were in want of employment, reduced to distress, and would be glad of the opportunity to cultivate the waste lands in America, where they might earn a subsistence for themselves, and aid to extend the trade, navigation, and wealth of England. The trustees were vested with the powers of legislation for twenty-one years, after which a permanent form of government was to be established, corresponding with the British laws, by the King or his successors. Lord Perceval was elected president of the corporation. As large expenditures were necessary, the trustees set an example of liberality by their private subscriptions; the directors of the Bank of England followed their example; the friends of humanity expressed their interest in the work by numerous gifts; the House of Commons, sharing the general enthusiasm, made a grant of nearly ten thousand pounds;* and the

* The grant for that Bermuda College which Bishop Berkeley had so persistently aimed at establishing, and in which he would no doubt have succeeded but for the indifference of Walpole—in which, as Swift told Lord Carteret, "he most exorbitantly proposes a whole hundred pounds a year for himself, fifty pounds for a fellow, and ten for a student," adding, "his heart will break if the Deanery be not taken from him, and left to your excellency's disposal" (Prof. Fraser's Berkeley's Life and Works, vol. iv. pp. 102, 186)—strangely

whole sum collected almost without solicitation amounted to thirty-six thousand. The trustees, to their credit, urged that a clause should be put into the Charter restraining them or their successors from accepting any salary, gift, or perquisites whatever; not even permitting them to receive a grant of land under any circumstances in the settlement proposed. Well may Mr. Peabody say that the perfect disinterestedness of their conduct distinguished the enterprise from all others of the kind yet recorded in history. *

"No wonder," as one writes, "that great Numbers of poor Subjects, who lay under a Cloud of Misfortunes, embraced the Opportunity of once more tasting Liberty and Happiness; that Jews, attracted by the Temptation of Inheritances, flocked over; that Germans, oppressed and dissatisfied at Home, willingly joined in the Adventure, some as Settlers, and others as Servants to the Trustees; and, lastly, that great Numbers of Gentlemen of some Stock and Fortune, willingly expended Part of

enough comes in here to connect Berkeley and Oglethorpe. Parliamentary influence soon after diverted the grant into another channel. The land in St. Christopher's produced £90,000. Of this £80,000 was granted as the marriage portion of the Princess Royal, on her marriage with the Prince of Orange. General Oglethorpe induced Parliament to vote the remainder for his new colony of Georgia, in America, after obtaining Berkeley's consent to this application of the money. (See Journals of the House of Commons, May 10, 16, and 17, 1732.) St. Christopher, or St. Kitts, was one of the Caribbee Islands, obtained by us in a dispute with the French.

* Sparks' Library of American Biography, vol. xii. pp. 228-9.

the same in purchasing Servants, Tools, Commodities, and other Necessaries, to *intitle* them to such respective proportions of land as the Trustees had thought proper to determine." *

While one committee of the trustees was engaged in visiting prisons for the purpose of examining and selecting the most suitable men for the enterprise, another was concerned to see that those who had been chosen were put through military drill and instructed in such things as might be most profitable to them in their new sphere of life. Oglethorpe, having resolved to give up ease at home and to accompany his *protégés* to Georgia, was named Colonial Governor. It adds to our respect and reverence for him, that he made it a strict condition that he should receive no payment in any form.

The following sentences are not drawn from the writings of enthusiastic friends and admirers of Oglethorpe, but from the State documents of the neighbouring State of South Carolina :—

"The benevolent founders of the colony of Georgia perhaps may challenge the annals of any nation to produce a design more generous and praiseworthy than that they had undertaken. They voluntarily offered their money, their labour, and time for promoting what appeared to them the good of others, leaving them-

---

* A True and Historical Narrative of the Colony of Georgia in America, pp. 26, 27.

selves nothing for reward but the inexpressible satisfaction arising from virtuous actions." *

It is of these heroic labours of Oglethorpe that Thomson writes in his poem Winter in "The Seasons"—

> " And here can I forget the generous hand,
> Who, touched with human woe, redressive searched
> Into the horrors of the gloomy jail,
> Unpitied and unheard, where misery moans,
> Where sickness pines, where thirst and hunger burn,
> And poor misfortune feels the lash of vice?
> While in the land of liberty, the land
> Whose every street and public meeting glow
> With open freedom, little tyrants raged :
> Snatched the lean morsel from the starving mouth ;
> Tore from cold wintry limbs the tattered weed ;
> Even robbed them of the last of comforts, sleep ;
> The freeborn Briton to the dungeon chained.
> Or, as the lust of cruelty prevailed,
> At pleasure marked him with inglorious stripes ;
> And crushed out lives, by secret barbarous ways,
> That for their coun'ry would have toiled and bled.
> O great design ! if executed well,
> With patient care, and wisdom-tempered zeal :
> Ye sons of mercy ! yet resume the search ;
> Drag forth the legal monsters into light,
> Wrench from their hands oppression's iron rod,
> And bid the cruel feel the pains they give !
> Much still untouched remains in this rank age,
> Much is the patriot's weeding hand required.
> The toils of law (what dark insidious men
> Have cumbrous added to perplex the truth
> And lengthen simple justice into trade),
> How glorious were the day that saw them broke,
> And every man within the reach of right !"

---

* Historical Collections of South Carolina, vol. i. p. 289.

Matters being brought to this favourable footing, it was but the work of careful administration to secure a vessel and make all the necessary preparations—details which, in Oglethorpe's hands, were accomplished with marvellous despatch; and so, as we have seen, the little craft set sail from the Thames in November 1732.

II.

The "Annie" reached the harbour of Charlestown on the 13th January 1733. The emigrants were kindly received by Governor Johnson, who invited them to settle down to rest for a time until Oglethorpe himself should go forward to explore the country. Governor Johnson was fully aware of the advantages of protection and intercourse that would arise to Carolina from this new colony, and he assisted and encouraged Oglethorpe in every way. Provisions, hogs, and cows were presented to the Georgian settlers by wealthy and kind-hearted Carolinians. William Bull, a man of knowledge and experience, agreed to accompany Oglethorpe and to assist him in the work of exploration. After a good deal of wandering and adventure, they found a high and pleasant spot of ground situated on a navigable river, and here they fixed the destination of the settlers. The locality for the first town having been agreed on, the colonists with their possessions were conveyed thither, and were speedily engaged in erecting houses.

them, and as they had been trained before by the serjeants of the guard in London, they went through their exercises in a manner little inferior to regular troops." *

The administration of the town was very strict. Strong drink was discouraged; only an English beer being allowed. Three bailiffs were appointed, whose duty it was to supervise the work, and to see that each did his due share; the laws were administered by the Recorder and Registrar of the Town Court; no lawyers were to be employed, but every one was to be heard in his own cause. Each freeholder was *at once* allotted fifty acres of land—five of which were near Savannah, and the rest farther off. The chief produce was to be wheat and flax, hemp and silk. A rent of twenty shillings was to be paid on every hundred acres of land; no settler could assign or transfer his lands (the whole was to revert to the trustees within a given time); and (a condition which turned out unfortunately) if a man died without heirs male, his daughters could not inherit—the property was forfeited, and liable to be granted to other hands. As Mr. Peabody remarks, "there is surely no sufficient reason for considering it a crime in a man not to have sons, nor for imposing a penalty on daughters." †
Though a power was lodged in the hands of the Govern-

* Historical Collections of South Carolina, vol. i. pp. 289, 290.
† Sparks' Library of American Biography, vol. xii. p. 239.

ment for dispensing with this requirement in special cases, still it was felt to be a source of dissatisfaction.

Great encouragement was to be given to the silk industry, one of the industrial teachers being Mr. Amatis, a Piedmontese, who had been engaged chiefly to instruct the colonists in rearing silkworms and in the art of winding silk. They had learned that the climate of the province was favourable to the silkworm, and that the mulberry grew wild. Though they knew that the industry of the men would be required for severer labours, they thought that the attention requisite during the feeding of the worms might be given by the aged and infirm, by women and children, without interference with any other duty.

It appears from Dr. Stevens' "Brief History of the Culture of Silk in Georgia" that the subject had engaged the attention of emigrants to Virginia as early as 1609; and in a pamphlet then published it is said, "There are silke-worms and plenty of mulberries, whereby ladies, gentlewomen, and little children, being set in the way to do it, may be all emploied, with pleasure, making silke comparable to that of Persia, Turkey, or any other."

Mr. Oglethorpe was before long visited by three or four gentlemen who had made a canoe voyage from Charlestown to Savannah. One of them published an account of what he saw, and in it is the following :—

"Mr. Oglethorpe is indefatigable and takes a great deal of pains. His fare is but indifferent, having little else at present but salt provisions. He is extremely well beloved by all the people. The general title they give him is *Father*. If any of them are sick, he immediately visits them, and takes a great deal of care of them. If any difference arises, he is the person that decides it. Two happened while I was there, in my presence; and all the parties went away, to outward appearance, satisfied and content with his determination. He keeps a strict discipline. I never saw one of his people drunk, nor heard one of them swear, all the time I was there. He does not allow them rum, but in lieu gives them English beer. It is surprising to see how cheerful the men go to work, considering they have not been bred to it. There are no idlers there. Even the boys and girls do their part. There are four houses already up, but none are finished; and he hopes, when he has got more sawyers, to finish two houses a week. He has ploughed up some land: part of it he has sowed with wheat, which has come up, and looks promising. He has two or three gardens, which he has sowed with divers sorts of seed, and planted thyme, sage, pot-herbs, leeks, skellions, celery, liquorice, &c., and several trees. He has done a vast amount of work for the time, and I think his name justly deserves to be immortalised."*

One of the great objects with which Oglethorpe had adventured in the colonisation of Georgia was, as we have said, the improvement, education, and religious

* South Carolina Gazette, April 23, 1733.

instruction of the Indians. He lost no time in devoting himself to this work. He was desirous that his friendly intentions should be speedily made known, as mischief might easily arise from delay. But he set about the task in a truly characteristic manner. He heard of an Indian woman, Mary Musgrove, who had married a trader from Carolina, and who could speak both the English and Creek languages. Finding that she had great influence with the Indians, and might be made useful as an interpreter in forming treaties of alliance with them, he sent for her and drew her to him in friendship by presents, and afterwards settled on her an annual small allowance. By her assistance he summoned a general meeting of the chiefs at Savannah, in order to procure their consent to the peaceable settlement of the colony.

Two widely-contrasted views of the American Indian have hitherto been the fashion. There is the romantic view, fed by the novels of Fenimore Cooper and others, and by poems innumerable, in which he stands not only as a picturesque, but as a noble, calm, and stately presence, high-minded, heroic, hospitable to a fault, and falling before civilisation to the loss of humanity and the regrets of those who knew him by most intimate contact. The other, which professes to be that of sober fact, regards him as greedy, cunning, idle, filthy, and deceitful; with the reserve of the diplomatist and the coolness of the paid assassin, able to plot to take your life even while entertaining you with all the aspect of placid and ingenuous friendliness. If this were true, it was strange why the Indians at first perished so pathetically under the treatment of the first adventurers and gold-hunters. Probably the truth lies between the two reports. Oglethorpe's experience, at all events, proves that they were susceptible of gratitude and faithful to pledges if treated with uprightness and honesty, and the great William Penn had already found them the same.

While Mary Musgrove was arranging the conclave, Oglethorpe was once more on the way to Charlestown, where he addressed the Assembly and received formal promise of support. Thomas Penn of Pennsylvania also came to his help, expressing the very deepest interest in the scheme and promising every aid he could; besides subscribing one hundred pounds himself, he was active in soliciting subscriptions from others.

Oglethorpe made no longer stay at Charlestown than courtesy demanded, and on his return he found the chiefs of the Lower Creeks in attendance at Savannah, for the purpose of forming a treaty with the colony. The deputation, which consisted of about fifty chiefs and leading warriors, was received with the utmost respect and kindness. Oglethorpe represented to them the great power, wisdom, and wealth of England, and the many advantages that would accrue to them from a connection and alliance with the English people. As they had plenty of lands, he hoped that they would freely resign a share of them to his people, who were come for their benefit and instruction to settle amongst them. He assured them that his intentions were only friendly to them, as he trusted the future would make clear; and expressed the hope that they would not only be friends, but always have the true interests of each other at heart. Ouechachumpa, an old chief, rose and replied in a friendly speech. He said that they were firmly persuaded that the GREAT POWER which dwelt in heaven and all around (and then he spread out his hands and lengthened the sound of his words), and which had given breath to all men, had sent the English thither for the instruction of them, their wives, and children. They therefore gave up freely their right to all the land which they did not use themselves. That was not only his opinion, but the opinion of the eight towns of the Creeks; each of which, having consulted together, had sent some of their chief men with skins, which is their wealth. He then stopped, and the chief men of each town brought up a bundle of buck-skins, and laid eight bundles from the eight towns at Mr. Oglethorpe's feet. He then said those were the best things they had, and therefore they gave them with a good heart.

A treaty was soon concluded, by which the Indians ceded lands on the Savannah River as far as the Ogechee, and all the lands along the coasts between the Savannah and Alatamaha Rivers, including all the islands, and extending west as high as the tide flows. A reservation was made of two or three islands, and a small tract on shore, the former for bathing and fishing, the latter for an encampment when visiting the country. The presents on the part of the English consisted of a laced coat, a hat, and a shirt to each of the chiefs, a gun with powder and shot to each of the war captains, and a mantle of coarse cloth to each of the men who accompanied them. The Indians departed, well pleased with the attention which had been shown to them. A special friendship was formed with one of the chiefs, Tomo Chichi, which, for reasons which will soon appear, must be made specially prominent. This Tomo Chichi, though he was only the chief of a small tribe established at Yamcraw, three miles from Savannah, was hereafter to exercise great influence. In a short time Oglethorpe is able to report to the trustees—

"The Lower Creek nation is within a short distance of us, and has concluded a peace with us, giving us the right of all this part of the country; and I have marked out the lands which they have reserved to themselves. Their king comes constantly to church, and desires to be instructed in the Christian religion, and has given me his nephew, a boy who is his next heir, to educate. The other two nations are the Uchees and the Upper Creeks; we agree so well that they have referred to me a difference to determine, which otherwise would have occasioned a war."

And later we find Oglethorpe writing, after further inquiry and exploration—

"The province is much larger than we thought, being one hundred and twenty miles from this river to the Alatamaha. The Savannah has a very long course, and a great trade is carried on by the Indians, there having above twelve boats passed since I have been there. There are some respects," he said, "in which the Indians are already exemplary. Theft is a thing unknown among the Creeks, though not uncommon among the Uchees. They abhor adultery, and do not approve a plurality of wives."

They were thus treated with such kindness that they were disarmed of the wish, not to speak of the power, to injure, and indeed were made to serve as a strong safeguard against other foes. The capacity to perceive the good points in savage peoples, and successfully to appeal to them, is one of the very rarest gifts in the class who regard themselves as called to be explorers; and much of the misery of colonisation has undoubtedly sprung from this. The extinction of the Red men and of the Maories is in great part due to it. In the historical documents of South Carolina we read—

"This generous and kind method of treating barbarians was better policy than that of overawing them by force, and was attended, as might have been expected, with the happiest consequences. To strengthen the frontiers of Carolina and promote the colony of Georgia, nothing could have been conceived more useful and effectual than a friendly intercourse with the savages of the neighbourhood."*

The combination of far-sighted statesmanship with lofty benevolent views, has seldom been better illusrated than in Oglethorpe's principle of dealing with the Indians.

Small parties of emigrants had been sent out from time to time, and, in June 1733, the whole number amounted to one hundred and fifty-two, ten being Italian and eleven German Protestants.

III.

Having seen the colony advanced to such a state of order, and a fair prospect of prosperity before it, Oglethorpe left it for England, with a view the better to arrange various matters with the trustees. Tomo Chichi, the Mico or chief of a branch of the Creek nation already referred to, was with him, as well as his wife and nephew and some other natives, whose appearance in England, it was hoped, would tend to increase the interest felt in the colony. Oglethorpe visited New England on the way, and was warmly received. Congratulatory addresses were voted to him by the Assembly of the province. On reaching home he found that the set of public opinion was in his favour. His supporters increased ; the newspapers recognised in him a hero and

* Historical Collections of South Carolina, vol. i. p. 293.

public benefactor. The following letter from the venerable Samuel Wesley, accompanying a copy of his work on the Book of Job, may be taken as an indication of the state of feeling towards him :—

"EPWORTH, *July* 6, 1734.

"HONOURED SIR,—May I be permitted, while such crowds of our nobility and gentry are pouring their congratulations, to press with my poor mite of thanks into the presence of one who so well deserves the title of *Universal Benefactor of Mankind*. It is not only your valuable favours on many accounts to my son, late of Westminster, and myself, when I was not a little pressed in the world, nor your more extensive charity to the poor prisoners; it is not these only that so much demand my warmest acknowledgments, as your disinterested and immovable attachment to your country; by your raising a new colony, or rather a little world of your own, in the midst of wild woods and uncultivated deserts, where men may live free and happy, if they are not hindered by their own stupidity and folly, in spite of the unkindness of their brother-mortals." . . .

Though now within a short period of his decease, Samuel Wesley took such an intense interest in the Georgian colony, that he declared that, if he had been ten years younger, he would gladly have devoted the remainder of his life and labours to the emigrants, and in acquiring the language of the Indians among whom they had to live. Among others who had gone to Georgia with Oglethorpe and had returned with him, was John Lyndal, one of Samuel Wesley's parishioners, of whom the venerable rector earnestly inquired whether the ministers who had migrated to the infant colony understood the Indian language, and could preach without interpreters.

Tomo Chichi went to court and presented eagle feathers to George II. Poems were written in many journals, and the "Gentleman's Magazine" offered a prize for a medal to commemorate Oglethorpe's benevolence and patriotism. Tomo and his friends were also presented to the Archbishop of Canterbury, and to him Tomo expressed the wish of his people for religious instruction. The visit of the Indians had the result intended. Fresh interest was awakened. Parliament continued its benefactions, the King expressed the deepest interest in the province that bore his name, and often inquired of his ministers respecting it. And when, after a stay of four months in England, the natives went home, it was inevitable that they should do good by spreading abroad among their brethren the impression they had formed of English greatness, and power, and culture, and kindness.

But success and appreciation did not lead Oglethorpe to lessen his activity. The cause of the colony was ever present with him. Scarcely had he landed when he was arranging for another relay of settlers. Some discontentment had been felt by certain of the emigrants at the embargo which had been put on the importation of rum and spirits, and avowedly on this ground a few had left the colony for other parts in America, efforts to smuggle in drink not having succeeded. In spite of this, we find the trustees firmly adhering to their policy.

While Oglethorpe was in England they passed an Act at once for preventing trouble with the Indians, and for preserving the health and morals of the people. It was entitled "An Act to prevent all importation of rum and brandies into the province of Georgia, or any kind of ardent spirits or strong waters whatsoever." A writer of the day makes this remark : "At the same time the trustees endeavoured to supply the stores with strong beer from England, molasses for brewing beer, and with Madeira wines; which the people might purchase at reasonable rates, which would be more refreshing and wholesome for them."

The news from Georgia continued to be encouraging. In September 1734 the trustees learned that Savannah was in a prosperous condition, and that the people had already reaped a crop of Indian corn, which produced upwards of a thousand bushels. The trustees also received a curious despatch from the Indians, expressing their sense of the greatness of the British nation, their thanks for the attentions shown to Tomo Chichi and his companions, and their attachment to Mr. Oglethorpe.

Meantime the colony had been swelled by new arrivals; for which the general had done his best to prepare before leaving. A body of Salzburgers—Bavarian Protestants who had been compelled to flee their country in the depth of winter, owing to the harsh treatment of their government—reached Savannah on the 10th of March 1734—a Sabbath day—and as they lay off the shore they heard the birds singing so sweetly that it seemed to them, after their many sufferings, that they had been conducted at last to a resting-place and a home. They were received with kindness by all; and the colonists provided for their wants according to the instructions Oglethorpe had given before he left. Some miles up the river from Savannah they found an attractive spot for a settlement, and with the Bible in their hands they marked out the boundaries, and significantly named it *Ebenezer.* The spot chosen was surrounded by vast forests of cedar, walnuts, cypresses, and oaks, with wild vines running to the top of the highest trees. As for game, there were eagles, turkeys, roebucks, goats, deer, wild cows, horses, hares, partridges, and buffaloes without number. The Salzburgers built tents made of the bark of trees, constructed roads and bridges, set up religious services, were furnished with domestic utensils and with cattle, and were soon a prosperous community. A short time later a band of Moravians were received, who fared equally well at the hands of the settlers; and later still, a yet more remarkable population, who far outnumbered the discontented who had removed to Carolina and other places. The proposal of the trustees had excited such interest in Scotland and been received with such favour that, in Inverness and its vicinity, no fewer than a hundred and thirty Highlanders and their families had been enrolled for emigration. These, with wives and children, making in all a party of about 200, arrived in Georgia in the month of January 1735; and with them came several private grantees, with their servants. The Scots were destined to settle on the frontiers, for the protection and defence of the province. After staying a few days at Savannah, they proceeded southward in periaguas; and, ascending the Alatamaha River about sixteen miles from St. Simons, they pitched upon a suitable settlement. Here they raised a little fort and mounted four pieces of cannon. They also built a guard-house, a store, and a chapel; for, with characteristic piety and foresight, they had brought a pastor with them—a Mr. Macleod, "a very good man, who is very useful in instructing the people in religious matters and will intermeddle with no other affairs." The district, at their desire, was called "Darien;" while the town was named "New Inverness," which, however, in later years was changed. It is refreshing to read—

"The costume of the Highland clansman, his cap and plume, his kilt and plaid, soon became very dear to the red man of the woods; they mingled in their sports, and hunted the buffalo together;—for the woods of Georgia were then as full of buffaloes as the plains of Missouri are now; and the writer of this notice was told when a boy, by General Lachlan M'Intosh, that when a youth he had seen ten thousand buffalo within ten miles of New Inverness." *

Meantime Oglethorpe was busy at home. He carried many measures for the future benefit of the colony. His concern for the Indians led him to interest the trustees in their moral and religious condition, and his proposition that efficient Christian teachers be engaged for the colony, some of whom should specially devote themselves to the Indians, was warmly supported.

They at once began to look round for fit persons to undertake this work. At the suggestion of Dr. John Burton, a member of the Board, they turned their attention to John Wesley, then a young man of great promise as a preacher. Wesley took counsel with his brother Samuel; asked the advice of William Law, and went to Manchester to consult his friends Clayton and Byrom. Thence he proceeded to Epworth, and laid the proposal before his widowed mother, who replied, "Had I twenty sons, I should rejoice if they were all so employed." † His decision was soon taken, and in a short time we find him writing to his friend Mr. Benjamin Ingham: "Fast and pray; and then send me word whether you

* J. Spalding's Memoir of M'Intosh, in "Portrait Gallery of Distinguished Americans," 1836, vol. iii.
† Tyerman's Wesley, i. p. 109.

dare go with me to the Indians." After a time Ingham answered that, though he had, on first getting the proposal, fancied that "we had heathen enough at home," the call had been made clear to him as he had dwelt on the prospect, and that he would go.*

Mr. Benjamin Ingham, above referred to, was a young Yorkshireman of great promise, and, as we have seen, he went to act as Wesley's assistant; while Charles Delamotte, who was the son of a wealthy London merchant, was so devoted to Wesley, that, in face of opposition from his family and the finest chances in business, he decided to go to Georgia as Wesley's servant. Another passenger at this time was the venerable David Nitschmann—the Moravian bishop—who, as Wesley said, "adorned the Gospel of our Lord in all things."

The ships were specially fitted out to carry the emigrants, and Oglethorpe would sail in company with them. The Government had offered Oglethorpe a vessel for his own accommodation; but this he declined, preferring to sail with the emigrants and to live as they did. The "Symond" and the "London Merchant," each about 220 tons, were the vessels that had been chartered; and they sailed from the Thames on the 21st of October 1735, but, owing to contrary winds, Cowes was not left till the 10th of December.

The Moravians went to join their brethren who had gone out the previous year. Most readers will remember

* Oxford Methodists, pp. 64, 66, 67.

something of the influence which was brought to bear on Wesley through his relationship with them on this voyage. Mr. Ingham describes them as "a good, devout, and heavenly-minded people. Almost the only time you know they are in the ship is when they are harmoniously singing the praises of the great Creator, which they constantly do twice a-day. Their example was very edifying. They are more like the primitive Christians than any church now existing, for they retain both the faith, practice, and discipline delivered by the apostles. They have regularly ordained bishops, priests, and deacons. Baptisms, confirmation, and the Eucharist are duly administered. Discipline is strictly exercised without respect of persons. They all submit themselves to the pastors in everything. They live together in perfect love and peace, having for the present all things common. They are more ready to serve their neighbours than themselves. In business they are diligent, in all their dealings strictly just; and in everything they behave themselves with meekness, sweetness, and humility."

In a storm that made many scream out for fear, and caused Wesley to tremble doubting if he were fit to die, the Moravians were perfectly calm and sang their hymns. "Are you not afraid?" Wesley asked one of them. He replied, "I thank God, no." "Are your women and children not afraid?" "No; our women and children are not afraid to die." No wonder that Wesley was deeply influenced by their conduct and the spirit of their life, having his idea of what a religious community should be elevated and spiritualised.

Oglethorpe, in preparing for the voyage, had given attention to the most commonplace details,—preparing tools, provisions, clothing, and other stores for the voyage ; and that not with any reference to himself, for we are assured by a fellow-passenger that, while he laboured incessantly at these preparations, he paid the passage of the gentlemen who were with him and his servants, and scarcely ever ate anything but the common provisions of the ship. We have a fuller account of this voyage than of any of the others, because of the attention of Messrs. Wesley and Ingham to their diaries, and from that of the latter we may make an extract specially throwing light on Oglethorpe's character. Mr. Ingham writes under date—

"*Friday*, December 19. Messrs. Wesley and I, with Mr. Oglethorpe's approbation, undertook to visit, each of us, a part of the ship, and daily to provide the sick people with water-gruel, and such other things as were necessary for them. At first we met with some difficulties, but God enabled us to persevere in the constant performance to the end of the journey. Mr. Oglethorpe himself went several times about the ship to comfort and encourage the people ; and, indeed, he had never been wanting in this respect. He is a pattern of fatherly care and tender compassion, being always ready, night and day, to give up his own ease and conveniences to serve the poorest body among the people. He seldom eats above once a day, and then he usually chooses salt provisions (though not so agreeable to his health), that he might give the fresh to the sick. But more will appear from the following instance. One Mrs. Welch, who was believed to be at the point of death, being big with child, in a high fever, attended with a violent cough, was, by Mr. Oglethorpe's order, removed into his own cabin, which was the best in the ship, he himself lying several nights in a hammock, till another cabin was got ready for him. He also constantly supplied her with all the best things in the ship. Some of the gentlemen seemed disgusted at this; but that made him only the more resolute. Yet, notwithstanding all possible care was taken of her, human means failed; the doctor gave her up, everybody thought she would die; Mr. Oglethorpe only continued in hope. Nay, he said, he was sure God would raise her up to manifest His glory in her. She had a desire to receive the Lord's Supper before she died; and lo! from the moment she received it, she began to recover, and is now safely delivered of a daughter, and in perfect health. 'Gracious is the Lord and merciful, long-suffering, and of great goodness; the Lord is loving to every man, and His mercy is over all His works.'"

The voyage from Cowes to the Savannah River was made in fifty-seven days. Oglethorpe seems to have always acted with great kindness. On one occasion, when some of the officers and gentlemen on board took liberties with Wesley and his friends, Oglethorpe indignantly exclaimed, "What mean you, sir? Do you take these gentlemen for tithe-pig parsons? They are gentlemen of learning and respectability. They are my friends, and whoever offers an affront to them insults me."

They had experienced a tempestuous voyage and had a rough passage, but now the weather was fine; the land breeze refreshed them as the ships lay quietly moored, and they hailed with delight the land of promise where, as Wesley said, "the groves of pines along the shores made an agreeable prospect, showing, as it were, the verdure and bloom of spring in the depth of winter."

The ships which bore this large accession to the colony passed the bar at Tybee, on the 5th of February 1736, and came to anchor. This island is at the mouth of the Savannah River; is five miles long, and three broad; and is the most easterly land in the State. Oglethorpe went immediately on shore, to see what had been done towards raising the beacon on the island, for the construction of which he had given orders. "It was to be an octagon building of squared timber; its dimensions twenty-five feet wide at the bottom and ten at the top; and its height ninety feet, with a flagstaff on the top thirty feet high. When completed, it would be of great service to all shipping, not only to the vessels bound to this port, but also to those bound for Carolina; for the land of the coast, for some hundred miles, is so alike, being low and woody, that a distinguishing mark is of great consequence."* To his disappointment and regret this most desirable enterprise had not been carried forward as he had hoped. The work had been neglected owing partly to unfaithfulness and partly to want of energy on the part of the contractors. But Oglethorpe's forecast and administrative talent is seen in his plans and in his future decision, for before a few months had passed the lighthouse was completed.

Oglethorpe was as much surprised as gratified to see the progress that had been made in his absence. The town now extended to nearly two miles in circumference. The ground on which it stood had only two years before been covered with dense woods. Two hundred comfortable dwellings occupied the space, some of them two or three stories high. To guard against the spread of fire, the houses were detached, each standing in its own lot of ground, sixty feet in width by ninety in length, and fenced in by stout palings. Each freeholder, in addition to his town-plot, had five acres outside the common, to serve as garden, orchard, &c. The streets were wide, and large squares were left at proper distances. A large public garden was now laid out under cultivation, which, beautiful as it was (and Ogle-

* Moore's Voyage, p. 18.

thorpe was a great garden lover), had other claims to admiration. It was meant to be a nursery for mulberry trees, many of which were already planted in it.

IV.

During Oglethorpe's absence some difficulties had arisen with a family of Indians respecting boundaries; and, in consistency with the principles on which he had from the first acted, he at once set himself to the settlement of this dispute. For this purpose he travelled a great distance through a trying country, hardly allowing himself ordinary rest or refreshment; but he arranged matters to the satisfaction of all parties without delay, making it clearly understood that no colonist on the slightest pretext must seem to overreach the natives. And, truly, Oglethorpe was no laggard. No sooner had he settled this matter, than he started to visit the Salzburgers, and having stayed with them for a day or two, he went on to see how the Moravians were proceeding with their works, and then southward to Darien. "He found the Scotchmen under arms," we are told, "dressed in their uniform of plaid, equipped with broadswords, targets, and muskets." Oglethorpe says they made a fine appearance; a remark in which perhaps he was the more justified that, in compliment to them, he wore their costume all the time that he was with them. They had provided him a soft bed, with holland sheets and plaid curtains; but he chose to lie upon the ground and in the open air, wrapped in his cloak, as did two other gentlemen; and afterwards his example was followed by the rest of his attendants. Fortunately such self-denials did not greatly try Oglethorpe. His constitution was hardy; he required little sleep; he could go a long time without food, and not feel any inconvenience or serious results from it. What would have killed many a man had hardly any effect upon him. A gentleman, who accompanied him on this and several other tours, says in a letter written on the 24th of February 1736—

"What surprises me beyond expression is his abstemiousness and hard living. Though even dainties are plentiful, he makes the least use of them; and such is his hardiness, that he goes through the woods, wet or dry, as well as any Indian. Moreover, his humanity so gains on all here, that I have not words to express their regard and esteem for him."

The record of Oglethorpe's travels fully justifies what has been cited above. Scarcely had he seen how matters were at Savannah when he set forth again, as the following passage from Wesley's life shows:—

"Ingham and Charles Wesley went off with Oglethorpe to lay out the town of Frederica; and Wesley and Delamotte, having no house of their own to live in, lodged, during the first month, with Spangenberg, Nitschmann, and other Moravian friends. Thus, from morning to night, were they mixed up with these godly people, and had ample opportunity to observe their spirit and behaviour. Wesley writes: "They were always employed, always cheerful themselves, and in good humour with one another; they had put away all anger and strife, and wrath, and bitterness, and clamour, and evil speaking; they walked worthy of the vocation wherewith they were called."

On January 19, 1737, Oglethorpe was able to tell the directors that during the past year, not only had Augusta, Darien, and Frederica been founded, and that a new town called Ebenezer had been laid out for the Salzburgers, but that there were several villages settled by gentlemen at their own expense. He was further able to give them the pleasing intelligence, that the remoter Creek nations, to a distance of some 700 miles, now acknowledged his Majesty's authority and traded with the settlers. As illustrative of the rough mode of life to which Oglethorpe gladly accommodated himself, the following passage from Mr. Ingham's diary must be given—

"*Monday*, February 16, 1736.—About seven this evening, I set forward with Mr. Oglethorpe and some others in a ten-oared boat, for the Alatamaha River, the southernmost part of Georgia. At eleven we arrived at a place called Skiddowa, where we went ashore into the woods and kindled a fire under a lofty pine-tree. Having written some letters, and eaten something, we lay down to sleep upon the ground, without either bed or board, having no covering besides our clothes, but a single blanket each, and the canopy of heaven. About eight next day we set forward again, passing several marshes, beset on both sides by trees of various sorts, whose leaves, being gilded with the glorious rays of the sun, yielded a beautiful prospect. About twelve the wind blew so high that we were driven upon an oyster-bank, where we could not get a stick to make a fire. Here we dined very comfortably. Near two we set forward again, and with great difficulty crossed over the mouth of the river Ogechee. The wind was exceedingly high, and the water very rough. Almost every wave drove over the side of the boat, so that every moment we were in jeopardy of our lives; and, truly, if Mr. Oglethorpe had not roused up himself, and struck life into the rowers, I do not know but most of us might there have made our exit. Towards six we got to a little place called Boar's Island, where we encamped all night, round a roaring fire, in a bed of canes, where the wind could not reach us. Here also we came up with a large boat, called a pettiangur, loaded with people for the Alatamaha, who had set out before us. Next morning after prayers, Mr. Oglethorpe, considering that our own boat was overladen, and also that I might probably be of some service to the people, asked me if I was willing to go on board the pettiangur, whereto I readily consented. Here, during the remainder of our passage, I read to the people, and instructed them as I had opportunity. This evening we lay upon St. Catherine's, a very pleasant island, where we met with two Indians a-hunting. I took one of them on board the pettiangur, and gave him some biscuit and wine, and he in return sent us the greatest part of a deer."*

Difficulties had already arisen in various forms upon Oglethorpe,—some of them, it may be said, in a measure, incident to such an undertaking, and others of a more special kind.

A proportion of the settlers had proved as idle and useless members of society in America as they had been in Great Britain; and as their material wants had been supplied from the common store, they felt no stimulus to industry and frugality. The trustees, as we have seen, had therefore begun to look round for a better class of emigrants. But still there were periodical expressions of discontent; now it was the exclusion of spirits; again the deprivation of slave-labour, the prevalence of which in the neighbouring colonies was held to put the Georgians at great disadvantage. Then, the mode of settlement, it must be allowed, though devised with the best intentions, did not give the settler a sufficiently close and permanent interest in the land he cultivated. Here, in Georgia, more than a century ago, the same principle was found at work as certain later educationists have dwelt on †—that unless associated

* Mr. Tyerman's Oxford Methodists, p. 76.
† See Dr. Rigg's Essay on National Education, *passim*.

with a fair prospect of free proprietorship, the education and moral advancement of the working classes must be slow, because they have really no fixed locality or home. It was an error of the trustees not to have given more of personal interest to the settlers. If any man could have overcome the disadvantages of such a settlement, we believe that Oglethorpe would have done it, and indeed he almost overcame them, but not quite.

We read in an official report: "By this time the colonists of Georgia had become fully convinced of the disadvantages of that plan of settlement framed by the trustees. However well intended, it was found to be ill adapted to their circumstances, and likely to prove ruinous to the settlement. In the province of Carolina which lay adjacent, the colonists discovered that there they could obtain lands, not only on better terms, but also liberty to purchase negroes to assist in clearing and cultivating them. They found labour in the burning climate intolerable, and the hardships and dangers to which they were subjected wholly unbearable. Instead of raising commodities for exportation, the Georgians, by the labour of several years, were not yet able to raise sufficient provisions to support themselves and families. Under such discouragements, numbers retired to the Carolina side of the river, where they had better prospects of success."

It was, above all, necessary that strong colonies should be planted along the frontiers. The service rendered by the Scotch people in virtue of their very position in the south was unspeakable; but detachments of the Germans on several occasions declined to move to the south to settle on the frontiers, on the very ground of possible trouble from the Spaniards, varied with excuses that they could not forego the enjoyment of the ministerial services at Ebenezer. This was unavoidable, perhaps, but it was in some sense a peril and a drawback, even though their steadiness and frugality and industry enabled them to plant new and flourishing settlements nearer to Savannah. As we may imagine, this was a delicate and trying circumstance to Oglethorpe in many ways.

The necessity of a stringent military service was another difficulty that increased just in the measure that the trustees were successful in finding the better class of settlers that they wished. The Scotchmen at Darien, it was true, were good settlers, and did not object to military exercises, but rather liked them; this, however, was not the case with the Salzburgers and Moravians, and their exemption from service out of respect to their principles was an apple of discord that became more and more obtrusive as time went on. For the Spaniards had not failed intermittently to annoy the colony; they had endeavoured in many ways to draw the Indians from their allegiance, and, failing, they had committed cruel outrages. It was necessary, therefore, that a force should be in readiness in case of any more effective demonstration being made. Skirmishes both on land and water were frequent ; and forts and drillings became more numerous and more necessary, as the events of the next few years fully proved.

In spite of the money invested and the time that had been spent, the silk industry did not succeed. Everything possible had been done to encourage it. But the climate did not prove so friendly as was anticipated. Sudden transitions from heat to cold destroyed great numbers of worms. Suitable labour, too, it was difficult to hire ; and as the colonists found that rice-culture and afterwards cotton required less labour and paid better, as a natural consequence they devoted themselves to these.

It was found hard, too, to keep out the drink. Drinking increased precisely as the schemes of the colonists failed. Such ingenuity was exercised to import it secretly as, had it been applied to legitimate trade, would have blessed the colony. The very same difficulties were experienced then as are being felt by many philantrophic legislators now, the chief being the rebound against an enforced sobriety and morality. One of the Indian chiefs, when urged to listen to the doctrines of Christianity, and become a convert, keenly replied, "Why these are Christians at Savannah ! These are Christians at Frederica !" and then exclaimed, "Christians drink ! Christians beat men ! Christians tell lies ! no, no; me no Christian !"

In addition to the treaty which Oglethorpe was confronted by, there now came all too decisive limits of discontent at the condition of the settlement in high quarters at home. "Misfortunes come not single spies but in battalions," Oglethorpe now fully verified.

From a letter which Wesley wrote to him on February 24, 1737, we learn that Sir Robert Walpole had turned against the general, and parliament had resolved to make a strict scrutiny into Georgian affairs.* Oglethorpe had been charged with misapplying monies, and with abusing his entrusted power. Wesley adds: "Perhaps in some things you have shown you are but a man; perhaps I myself may have a little to complain of; but, oh, what a train of benefits have I received to lay in the balance against it! I bless God that ever you were born. I acknowledge His exceeding mercy in casting me into your hands. I own you generous all the time we were at sea and since. I am indebted to you for a thousand favours here. Though all men should revile you, yet will not I." †

Though Wesley had been willing to consider the whole of the Georgian settlements as his parish, he was in some degree fettered in his work of ministering to the Indians through the unexpected absence of the Rev. Mr. Quincy in England. This made it necessary for him to stay and preach to the English at Savannah; and this circumstance

* Walpole would appear to have been moved by some personal dislike to Oglethorpe; for he uniformly tries to depreciate him. See Lecky's "History of the Eighteenth Century," vol. ii. p. 501.
† Tyerman's Wesley, vol. i. p. 136.

was perhaps unfortunate. His high-church views and his severity in several respects before long came into conflict with the feelings of many of the settlers, while meantime his one desire was to devote himself wholly to the Indians, as he had hoped to do when he left England. He was by and by joined by his brother Charles, who, with Mr. Ingham, did noble work both among the Indians and the settlers. By the Indians especially Mr. Ingham was received with much favour. They gave him a plot of fruitful ground, in the midst of which was a small round hill; and on the top of this hill a house was built for an Indian school. The house was named Irene.* The devotion which this group of men showed to those whom they had come to teach and to befriend shines out very cheeringly athwart difficulties, misunderstandings, and some imprudences it may be prompted by zeal. All were prepared to illustrate their teaching by example even in the minor details of life. Some of the boys in one of the schools went barefooted, and those who were shod looked down upon them. Wesley asked his friend to change schools with him for a time. He astonished the boys that had sneered at their barefooted brethren by himself coming to school barefooted; and bare feet soon ceased to be a mark for scorn.

Ingham was sent to England in the end of 1736, the chief purpose of his mission being to procure more help for the colonists. He faithfully executed the com-

* Wesley's Works, vol. i. p. 61.

mission; but he never returned to Georgia. He afterwards made himself a familiar name among the Methodists as the "Yorkshire Evangelist." He was only twenty-three when he went out to Georgia.

V.

In 1737 Oglethorpe, at the request of his brother-trustees, returned to England, in order mainly to represent personally to the British Ministry and those concerned the real causes of discontent, and also the necessity for a stronger force than the colony could furnish, or had been furnished, against the Spaniards. He urged his points well; showing, with respect to the latter question, that not only did the question concern Georgia, but Carolina and other colonies also. He returned in the end of 1738, with a commission to erect additional forts, and with certain supplies and aids. His calculations and his demands for yet more effective military organisation, were fully justified by the event.

There were now in Georgia the following settlements:—Frederica in St. Simon's Island, one hundred miles south of Savannah; Darien, at a distance of about eighty miles; New Ebenezer, about nineteen miles; Highgate and Hampstead, four or five miles south-west; and Thunderbolt, some six miles south-east.

Unfortunately, in some respects the discontent arising out of the necessity of increased military service had led to further departures from the colony, thinning the numbers of the Moravian brethren, every way good settlers; and these were soon to be followed by other departures. We read in a good and really unimpeachable authority—

"As the exemption from military service embittered the minds of the people against them, some of the brethren in 1738 left all their flourishing plantations, having repaid all the money which had been advanced towards their passage and settlement, and went to Pennsylvania. The rest were left undisturbed for a while; but in 1739, when the troubles of war broke out afresh, being again molested on account of military service, they followed their brethren in the spring of 1740, and afterwards begun the colonies of Bethlehem and Nazareth."*

Oglethorpe's care for the Indian people never lapsed; and proofs of it were continual. We may notice one or two in this place. Dr. Wilson, Bishop of Sodor and Man, who had had some conversation with Oglethorpe while in London in 1737, promised to complete a simple manual which might be translated into their language. This was not accomplished till 1741, when we find the bishop's son sending to Oglethorpe a copy of the manual which had been published by the Society for the Propagation of the Gospel in Foreign Parts. The bishop, after mentioning in his preface the circumstance in which the book was undertaken, says—

* Cranz's History of the United Brethren, pp. 193-229.

" Mr. Oglethorpe's great and generous concern for both the present and the future interest of these nations, and his earnest desire and endeavours, so well known, to civilise them first, and make them more capable of instruction in the ways of religion and civil government, and his hearty wishes that something might be done to forward such good purposes, prevailed with the author, however indifferently qualified for such a work, to set about the following essay for propagating the Gospel among Indians and negroes." *

In the midst of the most arduous labours, Oglethorpe always found time carefully to consider any request or complaint from the natives, and was ready to undertake the most troublesome journeys for their good. On the 17th of July 1739, we read that he set off on an expedition to Coweta, to hold a conference with the Creek Indians. On his journey, computed to be over three hundred miles, he and his attendants met with many and great hardships. They were obliged to traverse a continuous wilderness without roads, through tangled thickets and deep and broken ravines, across swamps and bogs where the horses sank and plunged to the great danger of the riders. They had to pass large rivers on rafts and cause horses to wade and swim, and to ford others. During most of the way Oglethorpe was

* The Knowledge and Practice of Christianity made Easy to the Meanest Capacity; or, an Essay Towards the Instruction of the Indians. London, 1740. 12mo.

under the necessity of sleeping in the open air, wrapped in his cloak or a blanket, and with his portmanteau for a pillow; or, if the night-weather was uncomfortable or rainy, a covert was constructed of cypress boughs spread over poles. For two hundred miles there was not a hut, not a human face to be seen, unless that of some Indian hunter traversing the woods. At length they arrived at Coweta, one of the principal towns of the Muscoghe or Creek Indians, where the chiefs of all the tribes were assembled, on the 11th of August. "Thus did this worthy man, to protect the settlement, which with so much pecuniary expense and devotedness of time he had founded, now expose himself to the hazards and toils of a comfortless expedition, that would have proved insurmountable to one of a less enterprising spirit and steady resolution."

We are not surprised when we learn that General Oglethorpe ingratiated himself highly with the Creeks by his great consideration for them exhibited in such a manner. The attitude of the Spaniards became only more and more threatening. It was evident that more help must be procured from the home country, else all might be lost. So serious did the crisis seem, that Oglethorpe—a man not apt to surrender to despondency, but to act with cool bravery and decision—gave orders that all who fancied they could better themselves by leaving the colony should do so. It speaks highly for the opinion—which in spite of some discontentment—the emigrants had formed of Oglethorpe, that not one availed himself of the offer.*

At length, in December 1739, the smouldering fire burst into flame. Oglethorpe had received orders from the Home Government to attack Florida, and would have done so had he been able to raise a sufficient force; but the Spaniards by an attempt upon the settlement of Amelia—in which they shot at and killed several unarmed Highlanders, afterwards hacking and mutilating their bodies—made this inevitable as an act of retaliation. Oglethorpe now determined, as soon as he could collect a sufficient number of boats, to make an incursion into Florida. With such a contingent as he could muster, he soon embarked and made his way to St. John's. Having taken and destroyed all the boats he found in that river, he landed and proceeded a day's march in the direction of Augustine. A troop of Spanish horse and a company of foot showed themselves preparing to attack, but the Indians advancing with the war-whoop drove them off. The war once begun went on with varying success, Oglethorpe's vigilance only sufficing to stave off disaster.

While these agents of disturbance were at work, Oglethorpe's wisdom and goodwill had supplied many counteracting elements. He had infected the better classes of emigrants with a complete trust in him, and such an enthusiasm for the objects he had at heart, as

* Harris's Memorials, p. 203.

enabled them to undergo many deprivations. The Indians too maintained towards him their first attitude, in spite of many endeavours on the part of the Spaniards to alienate them. One of his greatest disappointments had arisen from the conscientious manner in which he had endeavoured to provide for religious teaching. John Wesley, after a period of most devoted ministration, unfortunately became involved in a difference with some persons, who raised an action against him in the local court for defamation of character; and this led to his leaving Georgia, in circumstances that were not well calculated to further the end for which he had gone thither. He had shown zeal and self-denial more than prudence. He left Georgia in December 1737, and reached England in February 1738. Whitefield had left England for Georgia before Wesley's arrival. He reached Savannah in May, and for a time devoted himself energetically to the work which Wesley had begun. He sat by the deathbed of the chief Tomo Chichi, preached at Savannah, visited Frederica and other places. He sailed for England in about a year to receive priest's orders, and to obtain money for an Orphan Home on which he had set his heart. The vessel was caught in a storm, the officers lost their reckoning, and provisions failed. The daily rations were reduced to an ounce or two of salt beef, a pint of water, and a small cake made of flour and skimmings of the pot. Whitefield acted nobly: he was a power in comforting and cheering others. His diary tells of the calm Christian spirit his sufferings bred in him. Here is one passage—

"Blessed be God for these things; I rejoice in them daily. They are no more than what I expected, and I know they are preparations for future mercies. God of His infinite mercy humble and try me, till I am rightly disposed to receive them. Amen. Lord Jesus, Amen. It pities me often to see my brethren, lying in the dust as they have done, these many weeks, and exposed to such straits; for God knows both their bodies and souls are dear to me. But thanks be to God, they bear up well, and I hope we shall all now learn to endure hardships like good soldiers of Jesus Christ."

His return to Georgia was delayed, owing to the great religious revival which originated in his preaching at Kingswood; but in 1739 he returned to the colony, and preached and worked there with much success till the autumn of 1741, so that he was a witness to some of the most difficult and exacting labours the general underwent in a time of war, and his testimony has its own value. We find him writing thus to Mr. Ingham on March 28th, 1740: "How glad I should be of a letter from dear brother Ingham. When shall my soul be refreshed with hearing that the work of the Lord prospers in his hand? I suppose before now you have received my letters and seen my journal. I believe God is yet preparing great things for us. Many at

Charlestown lately were brought to see their wants of Jesus Christ. The Orphan Home goes on bravely. I have forty children to maintain, besides workmen and their assistants. The great Householder of the world does, and will, I am persuaded, nobly provide for us all. The colony itself is in a very declining way; but our extremity is God's opportunity. Our brethren, I trust, go forward in the spiritual life."

The ebb and flow of the wave of Spanish invasion it would be wearisome for us to follow out in full detail. Forts had to be raised, scout-boats kept perpetually afloat, to intercept Spanish cruisers bent on stopping the supplies of grain and other materials to Georgia. Even in the short intervals during which peace was maintained, efforts were constantly made to secure political advantages. We read that at one period the jealousy of the Spaniards was so inflamed, that through their ambassador they demanded that Oglethorpe should be recalled from Georgia. The "London Daily Post" of date says—

"If this be the fact, and there is no doubt of it, we have a most undeniable proof that the Spaniards dread the ability of Mr. Oglethorpe. It is, of course, a glorious testimony to his merit, and a certificate of his patriotism that ought to endear him to every honest Briton."

Seeing that no dependence could be placed on any pledges, the trustees petitioned his Majesty that a regiment might be raised for the defence and protection of the colony. This was granted. Oglethorpe was empowered to raise this regiment, and was appointed General and Commander-in-Chief of his Majesty's forces in Carolina and Georgia.

"This regiment he raised in a very short time, as he disdained to make a market of the service of his country by selling commissions, but got such officers appointed as were gentlemen of family and character in their respective counties; and, as he was sensible what an advantage it was to the troops of any nation to have in every company a certain number of such soldiers as had been bred up in the character of gentlemen, he engaged about twenty young gentlemen of no fortune to serve as cadets in his regiment, all of whom he afterwards advanced by degrees to be officers, as vacanies happened; and was so far from taking any money for the favour, that to convey them he gave, upon their advancement, what was necessary to pay the fees of their commissions, and to provide themselves for appearing as officers."*
"He carried with him also," says another writer, "forty supernumeraries at his own expense; a circumstance very extraordinary in our armies, especially in our plantations; and with a view to create in them a greater interest in the colony and to induce them to become settlers, every man was allowed to take with him a wife, for whose support additional pay and rations were offered.†

* London Magazine for 1757, p. 546.
† Gentleman's Magazine, vol. viii. p. 164.

This was in view of the expedition against Florida, which led to the unfortunate affair of St. Augustine. In a manifesto issued by Oglethorpe on April 1, 1740, he says—

"And I do further declare that whatever share of plunder shall come to me as general and commander of the said forces, I will apply the same totally towards the relief of such men as may happen to be maimed or wounded in the said expedition, and towards assisting the widow sand children of any of the said force that may happen to be killed in the said service; and for the rewarding of such as shall perform any distinguishing brave action. No Indian enemy is to be taken as a slave, for all Spanish and Indian prisoners do belong to his Majesty, and are to be treated as prisoners and not as slaves."

In spite of the utmost care and bravery the attack on St. Augustine's did not succeed, and Oglethorpe's forces had to withdraw. For his conduct in this matter Oglethorpe has been most unjustly blamed and criticised. He failed mainly because Carolina did not act in conformity with her pledges to supply a contingent of 800 men. Instead of 800 veterans, 400 raw youths were sent under Colonel Vanderdupen, from whom no efficient aid was derived. Those who had shared the "burden and heat of the day" in that unfortunate expedition, were the most forward to defend their general. We may listen to one witness and then leave this part of the subject:—

"The great cause of the Miscarriage was the Fewness of our Numbers, the Want of Pioneers, a proper train of Artillery and other Materials, which were promised by the Government of *Carolina*, but never sent. I may also very safely add the Badness of the Forces of that Province, among whom, I am very sure, there were not 250 Men fit to bear Arms, and even these all raw and undisciplined, and very often inclined to be mutinous, most of their officers, like themselves, being only Planters, and in Carolina on an equal footing." *

We have abundant testimony that Oglethorpe's statesmanship did not fail whilst he was overwhelmed with these military and other difficulties. In order that the burden of these harassing conflicts with the Spaniards should press more lightly on the settlers, he set himself resolutely to retrench wherever it was possible. He disbanded the troop of Rangers, who guarded the country on the land side, though they offered to serve without pay; but he deemed it improper that they should be on service without remuneration. The garrisons were relieved by the regiments, so that that expense ceased. He aimed to reconcile the dis-

* The *Spanish* Hireling Detected: Being a Refutation of the Several Falsehoods and Calumnies in a late Pamphlet entitled "An Impartial Account of the late Expedition against St. Augustine under General Oglethorpe. By George Cadogan, Lieutenant in General Oglethorpe's Regiment. 1743.

affected by his good offices. With very timely charity he assisted the orphans, the widows, and the sick; and contributed towards the relief of the most destitute. As the most efficient testimony that could be cited, we may quote a letter written by the German pastor, M. Bolzius, at New Ebenezer, to the Rev. Dr. Francke at Halle, dated 23d July 1741—

"The present War and the Burden of it hath not affected us yet, and we don't feel the least of it; and in the great Dearness the Colony suffered last Year, we have not been in want of necessary Provisions. As to the present Year, we have a very hopeful Prospect of a good Harvest, every Thing in the Fields and Gardens growing so delightful, as our Eyes have seen in this Country before. If *Isaac*, by the Blessing of the Lord, received from what he had saved an Hundredfold, I believe, I daresay, to the great Mercy of God over us, our Salzburgers will get a thousandfold, notwithstanding that the Corn, when it came out of the Ground, was eaten quite up two or three Times by the Worms. . . . Wheat, Rice, and other Grain must be sowed very thin, because each Grain brings forth fifty, an hundred, or more Stalks and Ears. The land is really very fruitful, if the Sins of the Inhabitants, and the Curse of God for such sins, doth not eat it up, which was formerly the unhappy Case of the blessed Land of Canaan. And I am sorry to acquaint you, that I don't find in some of the Inhabitants of the Colony, a due Thankfulness for, and

Contentment with, the many Benefits bestowed on them for several Years together; although those who are industrious, and will labour for their Maintenance, live contentedly and subsist under the Blessing of God."*

While Oglethorpe was thus ardently labouring for the public good, the malcontents of Savannah, under the leadership of a worthless but clever adventurer, Dr. Tailfer, were as busily endeavouring to ruin the province. Their schemes were chiefly directed to the obstruction of a respectable population in the colony, until the trustees should be forced, by its dwindling into weakness and insignificance, to gratify the eagerness of the most worthless of the people for slaves and spirituous liquors, so that they might indulge to the extent of their wishes in idleness and dissipation.

The difficulties with which General Oglethorpe now had to contend were peculiarly onerous and perplexing, not only with the Spanish foes,—with the restless Indians,—with the clamorous settlements,—with discontented troops,—with meagre supplies,—with the defection of Carolina,—with the protest of his bills, and with the refusal of a just naval protection; but the officers of his regiment were at enmity with him and with each other, and crimination and recrimination followed, disturbing the peace, and weakening the efficiency of the military corps.

* Historical Tracts and other Papers relating to the Colonies in North America. Collected by Peter Force. Vol. i.

For the unrest caused by the rumours of Spanish invasion still continued. Oglethorpe was making another great effort finally to attack and disperse the Spanish forces that hovered about the borders and the coasts of Georgia, when welcome news arrived that they had become dispirited and disunited under his well-maintained defence. The troops of Cuba and those of St. Augustine had fallen out and refused to act together, and this led to the complete withdrawal of the Spanish troops in 1742. The Spanish fleet had on one occasion approached very near to Frederica, but by admirable readiness, order, and organisation, was beaten back. Though there were rumours of a renewal of the war in 1743, nothing further came of them.

Thus we see that Oglethorpe, by unceasing vigilance, and by the skilful disposal of small forces, kept the Spaniards at bay. He knew the points at which alone it was possible for them to make entry and overrun the province, and he skilfully concentrated strength on these. For several years amid such obstacles as would have wholly overpowered a weaker man, he withstood assaults without and divisions within; and at length the Spaniards, baffled, wearied out, and wasted in their long-continued efforts, withdrew from the contest, greater losers even than those they had endeavoured to overthrow.

Whitefield writes on this point: "The deliverance of Georgia from the Spaniards is such as cannot be paralleled out of the Old Testament. I find the

Spaniards had cast lots, and determined to give no quarter. They intended to have attacked Georgia; but they were wonderfully repelled, and sent away before our ships were seen."*

In 1744 Oglethorpe was summoned home to answer an impeachment from one Lieutenant-Colonel Cook, relating to his conduct of the war with the Spaniards. Under pretence of requiring witnesses from Georgia, Cook secured delay after delay, much to the trouble of Oglethorpe. When at length the trial did come on, the court sat only two days; and, after a strict scrutiny into the complaint article by article of the nineteen specific charges, the board were of opinion that the whole and every article thereof was groundless, false, and malicious. On the presentation of the report to his Majesty, he was pleased to order that Lieutenant-Colonel Cook should be dismissed the service.

"When I reflect," says one who was an eyewitness of the scenes at the siege of St. Augustine, "upon General Oglethorpe's *great* Qualities, and his indefatigable Zeal in serving his Country; his many hazardous and painful Expeditions (particularly that of the Siege of Augustine, in which he was betrayed and neglected by the mean Carolina Regiment, and many of the Men of War); and his late Glorious Defeat of the Spanish Invasion of *Georgia:* When I reflect on his breaking a good and vigorous Constitution, to render the Persons under his

* Whitefield's Letters, vol. i. p. 467.

Command easy and happy; his extending his compassion to the miserable of all Sorts, and in short his Possession of every Civil and Military Virtue ; I am shock'd, that Envy itself dare mean to taint his Character with its foul Blast. But what Merit is Proof against some foul Tongues and fouler Hearts, when God Himself cannot escape them? . . . From an impartial survey of his actions, the Tendency of which I have perhaps had more Opportunities than most others to contemplate, I can't forbear to say with *Addison*, only with the variation of the Person,—

> ' Oglethorpe's Acts appear divinely bright
> And friendly shine in their own native Light,
> Raised of themselves, their genuine Charms they boast,
> And those who paint them truest, praise them most.' " *

And companion verses appeared at the time in the " South Carolina Gazette "—

> " The fame of tyrants should, if justice swayed,
> Be howled thro' deserts their ambition made ;
> But Oglethorpe has gained a well-earned praise,
> Who made the heirs of want the lords of ease :
> The gloomy wood to plenteous harvests changed,
> And founded cities where the wild beasts ranged.
> Then may the great award assigned by Fate
> Crown her own wish to see the work complete."

---

* A Relation and Journal of a late Expedition to the Gates of St. Augustine in Florida, conducted by the Hon. General James Oglethorpe. By a Gentleman Volunteer in the said Expedition. P. 34.

VI.

Having performed such conspicuous service—done more than any other man to curb the power of Spain in America—Oglethorpe returned home, not to rest and to honour, but to new labours and trials, in order to relieve himself from the encumbrances brought on his estates by the liabilities he had so generously incurred in the public service.

On the 15th of September 1744 he married a daughter of Sir Nathan Wright, Bart., of Charham Hall, Essex, and would probably have retired from the army and devoted himself to his own affairs, had not the rebellion of 1745 made occasion for his services. He took the field at the head of four companies of cavalry, which, out of respect to his former grand achievements, were called "The Georgian Rangers." Especially was he concerned in an engagement near the village of Clifton, where, owing to his failing to force an advance, it was said that he was the occasion of loss, though his friends urged on his behalf that he had only exercised a proper prudence; that if he had advanced in the circumstances, it would only have shown rashness and led to needless bloodshed. This was the view taken of the affair by the court-martial before which Oglethorpe was brought in 1746. The decision, after the most careful consideration, was, as might have been expected, that the necessities of the halt were evident; that it was clear an attack, under the circumstances, would have implied both inhumanity and rashness ; and the General was honourably acquitted. And not only honourably acquitted of the charge which enemies had tried to fasten upon him in order to clear themselves, he was promoted in the army in 1747, sufficiently showing that his superiors and the crown did not cherish any grudge against him. When the British Herring Fishery was established in 1750 he took an active part in it and became one of the council.

He never forgot the causes which, in earlier days, had engaged his mind and heart. He succeeded, in 1749, in carrying a bill through Parliament exempting the Moravians in England from the necessity of violating their religious sentiments by taking oaths or bearing arms.

In spite of his honourable career and his great usefulness, his public life was brought to a close in 1754 by his being defeated in a contest for the representation of Haslemere, which he had represented in Parliament for the long period of thirty-two years.

In February 1765 he received the rank of General of all his Majesty's forces, and for many years before his death was the oldest general on the staff.

The spirit of Oglethorpe's last days was quite in keeping with his earlier life, though now he moved on a less conspicuous stage. He sought out and relieved many who needed aid; he was the intimate friend of the best and wisest men of his day. He exercised a genial and benignant hospitality, and was ready, as he had been in younger days, to aid the ascent of genius striving amid difficulty and discouragement. This, indeed, was one of the ties which bound him in brotherly regard to Dr. Samuel Johnson, who was wont to speak of him with the utmost love and reverence. Boswell, in his own characteristic, gossipping way, tells us of the first kindly contact of Oglethorpe with Johnson—

"One of the warmest patrons of this poem ['London'] on its first appearance was General Oglethorpe, whose strong 'benevolence of soul' was unabated during the course of a very long life, though it is painful to think, that he had but too much reason to become cold and callous and discontented with the world, from the neglect which he experienced of his public and private worth, by those in whose power it was to gratify so gallant a veteran with marks of distinction. This extraordinary person was as remarkable for his learning and taste as for his other eminent qualities; and no man was more prompt, active, and generous in acknowledging merit. I have heard Johnson gratefully acknowledge, in his presence, the kind and effectual support which he gave to his 'London,' though he was then unacquainted with its author." *

We have many glimpses of Oglethorpe in the course

* Boswell, vol. i. p. 140.

of Boswell's Johnson, and in all of them he appears in the most flattering aspect. Johnson, it would seem, was never tired of asking him questions about his earlier experiences in field and camp, as well as about Georgia; and indeed seemed exceptionally anxious to have had it in his power to write a memoir of him. How different might have been Oglethorpe's fame if Dr. Johnson had overcome the General's reserve, and been favoured with those materials for which he asked!

Boswell tells of one meeting, that "Johnson urged General Oglethorpe to give to the world his Life. He said, 'I know no man whose Life would be more interesting. If I were furnished with materials, I would be very glad to write it.' The General seemed unwilling to enter on it at this time," adds Boswell in a footnote; "but upon a subsequent occasion he communicated to me a number of particulars which I have committed to writing; but I was not sufficiently diligent in procuring more from him, not apprehending that his friends were so soon to lose him; for notwithstanding his great age, he was very healthy and vigorous, and was at last carried off by a violent fever, which is often fatal at any period of life."—*Boswell*, p. 296.

This is a specimen of the anecdotes with which Oglethorpe was wont to regale the meetings at Dr. Johnson's—

" The General told us that when he was a very young man, I think only fifteen, serving under Prince Eugène of Savoy, he was sitting in a company at table with the Prince of Wirtemburg. The prince took up a glass of wine, and, by a fillip, made some of it fly in Oglethorpe's face. Here was a nice dilemma. To have challenged him instantly might have fixed a quarrelsome character upon the young soldier; to take no notice of it might have been considered as cowardice. Oglethorpe, therefore, keeping his eye upon the prince and smiling all the time, as if he took what his highness had done in jest, said, '*Mon* Prince'—I forget the French words he used; the purport, however, was—'that's a good joke; but we do it much better in England;' and threw a whole glass of wine in the prince's face. An old general, who sat by, said, '*Il a bien fait, mon Prince; vous l'avez commence;*' and thus all ended in good humour.

"Dr. Johnson then said, 'Pray, General, give us an account of the siege of Belgrade;' upon which the General, pouring out a little wine upon the table, described everything with a wet finger: 'Here we were; here were the Turks,' &c., &c. Johnson listened with the closest attention." *

With Edmund Burke, Goldsmith, and Dr. Warton, also, he was on terms of intimacy. Pope devoted to his praise some well-known lines—

"One driven by strong benevolence of soul
Shall fly, like Oglethorpe, from pole to pole."

---

* Boswell, vol. iii. pp. 217, 218.

Hannah More, in a letter to her sister, thus celebrates her introduction to Oglethorpe, in 1784—

"I have got a new admirer; it is General Oglethorpe, perhaps the most remarkable man of his time. He was foster-brother to the Pretender, and is much above ninety years old; the finest figure you ever saw. He perfectly realises all my ideas of Nestor. His literature is great, his knowledge of the world extensive, and his faculties as bright as ever. He is one of the three persons still living, who were mentioned by Pope; Lord Mansfield and Lord Marchmont are the other two. He was the intimate friend of Southern, the tragic poet, and of all the wits of that time. He is, perhaps, the oldest man, of a gentleman, living. I went to see him the other day, and he would have entertained me by quoting passages of Sir Eldred. He is quite a preux chevalier, heroic, romantic, and full of gallantry."

She remarks of another meeting that Mr. Burke talked a great deal of politics with General Oglethorpe.

Dr. Warton, speaking of Oglethorpe, said, "I had the pleasure of knowing him well;" and, in reference to Pope's well-known couplet, he remarked: "Here are lines which will justly confer immortality on man, who well deserved so magnificent a eulogium. He was at once a great hero and a great legislator. The vigour of his mind and body has seldom been equalled. The vivacity of his genius continued to great old age. The variety of his adventures, and the very different scenes in which he had been engaged, made me regret that his life has never been written. Dr. Johnson once offered to do it, if the General would furnish the materials. Johnson had a great regard for him, for he was one of the first persons who, in all companies, praised his 'London.' His first campaign was made under Prince Eugène against the Turks, and that great general always spoke of Oglethorpe in the highest terms. But his settlement of the colony of Georgia gave a greater lustre to his character than even his military exploits."

General Oglethorpe was, in some respects, advantageously distinguished from common philanthropists; who are too apt to fix their whole attention on a single point, failing to see it in its relation to others, and exaggerating it to such a degree that humanity itself takes testimony against them and refuses to accept their well-meant panacea. Oglethorpe's practical education saved him from this. He has been blamed for irritability and impatience; but he belonged to the class of rapid, originating intellects, who never can keep pace with the purposes that seem to be easily realisable. To such men some impatience may well be forgiven in view of the impulses they impart to others, which else were wanting; and surely the man who showed such contentment amid circumstances of trial and hardship, and carried his great purpose in face of such overpowering odds, cannot be denied some share of the quality of genius which Mr. Carlyle has called patience.

"His great powers," says one, "could not fail to make a deep impression even on those who did not understand his lofty self-consecration and devotion to others. Neither could they help respecting the apostolical zeal which enabled him to despise all ordinary comforts—fording rivers, crossing swamps, sleeping on the ground, and exposing himself to all kinds of hardship for the good of others."

Oglethorpe died in 1785, at the ripe age of ninety-six.

History has been figured as a great Morgue, where the dead lie waiting recognition and an impartial verdict. A few names dwell unchallenged on the lips and the minds of men. They sum up, as it were in abstract, the element, the quality, the great event; some phase of truth is, so to speak, polarised in them, and this suffices for the general need. But the careful inquirer soon finds that, however great, no man stands by himself; that his path was prepared for him; that he cannot be seen completely save in a perspective, which is formed by the figures that surrounded him or went before him. From this arises one of the great difficulties of biography—to isolate, and yet not to isolate too much —to fetch the chief figure forward, and yet not wholly to ignore the influences to which he was indebted and which enabled him to play the precise part that he did. There were reformers before Luther; John Howard and Elizabeth Fry had their forerunners, who, in effect, made their work possible. Oglethorpe was one of these—one of the most prominent and essential of these; and, though it is not intended to lessen by a leaf the laurel of later heroes, yet it is claimed that Oglethorpe deserves more recognition than he has got, and ought to have a fitting monument—the tribute of loyal remembrance—in English minds and hearts. He was politician, soldier, reformer, and founder of a colony, and in all of these capacities he did his country signal service; but in neither aspect would he have claimed the regard we crave for him had he not been first and foremost a philanthropist and prison-reformer.

DAVID ZEISBERGER AND THE INDIANS.

VERY few, we believe, beyond the circle of the Church of the Moravians, or Bohemian Brethren —the "Unitas Fratrum," as it still loves to style itself— have read, far less studied, those " Periodical Accounts of Missions among the Heathen," which are regularly issued in the easily-recognisable dingy-blue paper covers. Yet, beyond most reports, they are richly interesting, and beyond most they carry the imagination to distant places and scenes, fragrant with Christian associations. Before any of the modern missionary societies now in successful operation had been instituted, or British Christians generally had awakened to the necessity of taking practical action in the matter, the Moravian Brethren had established missions in both hemispheres. Their mission to the West Indies was undertaken as early as 1732, and in 1733 the first missionaries went to Greenland. The name and work of Leonard Dober yet survives in several of the West Indian stations, and Greenland still has its New Herrnhut, making us think of many heroic labours. There are stations also in Labrador, in South Africa, in South America, on the Mosquito Coast, among the Indians, in Australia, and in Central Asia—all carried on by men who inherit much of the apostolic spirit which imbued the first founders of the Church. What is perhaps the most remarkable trait in the Moravian missionaries, is the power they have to adapt themselves to the most trying conditions of life, labouring with their own hands as they yearn and strive to bring those around them within the fold of Christ. Wherever they have set foot, they have called beauty and fruitfulness out of sterility, frequently triumphing over the very elements. Mr. Andrew Wilson, in his "Abode of Snow," eloquently tells how the Moravian missionaries have created an oasis amid the wilds of the lower Himalayas. They have made the wilderness (Lahaul is literally 'Wilderness') to blossom as the rose, materially as well as spiritually. Out of the barrenest tracts they have created blooming farms and gardens, and have produced such effects upon the people as, he avouches, are not to be judged by the number of their converts. The immense work done in the far North, as in the far East, with such scanty means and with on the whole so little stir, would be almost incredible did we not know the traditions which they have inherited, and the training which they have undergone. The men of to-day, though not bound hard and fast by dead rules, yet do abide by certain principles long ago developed, applied, and found worthy. Hence, in a great measure, the secret of their success. If we are at all right in this, it cannot be unprofitable to glance for a little at the life of one of their earliest and greatest missionaries—from which we will see how the seeds of the harvest that are now being reaped in many latitudes were sown in the first mission-fields cultivated by the Moravians.

Among the band of devoted men and women who for conscience' sake fled from Moravia, in many cases sacrificing worldly wealth, to seek shelter in Count Zinzendorf's Herrnhut, or "watch of God," were a worthy couple, David and Rosina Zeisberger, who carried with them several young children. The Saxon Government, ill-advised in this regard, soon began to look with such disfavour on the religious settlement, as made its maintenance doubtful, and the Zeisbergers were of the party who went with the noble Nitschmann to Georgia, where, a Church having been founded, our own John Wesley was present to witness the ordination of their pastor, Anthony Seyfert, and thought himself transported back to the times of the apostles, by the impressive simplicity of the act.

The Zeisbergers left behind them a little boy, David, whose diligence and love of study had attracted the attention of his superiors, in order that he might the better finish his education; and this circumstance may be said to have determined to a great extent a very remarkable history. When fifteen years of age, David Zeisberger, having gained the favour of Count Zinzendorf, was taken by him to Herrndyk, a Moravian settlement in Holland, where he was employed as an errand boy. But the rigid rules, the want of sympathy, and the mistrust showed towards him, rendered him very unhappy.

He was sometimes beaten for acts of which he was innocent, and, notwithstanding his resolve to bear with the injustice rather than run the risk of grieving his parents, matters were brought to a crisis by a circumstance which deserves to be fully told, as it is very characteristic both of the rulers of Herrndyk and of the young errand lad. One day a gentleman of rank visited the place, and wishing a guide to Ysselstein, Zeisberger was sent with him, and so won his good opinion that, when parting, he offered the lad a present. David had been forbidden to accept presents, and therefore declined it. "You must take it," said the gentleman. " Keep it to yourself, it is yours !" and pressing the gold into the boy's hand, rode away. Zeisberger was now in great perplexity. "If I conceal this occurrence," he said to himself, "it will be an act of disobedience; if I make it known, and deliver the fee, my story will not be credited." At last he concluded to keep one half, and to carry the other to his employers. But the very suspicion he thus thought to avert, was aroused. "No stranger," said the frowning brethren, "ever gives so large a reward to an errand boy ! You have not come by that money honestly. Hold! we will expose your wickedness!" Two persons took him back to Ysselstein, to find if there was anything in the story. But the gentleman had left; no one knew where he had gone; and Zeisberger returned to Herrndyk, stigmatised as a liar and thief. And, though he had bravely borne the beating with rods, he was determined not to brook this treatment. An opportunity ere long arose for his acting on this resolution.

In these days—that is, in 1737—news did not travel fast; but Zeisberger somehow learned a fact that suddenly settled what had become a pressing problem with him. He had only remained at Herrndyk for some time past, because he did not know where to go, and had no means of transit. It seems that, in spite of what he had undergone, any other place than a Moravian colony never suggested itself to his mind; and to get to his parents in Georgia he regarded as wholly hopeless. The fact he now learned threw light on his mind, and determined his future. General Oglethorpe, who, as we have seen, had a few years before carried his motley band of broken-down debtors and other hopeless persons to Georgia, and had by this time founded not only Savannah, but several other towns, under sanction of the Charter of George II., was then back in England for the second time, arranging various matters respecting the new colony.*

* The General had shown more than ordinary sagacity in laying out the plan. To the fortunate arrangement of wide streets, houses

Zeisberger, once aware of this, lost no time, but with another lad, who, like himself, was discontented, set out for England to beg General Oglethorpe to aid them in getting a ship for Savannah. On hearing their story, the General must have been interested in them, for he procured them passages.

Landing in America, Zeisberger took up his abode with his parents. Many were the privations which he endured here, many the adventures in which necessity compelled him to share, for the settlers lived more like backwoodsmen than aught else; but of still more importance was the influence which Peter Boehler, now the pastor, exercised over the young Zeisberger, as he had done over John Wesley. For months Zeisberger was his only companion in a mission to the negroes in Carolina, and we can well imagine how Boehler would combine practical work with pious inspiriting converse. War caused the Moravians to break up their settlement in Georgia, and a section, the Zeisbergers in it, went to Pennsylvania, where, with Whitefield, they engaged in improving a tract in the "Forks of the Delaware." Bishop Nitschmann shortly after returned from Europe with a commission to buy land in Pennsylvania, and a tract was selected some miles to the south of Whitefield's. The name of Bethlehem was given to the new settle-

built at a pretty large distance from each other, with great squares at proper spaces, the town owes its beauty to-day. See the opening sketch, "General Oglethorpe," p. 46.

ment, and it has been ever since the chief seat of the Moravians in America. Chosen to accompany Count Zinzendorf to Europe, young Zeisberger was full of regrets, because the idea of becoming a missionary to the Indians had already risen in his mind. Just as the vessel was about to sail, the Count noticed his dejection and questioned him, and finding the young man's heart set on so noble an object, he was sent ashore, and immediately made known his determination. From henceforth he was as truly the Apostle of the Indians of the West, as John Eliot had been of those of New England.

The Indian till recently had maintained much of his original simplicity. He was a hunter, a warrior, full of superstitions, and often given to cruelty, yet with a certain frankness and love of truth, which, it is mournful to think, were soon so largely lost by contact with the white man. France already claimed to have control over no less than one hundred and three nations, comprising sixteen thousand four hundred and three warriors, and eighty-two thousand souls, and this claim and the effort to extend her influence led to difficulties ere long. The steady advances of the "pale faces" had caused the Indians to retreat deeper and deeper into the recesses of the western wilderness.

"Around the western head of Lake Erie, in Canada, and Ohio, lived a remnant of the Hurons, or Wyandots; about Saginaw Bay the Ojibways had their wigwams; the waters of Lake Michigan reflected the council fires of the Ottawas and Potawatomies on the east, and of the Menomonies, Winnebagoes, and Kickapoos on the west; the Chippeways—a powerful nation, mustering many braves—were scattered in Canada, along Lake Huron, and south of Lake Superior; the towns of the Sacs, Foxes, and Ottigamies lay between Lake Michigan and the Mississippi, and farther down the river were domiciled the Illinois."

Rome had sent missionaries amongst them, who had worked with but little result. Eliot and Rauch had been more successful; but they had only touched the outer fringe. Zinzendorf had made journeys into native territory, and lodging in a bark hut at Shekomeko, had baptized ten persons—Mohicans or Wampanoags—and had thus formed the nucleus of the first native Moravian Church. Very soon the membership increased; and when Zeisberger, who had described himself as " destined to be a messenger to the heathen," arrived there on his way to the Mohawk valley to perfect himself in the knowledge of the Mohawk tongue, the Church had increased to some sixty-five souls, to whom he preached. Passing onwards, the suspicions of the garrison at Williams Fort were aroused, and the party were detained and questioned, but finally allowed to proceed. At Canajoharie they were well received by the chief of the Mohawks, but had only enjoyed his aid and instruction a few days, when constables arrived bearing the warrant of the mayor of Albany to apprehend them. They were brought back, examined before the magistrates, and remanded to jail, where Zeisberger devoted the time to the study of Mohawk. "We count it a great honour," he writes, "to suffer for the Saviour's sake, though the world cannot understand this." At length, on the arrival of papers, they were released; and a project having been set on foot to transfer the mission at Shekomeko to the valley of Wyoming, Zeisberger was appointed assistant to Bishop Spangenberg, on a visit to Onondaga to negotiate with the Iroquois or Six Nations to whom the territory belonged. This embassy was successful; the Sachems said they were glad to renew their compact with Count Zinzendorf and the Brethren, and they gave their consent. Returning by a new route, the missionaries encountered several dangers, which gave Zeisberger experience in travel, as his contact with the Indians added to his knowledge of their manners. But to their surprise the Indians of Shekomeko refused to move to Wyoming. They were as loath to leave their pleasant homes at the foot of the Stissing, as they were afraid of the savages of the Susquehanna. The animosity of the settlers so increased, however, that a removal was made inevitable, and a tract of land on the Mahony Creek was selected as a permanent settlement. The charge of the mission of which this was to be the centre, was given to Mack, and he, with Zeisberger and some others, proceeded there to lay out a town, which became the historical Gnadenhütten, or "tents of grace."

This accomplished, the board devoted its attention to the founding of a mission at Shamokin, which, with its smithery, had become a kind of centre for the Indians since they had begun to adopt firearms. Zeisberger's fluency in the Mohawk language led him to be appointed assistant there. With others he made explorations in the branches of the Susquehanna, and found the natives being decimated by smallpox and by famine—their sorrow only deepened by their helplessness to render effectual succour. After spending a couple of months at Bethlehem, Zeisberger once more devoted himself to labour at Shamokin, but drunken revelries and bloody brawls were so frequent that he was much discouraged, and on the meeting of the board it was arranged that he should go as interpreter to a Council of the Six Nations at Onondaga, to arrange for sending a mission into the country.

While the Sachems—hindered by the intoxication of some of their brethren—were deliberating, the missionaries resolved to visit the Senecas, and taking a trail west by north, they entered a fearful wilderness full of swamps. Here Bishop Cammerhoff fell ill of fever, and while Zeisberger ministered to him in a village, he was summoned to a conference of the Indians, who, he found, were drunk here also. When he left them, they followed him, and came trooping, yelling, and dancing round the hut where the sick man lay. It needs not to be said that Zeisberger, at risk even of bodily injury or of death, boldly urged them to give up strong drink—but with small result; and as soon as Bishop Cammerhoff was able to crawl, they anew set forth for the capital of the Senecas. Drunken revelry reigned here also; Cammerhoff's fever increased, and the prospect was, indeed, terrible. They were assailed not only by men, but by women, drunk and infuriated. As no good could be done, they escaped, secretly creeping forth from the village during a heavy fog, though Cammerhoff was hardly able to walk. The story of their return is a series of remarkable escapes, as thrilling as any ever chronicled.

"Without provisions and unable to find any game, for it seemed to have disappeared from these hunting-grounds, they suffered greatly from hunger. In attempting to wade across the outlet of Lake Seneca, they missed the ford and were carried into deep water, struggling for their lives. After superhuman exertions, Zeisberger gained the shore; Cammerhoff, whose strength the fever had greatly reduced, sank, and remained so long immersed that his companion gave him up as lost. At last he rose, and almost by a miracle, himself could not tell how, he reached the land. Barely sustaining life on a pheasant which Zeisberger shot, they proceeded to Onondaga."

Arrived there, the news was not encouraging—various difficulties were raised; but, finally, the Six Nations agreed to let any two of their Church come among them and learn their languages. This settled, through many difficulties, they made their way back to Bethlehem, having travelled more than sixteen hundred miles on horseback, on foot, and in their canoes.

Notwithstanding the frightful ravages drink had made among the Indians, the settlement at Gnadenhütten began to have its own effect. A spirit of inquiry had sprung up among the Delawares and other tribes along the Susquehanna; many visitors had come to hear the Word of God, and heathen Indians had even assembled voluntarily to talk of Christ. Zeisberger's one wish was to take advantage of this condition of affairs, and to follow up the news these visitors carried to their own tribes, by penetrating still farther into the wilderness. But various complications led to his being sent at this stage to Europe, where he remained for some time. On his return he found that Cammerhoff was dead, never having recovered from the fever of the swamp. Without loss of time he set off for Shamokin, preaching the Gospel wherever opportunity offered, as he went thither. At Shamokin he laboured for a while, but his heart was with the Six Nations, and as soon as possible he arranged to go back to Onondaga—this time not to study languages chiefly, but to teach and preach. He soon conciliated the Sachems, and so thoroughly secured their goodwill in his work, that great progress was made. His biographer may well say—

"Considering the inordinate pride of the chiefs of the Six Nations, and the suspicion with which the aborigines regarded every attempt of the white men to gain a foothold in their country, the results of the council's deliberations were remarkable, and proved the high esteem in which the Church of the Brethren was held at Onondaga, and the personal influence which Zeisberger had acquired among the same tribes, whose favour the Colonial Government purchased with much difficulty and by constant presents of great value."

Here Zeisberger had full opportunity for studying the ways of the Indians, and, as one wise for God, he made good use of his time. He gained more and more influence over the Sachems, and through their help was able to finish his Iroquois dictionary. He was even adopted into the nations, receiving the name of Thaneraquechta. He made various journeys into the territory of other Indians, in one of which he was severely wounded; the Indians having been encouraged in their onset by a Dutchman, who fancied the missionaries were rival traders,—so that we see similar difficulties to those of our times were sometimes met with then. After a short stay at Bethlehem, made necessary in various ways, Zeisberger returned to Onondaga, where a famine before long broke out. The missionaries took a large share in bringing supplies from a distance, and when, owing to bad food and neglect, various diseases spread, their knowledge of simples stood them in good stead, in spite of the tricks of the native doctors. After a short absence at Bethlehem to attend a great congress, Zeisberger returned, and, with the cordial help of the Indians, succeeded in erecting a large loghouse for the mission. Meanwhile the war with the English broke out, and the Moravians were accused of secret understandings with the French. This idea was made use of, and fomented by agents, till some Indians were led to make an attack on the premises at Gnadenhütten, while Zeisberger, who would most probably have been killed had he been found, was providentially absent. He at once made his way to Bethlehem, reporting this attack, in which the buildings were burned, ten persons killed, and one woman carried away captive.

This was but the prelude to a new series of horrors; the fatal Indian wars followed. During a lengthened period no missionary work could be done, but Zeisberger devoted himself to study, going here and there to stir up an interest in the Indians.

After these wars came the dawn of a new epoch to America and the world. England had been victorious, and America was hers, from the Gulf of Mexico to the ice-fields of the Arctic lands. But the wars had in effect swept away most of the stations that had been founded at cost of so much labour and anxiety. Zeisberger was now despatched on another journey to the Indian country as envoy to Sir William Johnson and Governor Hamilton. It was winter, and the snow lay on the ground. He preached to several settlements of Delawares with decided effect, for he did not cease to be a missionary when he became an envoy, and his heart was strangely stirred within him at once more seeing the Indians. Before returning home he visited two of the stations—Nain and Wechquetank, and from there passed over the Broad Mountains to Wyoming, and from that to Machiwihlusing, where we note that he preached with more than his usual fervour; and that whilst so engaged, one John Woolman, a Quaker evangelist, arrived. A council was called to receive this Quaker missionary, whose name will not soon die. He spoke to the people at first by the mouth of an interpreter, but afterwards feeling his mind covered with the spirit of prayer, he expressed a wish that the interpreting should be omitted. Divine love was shed over the meeting; and when he left he prayed that the great work which Zeisberger had undertaken might be crowned with success.

The meeting of these two men, and the spirit in which they regarded each other's work, their tolerance and goodwill and true Christian fellowship, are such that we may well pause over it, in view of many of the divisions and jealousies of our day.

Before Zeisberger left, the whole town gathered to a solemn assembly, when one Papunhank, "the first prophet Zeisberger had brought into the Church," and another were baptized. But even while these things were being done, what was called the Pontiac Conspiracy broke out with its bloodshed and woe, and led Zeisberger to be recalled, as already Pontiac's spies were visiting the town. He was soon once more in Bethlehem. The war spread, and tribe after tribe were involved in it; so that, though he as soon as possible left Bethlehem, and took up his abode at Christiansbrunn, little missionary work could be done. The settlers "breathed vengeance against the 'Moravian Indians,' as the converts were called, and blamed them for being in league with the savages." These converts had to claim the protection of the governor, which he promised; and for some weeks after he had issued articles to that effect, they were undisturbed; but a band of Christian Indians —men, women, and children—were at last cruelly set upon and murdered, which was the signal for new attacks and outrages of all kinds. Terror and surprise were the rule; there were mobs in the towns—the panic spread, and there seemed no way to end the frightful distress and bloodshed. Zeisberger betook himself to Province Island, where he acted as minister and superintendent, going between it and Bethlehem, and doing all he could for the Indians who, escaping after him, sought his succour. The Assembly voted one thousand pounds to protect the Indians, and it was determined to devote this sum to sending them under escort to Philadelphia. But unforeseen difficulties arose from the authorities of the provinces, through which they must pass, refusing to receive or to recognise them. "This unprecedented pilgrimage of nearly three weeks, undertaken by the Indian Mission and its teachers, through one of the most thickly populated parts of the country, seems to have been permitted by God, in order to establish the glory of His Gospel. The bearing of the converts was so extraordinary, so humble, and yet manly, so clearly the result of the Christian faith which they professed, that the reviler forgot his revilements, and the scoffer looked on amazed. Even their escort of soldiers, among whom were such as had been at Detroit during the siege, and hated Indians with all the bitterness of their past experience, began to show them respect."

Their return was simply the signal for fresh outbreaks. Riot followed riot—Pontiac's cruel warriors were still identified with patient Christian men and women, who had given such testimony of incapacity for the brutal deeds of Pontiac's followers; and the settlers refused to be convinced. The war went on for a while longer; but expectations of French aid were not realised, and without that, the inducements to carry it on were greatly weakened. In March 1765, Governor Penn proclaimed that the way to their own country was now open to the Christian Indians. They accordingly set forth, after having passed sixteen months in Philadelphia, and after having borne nearly one-half their number to Potter's Field. Zeisberger here as always showed all that zeal and prudence which, brightened by Christian self-denial, illumined his life. His one aim now was to keep the Christians together, so that they might not be exposed to the special perils likely to beset those who were but recently heathens in habit and belief, suddenly set free to find homes where they would. It was therefore resolved to found a mission settlement at Machiwihlusing, near to which lay extensive hunting-grounds, with several tracts already cleared. The converts themselves had suggested the choice of this site; and, to their inexpressible joy, Zeisberger was appointed resident missionary, with Schmick for his assistant. Now began his true work, for which he had undergone such thorough preparation. After many difficulties in the journey, through thick woods and swamps, where no greater rate of progress than five miles a day was possible—their journey from Nain having occupied five weeks—they at length reached their destination. Without loss of time, Zeisberger, Schmick, and Papunhank, of whom we have already heard, proceeded to lay out a town. The permission of the Iroquois Sachem at Cayugu Town had been accorded, and though some difficulties arose by and by, these were soon overcome by Zeisberger's signal tact.

"The new town which came into existence rang with the melody of praise even while it was being built. In every place the feelings of the people burst into song. And when they went out to the chase, or fished in the rivers, when they roamed through the woods gathering roots or herbs, the game that they found, the fishes that they caught, and everything that grew upon the ground, seemed given to them by a special act of Providence. 'Behold,' says Zeisberger, as he saw this general happiness, and heard some of his own Delaware hymns echoing through the forest, 'this is making good use of their liberty! Beginning their work in this way, God will richly bless them. Under such circumstances it is joy to be among the Indians.'"

In spite of illness and weakness, brought on by anxiety and the great efforts he had made, Zeisberger no sooner saw the loghouses built, than he began to devote himself to the Indians that visited the settlement, or to those whose grounds lay near it. "It often happens, while I preach," he says, "that the power of the Gospel takes such hold of them that they tremble with emotion and shake with fear, until consciousness is nearly gone, and they seem to be on the point of fainting. As soon as such a paroxysm is over, they generally begin to weep silent tears. We have many candidates for baptism." A code of municipal laws was drawn up, which forbade heathen Indians who came merely for the sake of outward advantage, to build lodges in the town, or traders to stay longer than three days. The appropriate name of Friedenshütten, or Tents of Peace, was given to the new settlement. Friedenshütten very soon excited the admiration of every visitor. It embraced twenty-nine loghouses, with windows and chimneys like the homesteads of the settlers, and thirteen huts, forming one street, in the centre of which stood the chapel, thirty-two by twenty-four feet, roofed with shingles, and having a school-house as its wing. Opposite, on the left side of the street, was the mission-house. The converts had large herds of cattle, and hogs and poultry of every kind. They devoted more time to tilling the ground than to hunting, and raised plentiful crops. They did a considerable trade with the heathen Indians in corn, maple-sugar, butter, pork, &c.

A report having reached the settlement that the Iroquois Council had declared the grant of the site made by the chief Togahaju null and void, Zeisberger was despatched to represent the matter to them. He was received with great honour, assured that the report was utterly false, and invited to visit them at Onondaga again. His work done, he then went to Bethlehem, having concluded that as Schmick could now manage the settlement at Machiwihlusing, he was free to prepare for another exploratory tour on which his heart had long been set. Anthony, a recent convert, and Papunhank, consented to accompany him. Crossing the Susquehanna, they proceeded up the Chemung to its confluence with the Tioga, when they followed it to the mouth of the Cowanesque Creek. Up this they proceeded a day's journey, and then entered a dense swamp. They forced their way through the underwood to the head waters of the Alleghany, through well-nigh impenetrable spruce forests, into regions till then untrod by white men, and even now largely waste. The Senecas here were at first inclined to treat the "pale faces" with suspicion, but whenever Zeisberger said, "I am Ganousseracheri," their whole demeanour changed; showing how widely the news of his goodness had already travelled. When he told the Seneca chief that he meant to make his way to the Indians at Goschgoschuuk, the old man gravely shook his head and said, "They bear a bad character, they are sorcerers, and will not hesitate to murder you. Go not thither." But to this Zeisberger replied, "No harm can befall me if my God, in whom I believe, does not permit it. The wickedness of the Indians there is just the reason why I ought to go and preach to them." And with the chief's serious warnings in their ears they pressed forward.

It is one of the greatest tributes to Zeisberger's influence, that already the news of his work and his love of the Indians had been carried far and wide. In the most remote villages his name was known. In the next Seneca town to which they came they found two old acquaintances, Onondagas, who welcomed them there, and they preached to the people with great acceptance. Even at Goschgoschuuk, which they reached in the month of October, they found friends of Papunhank, who were ready to entertain them. At the earliest moment Zeisberger appointed a religious service, when he spoke with great eloquence and earnestness, telling them that he brought to them the same Gospel as their friends at Friedenshütten had received, and had been made happy by receiving. We are told that his hearers —men who were, above all the Indians, superstitious, wicked, and bloodthirsty—were spell-bound. "Never yet," he himself writes, "did I see so clearly depicted on the faces of Indians both the darkness of hell and the world-subduing power of the Gospel." Next day all the three villages were represented, and a yet more powerful effect produced. In spite of the efforts of some, Zeisberger was warmly invited to establish a mission settlement there. Nothing had as yet produced a deeper impression on the board than his success in this enterprise. It was necessary for him to return to Bethlehem to report and make arrangements with the board, who deemed it expedient that he should spend the winter at Christiansbrunn. But to show that the impression had not vanished from the minds of the people of Goschgoschuuk, in April runners reached Friedenshütten to inquire if the teachers that had been promised were coming. A few days later Zeisberger arrived at Friedenshütten, and, naturally, on account of this message, he hurried on the more quickly to his destination.

In spite of some marked changes for the worse during his absence, Zeisberger set himself resolutely to work, raised a log-building, twenty-six by sixteen feet, about half a mile from the town, round which the converts were to rear their cottages. But they were not allowed to proceed long without difficulties of a special kind.

All the Indians, as we have said, were much given to sorcery; but the Seneca chief was right in saying that the Indians of Goschgoschuuk surpassed all the rest. Zeisberger, who was not "inclined to start at shadows," was compelled to allow the depth of their degradation and superstition. "Some existed," he said, "by whom Satan himself worked, with all powers and signs and lying wonders." He said that he disbelieved the stories he heard of what they could do until several of them were converted. These unfolded to him things from their own past experience, which forced him to acknowledge the reality of Indian sorcery, and to adopt the opinion, which was universal among the early Church Fathers, that the gods of heathenism were not visionary beings represented by idols, but satanic powers and principalities, to worship whom was to worship demons and be under demoniacal influences."

The sorcerers of Goschgoschuuk, like the image-makers of Ephesus, felt that if Zeisberger thus went on gaining influence with the people, their source of wealth and power would be gone. They therefore declared that worms would destroy the crops because there were white teachers in the town, and sent abroad many similar rumours. Other tribes rose up, threatening also. The meetings were disturbed; Zeisberger was threatened and watched by bands of young people, resolved to injure or to murder him. Nevertheless, he and his friends went on preaching, and he even managed to get the people to agree to prohibit the bringing of "fire-water" to Goschgoschuuk.

"Nor was it less an evidence of Christian power in so notorious a nest of murderers that, after the second attempt had been made on Zeisberger's life, those Monseys who attended his preaching held a council, and appointed two of their number to administer a public reproof to the young men engaged in the plot. That God's word was not proclaimed in vain its most vindictive opponents had to acknowledge. Goschgoschuuk separated into a Christian and heathen party. At first the former timidly succumbed to every persecution. By and by, however, it gained courage, and stood forth openly on the side of the Gospel, whilst several of its adherents built themselves huts around the mission-house. The accession of Allessrewi and of Gendaskund, a distinguished head-man, was the crowning triumph of this party."

More and more the Christian party separated themselves from the heathen; and when the hunters of the clan returned from their autumnal chase, they nearly all joined the mission, and the wrath of the heathen was thus excited anew. Feasts and all kinds of attractions were set on foot by them to wile the converts away, but without effect. The persecution at length grew so bitter that Zeisberger determined to remove the mission premises to Lawunakhanck, some three miles farther up the river, not far from a petroleum spring, which was found to be of great value. The Christians removed, the heathens at Goschgoschuuk lapsed deeper into drunkenness and all kinds of wickedness; but Zeisberger did not despair of converting some, and lost no chance of appealing to them, being energetically aided in these efforts by Anthony, of whom Zeisberger at this time wrote, "Anthony is as eager to bring souls to Christ as a hunter's hound is eager to chase the deer." The friendship of a chief, Glikkikan, who had great influence at Goschgoschuuk, proved of signal service now; and in union with other two chiefs, Zeisberger was invited to found a mission at Kaskaskunk, on the Beaver River in Ohio, whither he went. There he founded a town Friedenstadt, or City of Peace, which soon became a centre of great changes. Chiefs who had lived in life-long feud became reconciled, "one haughty war-captain weeping publicly at thought of his past deeds in the presence of his former associates." Zeisberger writes, "This is marvellous! Thus the Saviour, by His word, breaks the hard hearts and humbles the proud minds of the Indians." One of the greatest achievements of the missionaries at this settlement was the appointment of an umpire to settle all differences between the Christian Monseys and the rest, Zeisberger being at the same time enrolled as a Monsey. The Church increased day by day; but in the midst of his success he was summoned to Friedenshütten, where difficulties had arisen. It had been found that the land granted by the Iroquois

Council to the Susquehanna converts formed part of the tract sold to Pennyslvania at the treaty of Fort Stanwix, and Zeisberger, after much consideration, came to the conclusion that the proximity of settlers would be detrimental, and suggested to the board that the unreclaimed wilderness of Ohio would form the best field for the future operations of the Church, and advised the removal of the whole body of converts to that country. Very shortly he was on his way with the first detachment, five families, numbering twenty-eight persons. Having committed the mission on the Beaver to the charge of Jungman, he now went on hopefully with the building of the first Christian town in Ohio. The district chosen was fair and fruitful; the chief had made a grant near the "Big Spring" of all the land from the Gekelemukpechunk northward to Tuscarawas; and in an incredible short time things were in such order that Zeisberger, in spite of the return of ill-health, felt himself free to resume his explorations, in which he took much delight. He visited the Shawanese of the Muskingum, and was well received, though they were one of the most superstitious and perfidious tribes. The religious interest spread even to the Delaware capital. Eckpalawehund, a noted chief, became a convert, and exercised a wise and beneficial influence over his people. Zeisberger at this time made sundry translations of passages of Scripture, and of a liturgical service. Shortly after he accompanied one of the chiefs to New Orleans. In spite of the outbreak of Dunmore's war—a mere pretext for extension of territory, which did great mischief—and the self-interest of the chiefs who had favoured the settlement in the Tuscarawas, in the hope of adding to their influence, and having learned as much as they wanted, now wished to get rid of the teachers, the missions prospered. The chiefs were caught in their own toils, one of their number, "White Eyes," so far the superior of the others that they could not do without him, having resolved to stand by Zeisberger. This chief undertook a circuit of visitation to his brother chiefs, to represent to them the real objects of the missionaries, and to beg for a proper recognition of the Christian converts. He even developed a great scheme of union. So the villages on the Tuscarawas increased, and not only so, but exhibited more and more the lofty ideal of the missionaries.

"They were remarkable not merely as towns built with surprising regularity and neatness, but also as communities governed without the aid of colonial magistrates, by a complete code of laws. In order to administer these, a council was set over each village, consisting of the missionaries and national assistants or 'helpers,' as they were called. In such a council, the influence of the white teachers properly and necessarily continued supreme; but a native element was, at the same time, brought out that reconciled personal liberty, which the Indian prizes so highly, with restrictions tending to the common good. But, from one point of view, perhaps the most remarkable feature of these towns will appear in this, that they were centres of agriculture, and not a collection of hunting-lodges. The chase was by no means abandoned, but it had become a secondary object. To raise grain, cattle, and poultry formed the principal employment of the converts. Their plantations covered hundreds of acres along the rich bottoms of the valley; herds, more numerous than the West had ever seen, roamed through the forests or were pastured in the meadows; while few farmyards in Pennsylvania had poultry in greater variety. Men of judgment and distinction coming from the eastern colonies were often filled with astonishment when they here beheld Indians not only civilised, but changed in all their habits, and growing rich."

Though the revolution was now drawing near, and disturbances were already felt all over the land, Zeisberger went on with his work unmoved. His next great enterprise was the founding of a mission at Lichtenau, on the Muskingum. Papunhank, who had formerly assisted him well in such work, had passed away at a ripe age; but new helpers sprang up, and though "White Eyes" for a time yielded himself to ambitious projects, he soon awakened to his blunder. More distressing and injurious to the mission work were the efforts which the British now made to stir up the Indians—a policy so persistently pursued that by and by the mission stations were nearly all broken up. When all the others, save himself and Edwards, had been withdrawn from Lichtenau, Zeisberger wrote in a letter to the board—

"My heart does not allow me even so much as to think of leaving. Where the Christian Indians stay, I will stay. It is impossible for me to forsake them. If Edwards and I were to go, they would be without a guide and would disperse. Our presence gives authority to the national assistants, and the Lord gives authority to us. He will not look upon our remaining here as foolhardiness. I make no pretensions to heroism, but am, by nature, as timid as a dove. My trust is altogether in God. Never yet has He put me to shame, but always granted me the courage and the comfort I needed. I am about my duty, and even if I should be murdered, it will not be my loss, but my gain; for then will the fish return to his native element."

They were equal to the position. Zeisberger went from place to place, counselling the Indians to be at peace, to refrain from declaring war, and to be guiltless of bloodshed. As soon as the position of affairs would admit of it, he set forth to found three new missions, as the inrush to Lichtenau had overcrowded it. This accomplished, he went to Bethlehem to confer with the board, and found on his return that both Goschgoschuuk and Lichtenau had been destroyed by Colonel Broadhead's soldiery. With immense labour the settlements were restored. But Zeisberger, though now patriarchal, would not rest. He was in danger of death from heathen sorcerers more than once, was more than once taken prisoner, and always displayed the same high heroism. It would be impossible to recount all his brave deeds—his wanderings in peril and solitude, and his constant witness, borne amid all manner of threatenings and privations, to the Gospel of his Saviour. One of the most touching episodes of his later days was the massacre at Gnadenhütten by the heathen Indians, in which twenty-nine men, twenty-seven women, and thirty-four children were barbarously murdered.

"Their death was the beginning of the decline of the mission, but it was also the most illustrious exemplification of what the Church and Zeisberger had accomplished among the aborigines. Their very murderers confessed that by their faith and patience, by their fearlessness and resignation, they had glorified God. Even at this late day the traveller, as he passes through the blooming valley of the Tuscarawas, stops to see the spot where they suffered."

From this date the fire of Zeisberger's zeal began to decline, though he still fought on nobly. He visited the Chippeways, and began a mission amongst them, and led his own remnant farther westward to find a new and a safer home, only, however, to gain further experience of massacre, the horrors of which were implicitly confessed to by Congress when it " made a grant of land to the Christian Indians," as an indemnity. He planted new towns at Detroit, and founded Fairfield in Canada, and Goschen in Ohio; he rallied the scattered converts and pled their cause before those in power. Though the infirmities of age had crept on him—his hearing being impaired and his eyesight dim—he still abode with the Indians and ruled them, dealing decisively with intemperance and rebuking it. As the weakness increased, he felt death was not distant, and, sitting up in bed, in spite of the cramp in his bowels, solemnly bade the mission family farewell. He lingered a few days more, suffering great pain, then passed away peacefully, responding to the singing of the converts by signs expressive of his joy and peace. He died in 1808, at the patriarchal age of 82.

He was learned as well as brave. He translated many works into the native tongues, and composed many hymns and tales. His idea of weaning the Indians from their wild mode of life and attracting them to the labours of agriculture, and settling them in Christian communities, well deserves note, as from the process he followed hints may still be drawn for our missionaries who labour among certain savage peoples. Not only bold, daring, and self-denying, but discreet, sagacious, and reticent, never acting precipitately, and yet never found wanting in a crisis, Zeisberger deserves to rank amongst the very greatest Christian missionaries of his own or of any age.

BASLE INSTITUTE.

Master Missionaries.

p. 118.

SAMUEL HEBICH AND THE HINDUS.

ON Christmas Eve, in the year 1831, the students at the Basle Missionary Institute were surprised in midst of a distribution of Christmas gifts, by the somewhat unceremonious advent of an important looking but rather roughly-attired visitor. He had come right from Finland, where he had successfully discharged responsible duties, in superintending a large estate and a factory, to undergo training for missionary work. He had for some time regarded himself as destined to this field; but one thing after another had arisen to hinder him; and now as he looked round on those who were to be his fellow-students, he must have been struck by their youthfulness compared with his own maturity, as the good Director Blumhardt introduced him to them as "Dear Brother Hebich." Some men might have been so vexed and disappointed at the sight as to feel that it was too late for them to persevere. But Samuel Hebich at no time was afraid to be singular, and in his earliest, as in his latest days, was noticeable for independence and decision of character. He was the fourth son of a Lutheran pastor at Nellingen, a good man, but more eccentric than evangelical, who had caught hold of rationalistic ideas, but believed it well for the sake of the common folk to keep to the old teaching, and who probably exhibited more of the real spirit of his life than he was aware of, when, after his son Samuel's confirmation, he gave him the present of a tobacco-pipe !

The boy was sent in his fourteenth year to an elder brother who had succeeded in business at Lubeck, that he might assist him. Young Samuel did his best to be useful to his brother, and to learn the business; devoting his evenings to make up for deficiencies in school-learning. After three years thus spent, he was bound to a merchant for four years. During this time he became subject to deep religious experiences—underwent Bunyan-like struggles, till suddenly when out walking during a popular festival in 1821 great peace fell upon him. Finding much in the preaching of Pastor Geibel, of the Reformed Church, he left the Lutherans and joined that congregation, and his close study of Scripture, and what his brother regarded as religious vagary, soon brought painful protests.

"Samuel's brother was not a little put out at finding him spending every available quarter of an hour in poring over the Bible. He said he would not put up with all this hypocrisy; and there was a great to-do in the house. Nor was the father less displeased: amongst others, he wrote what his son calls 'a terrible letter:' 'Son, thou hast chosen the downward path,' &c., and finished by subscribing himself 'faithfully your father, a respected Lutheran clergyman, neither a tailor nor a cobbler.' Samuel, who dearly loved his father, had now been parted from him for four years, and was on the point of returning home. As he read this letter, all that he had received from God seemed in a moment gone, a heavy weight oppressed him, and the language of his heart was, 'You foolish lad, you! Barely twenty years old, while your father is over seventy, a learned and experienced clergyman, your brother held in universal esteem, can it be that both these are mistaken and you only right? Surely not!' He adds: 'Sorely I grieved, the day was wild and stormy, I could yet show the spots where, on my way home through the market place, I seemed to hear a voice, 'If thou lovest father or mother more than Me, thou art not worthy of Me.' At once I knew what I had to do; all my father's and brother's reproaches fell off from me like the rain which was then falling."

It should be said, however, that when the lad paid that expected visit shortly afterwards, the father saw that he was really in earnest, and said that he would not maintain his opposition. Samuel was now seized with a strong desire to devote himself to missionary work, and became a member of the Lubeck Missionary Society;

but a friend, whose prudence he trusted, advised him meanwhile to remain at his business; and his indentures having expired, in 1824, he became clerk and traveller to another mercantile house in Lubeck. It was whilst on a business journey for this house, that he made the acquaintance of Madame Lefrén, a Christian lady, who by-and-by invited him to undertake the management of some estates of hers in Finland. In this position he met with great success; but Madame Lefrén sympathised with him in his yearnings towards missionary work, notwithstanding that she was likely, by his obtaining it, to lose a good steward; and she backed his applications to Inspector Blumhardt, by an offer to bear the expense of his training at the Basle Institute. From one cause or other, however, his acceptance was still delayed for more than a year—the desire deepening as his prayers grew more earnest. Thus it came about that the students at Basle, on Christmas Eve, 1831, were set wondering at the advent of a man of the ripe age of twenty-seven, who had come direct to them from Finland.

He was not very successful as a student, we are told. "Hebich has little aptitude for grammatical studies," said his teacher; "probably he would pick up languages more readily, colloquially; he shows, however, much maturity of spiritual judgment, and his conduct and demeanour are excellent." These qualities had soon opportunities for showing themselves—particularly when confederate troops occupied the town, in the strife between town and country. Hebich showed the officers who visited the mission-house through the museum, and took occasion to speak earnestly to them of Christ. In short trips here and there, he was always ready to bear his testimony—to speak or to preach. " In Geneva he heard the preachers Bost and Malan. The latter, at the close of his sermon, came up to Hebich and inquired, 'Who are you? Why do you wish to join us at the Lord's table? Do you love the Lord Jesus?' to which Hebich replied, 'The Lord Jesus is my only hope, my all in all.' Whereupon Malan took him by the hand, saying, 'Be thou heartily welcome, brother!' and kissed him." Hebich continues: " We afterwards spent three hours with him, in intimate conversation; we spoke of the only foundation of all blessedness, and enjoyed sweet communion of spirit. The believers of Geneva have done quite right in separating themselves from the National Church, for the rulers (or, which in this case is the same thing, the State clergy) had forbidden them to preach the Divinity of our dear Lord."

In August 1833 the Act for the renewal of the Charter of the East India Company passed through Parliament, granting the right of entry into India, and residence there, to Europeans of all nations, with the privilege of holding land. This decided Hebich's choice of a field of work, and all that now caused delay was the question of funds. Fortunately, Prince

Victor of Schomberg had been led to interest himself in the condition of India, and in 1834 he gave ten thousand thalers towards the founding of a school for catechumeni. Hebich and two other Basle students, Lehner and Greiner, were selected to open this new field. Hitherto the Basle Society had had no intercourse with India, and were so little acquainted with it, as to be unable to assign a definite station to these pioneers; but they set forth full of hope, with instructions to avail themselves of any suitable offering on the borders of any of the older mission districts in South India; their thoughts more particularly turning to the neighbourhood of the successful Tinnevelly mission. On his way through London, Hebich attended the May meetings, and, owing to some differences between two societies already established in India, representations were made to the Basle Society, and he was instructed to fix upon " some healthy town, between Cochin and Bombay."

Accordingly, Mangalore was chosen as the best point where they might settle and learn the Canarese tongue. During the voyage Hebich's ministrations to the crew of the " Malabar " were so highly beneficial and so much appreciated that we are told the mate, who was afterwards made captain, on his visits twice a year to Cannanore, always gave Hebich the opportunity of carrying on his work of dealing with men, officers, and passengers on board his vessel up to the last moment.

And in that form of prayer, which, though unwritten, had become by force of usage as stereotyped to him almost as a liturgy, Hebich always remembered that ship every Sunday.

On the 14th of October they reached Calicut, and were warmly welcomed by Mr. Nelson, then judge there, who procured them a boat to their destination. There they found a true friend in Mr. Finlay Anderson, the sub-collector, to whom Mr. Nelson had recommended them. The whole coast from Bombay to Cochin was as yet unoccupied; and, looking inland, Bangalore, Bellary, Belgaum, were the nearest stations, each between one and two hundred miles distant. All these stations were within the Canarese-speaking district, and they therefore opened correspondence with the brethren of the London Missionary Society who were stationed there. Greatly did they rejoice, we are told, over the cordial letters of welcome, and over the first Canarese tract received from these stations in reply.

They found the races so mixed that they decided it would be necessary for them to master another language besides Canarese. It was therefore agreed that Lehner should devote himself to Konkani. In December they entered a hired house on the hills, where they worked away undisturbed, with two native teachers. The population of Canara at that time was estimated at 20,000 Roman Catholics, 651,000 Hindus of various castes and sects, and 46,000 Mohammedans. The English in the station itself numbered about 18; they were visited twice in the year by a chaplain from Cannanore; so they begged to have divine service on Sundays.

Hebich soon found himself at home in his new sphere; but he was sadly dismayed when he was told that he had better not begin anything for two years. Never, perhaps, was the patience of man more severely tried; he was consumed with pity for the idolaters around him, and was eager to speak to them of Christ. The Roman Catholics, he says, were in almost as deplorable a condition as the heathens, having retained caste and most of their heathen habits. The Bible was absolutely forbidden to them. It was, therefore, very hard for him to wait. Action of some kind had always been necessary to him, and never more so than now. He hit upon a happy way of relieving his depression.

Correspondence with the brethren of the English mission stations led him to desire to see their work; and he therefore set out in October 1835, travelling in a palanquin. He first visited Cannanore, then Mysore, Bangalore, and Bellary, where Mr. Hands had founded the first Canarese mission in 1810. Here he spent three happy weeks, and then pursued his way towards Harrihar, which had been recommended to him as very suitable for a mission; but he preferred Hubli, the next station to Dharwar.

What he had seen made him sure of one thing—that they must "go out among the people." This was now his aim, and, accordingly, a house was taken near to the bazaar, which was constantly visited. Then a Canarese school was built, and the parents were waited on and urged to send their children. It was uphill work; but Hebich writes—

"What a joy it is, when we feel all the difficulties of our way, and remember that it leads heavenwards! In all the press of work that comes upon us, all seems at times only darkness before me, but I press on in the Lord's name, and lo! a ray of light shines through my night, and with that light come strength and courage for the contest. Many consider me a fool or an enthusiast; others say, nay, but I am a pious man. But what avails the judgment of men unless we have the seal of God, the witness of His Spirit in ourselves? The Lord acknowledges my weak efforts, and that humbles me."

The work was persevered in faithfully; but he needed all the heartening and strength to be derived from such considerations as the above extract refers to, as our readers will acknowledge in thinking over the following:—

"'We do not want you here,' a high and mighty Brahman once said to the missionary. Pelting with stones or with filth became almost a matter of course, till one day Hebich roundly rebuked a lazy policeman who was looking on unconcerned, and after much consideration, Mr. Anderson gave a hint to the police that when they happened to see such disorderly conduct they were to put a stop to it. It would have been too unreasonable to tell the police that they were to be on the look-out for such disorders. When the Brahmans asked whether the Government had ordered them to preach, Hebich replied, 'No! but the God of heaven and earth alone has commissioned me to do it.' Then a Brahman held up four nails which he happened to have at hand, exclaiming, 'A God who was nailed to a cross with nails like this!' a piece of wit which was rewarded by loud applause from the crowd. But when Hebich, in full earnest, threatened them with the wrath of God, telling them that they were deceivers of the people, and calling heaven and earth to witness that he was only speaking the truth, which they themselves would have to acknowledge when perhaps too late—these wiseacres and witlings shrunk away home. From this time forth a certain intimacy was established between the missionary and the inhabitants of Mangalore. They were freely visited by men of the highest castes, and on the other hand they found their way into the cottages of poor palm-climbers and fishermen. . . . Meanwhile the English residents induced Hebich to undertake a new line of work; they had a poor-fund, with a monthly income of about eighty rupees, of which he became the manager. This involved a weekly distribution of rice to paupers; and the care of a number of lepers and cripples, gathered in a poorhouse near the gaol; these opportunities were used for preaching the Gospel to them. Hebich divided his evenings between bazaar-preaching and the schools; thus, as much as his knowledge of Canarese would allow him, dealing in one case with those still far off, and in the other, by lamplight, to those who had already been drawn somewhat nearer."

A reinforcement of four brethren having been sent out from Basle, Hebich at once proceeded vigorously to dispose of them by planting them at the points most available. With H. Mögling from Wurtemberg, he proceeded by Goa to Dharwar, where he began a great work, which necessitated his very soon being joined by two of those who had come out from Europe with him. One trait, which in spite of some eccentricity and reserve in council, Hebich had in common with most of the great organisers and leaders of men, was the gift of discerning what a man was fit for. His judgment in the settlement of Mögling amply justified itself, in spite of one error on Mögling's part, which shall be referred to by and by. With them, before returning home, Hebich visited Hubli, and decided that very soon it must become the centre of a new mission.

"Hebich," we are told, "set out alone to travel slowly towards Mangalore, preaching to the heathen by the way. He received a letter from the collector of Dharwar, warning him of possible danger, and begging him to be very guarded in his intercourse with the natives; but he did not allow this to hinder him in delivering his message. The collector in his letter urged him to be particularly careful not to speak of the vanity of the heathen gods. His comment was—'Poor fellow! he knows nothing about what I preach; but I have God's Word to declare, and I dare not keep silence. Amen.'"

The insurrection, which shortly after this arose, filled Mangalore with soldiers. Hebich became only the more convinced of his call to declare God's Word to English as well as to heathens. Some friends represented to him that there was great danger of falling into by-paths, and that to the heathens only should he look.

"Am I a servant of God for the heathen only, and not rather for all men?" he urged in reply. "I feel that the British have claims upon me; first, because our way is opened to the natives by the fact that God has committed this country to them; secondly, because God bestows upon us unnumbered benefits through their rule; thirdly, because our mission could never have attained its present state but for their liberality. And shall nothing be done for them in return? In their case it has been found true that we ourselves have been the first to enjoy the fruits brought forth by our own kindness. . . . Yet we may well be thankful for the warning against all wandering in by-paths. If, at a station where there is no chaplain, we missionaries give the English a weekly service, it is no more than we ought to do. If the heathen have a mind to be saved, there is no lack of opportunity for them to hear the word. Of course, we must not allow such occasional services to keep us back from preaching-tours. For myself, so far as I can perceive the Master's will, I should not grudge to give up a month or two every year to work among the English."

In the end of 1836 several men of lower caste were baptized; in the beginning of 1837 there were twenty-two boys in the orphanage; building operations went on vigorously; and the brethren were ceaselessly itinerating and preaching in country places. In July, to Hebich's great joy, both the Canarese teachers and three palm cultivators asked for baptism and broke caste, in spite of what they had to suffer from their relatives. The new station at Hubli had to be organised, and thither Hebich went. He even prevailed on Mr. Mills, the collector, to grant a site, and preparations went on apace. Meanwhile, at the festival of the goddess at Sandidi, he camped out, like the rest, in the open field, living among the people as he had never done before. Here he preached and conversed, and produced a powerful effect. Returning to Hubli, and finding that building could not commence for some time, he set out on another missionary tour, going to Püttoor, Coorg, Chinnapatam, Bangalore, and Chittoor. In the course of this journey various remarkable adventures befell him, and he had some original encounters both with Europeans and with natives. At Mercara we learn that his horse fell with him.

"The accident might have been serious, but from that moment, even when in suffering, he was able to testify boldly. His principal opponent was an officer of engineers, who, denying any freewill in man, sought to cast on God all the responsibility of sin. Hebich one day forced him down into a chair, saying (to convince him that he had the power to sit or rise), 'Sit you there!' A lady once said to him, in the presence of her husband, a surgeon and philosophist, 'You do preach such terrible things!' to which the husband remarked, 'Well, I am able to laugh at all Mr. Hebich tells us.' 'Yes,' said Hebich, 'you laugh now. Wait till you come to your deathbed, and then tell me where the laugh is.' Thus, in the houses of the gentry, he had what he styles 'lively encounters,' but he was also diligent in seeking to lead the ill-educated half-castes into the doctrine of justification, on which important doctrine he says he found the people very badly grounded. He had the joy to baptize a few of these in the regiment stationed there, who had been moved to earnestness by his ministry, and thus to constitute a little church, which he put under the care of the apothecary."

At Chittoor he hired a bullock-cart, and in it he passed slowly from village to village, declaring the glad tidings.

"In this fashion he reached Nandidroog, where he was exposed to a peculiar danger. A Mohammedan state-prisoner was confined in a hill fort at this place, who invited Hebich to visit him. During the interview the missionary taxed the Koran with falsehood; whereupon the Mohammedan first threw his slippers at him, and then ran at him with a drawn dagger; a precipitate retreat over the slippery granite rocks alone saved his life. On another occasion he was pelted with stones; but these were rare exceptions; for the first declaration of the truth generally met with a glad hearing: at times also only with a stare of stupid astonishment."

At Toomkoor Hebich learned that Mögling, who had gone to Mangalore to take his place, had been caught in the toils of self-will, and that the mission was threatened with danger. Warnings from another quarter had, however, sufficed to bring Mögling to a sense of his danger before the evil was irremediable. Hebich hurried to Dharwar, and, like a true bishop and missionary, wrote to him from there such a letter as not only restored its old harmony and prosperity to the mission, but brought Hebich and Mögling into yet closer union.

Far from being an ascetic, Hebich had frequently to protest against a tendency to it in his fellow-workers. When he first began to fear that there was too great a bias that way amongst his associates at Dharwar, he wrote to them in the most sensible terms. They were thinking of purchasing a house, and had, as he thought, underrated or ignored considerations of their own health and comfort, and thus he protests—

" I would certainly not do without the verandah; and

especially do not cramp yourselves too much for room, it will only be a loss in the end. I have learnt some lessons from my own experience in building; I often wax warm over it; but when my courage is ready to fail, the Lord lifts me up again, and the work goes on all the more cheerily. Even in such dull work He ever makes me 'more than conqueror.' Again I hear that you deny yourselves the Lord's good gifts, such as butter, milk, sugar, &c. Now I do not mean to lord it over you; do as you judge right; let me only say, Be wise, enjoy with thankful hearts any refreshment you can fairly attain to; our Master is not so poor as to grudge these things to His servants; in India a more strengthening diet is needed than in Europe: I write this only out of affection, so forgive me!"

His stay in Mangalore was now drawing to a close. He felt that the mission there would be left in good hands, and that he could move to a new field. His attention was therefore turned to Cannanore, whither he went, and repeated, with some variations, the Mangalore story. The town, which lies along the sandy beach of the bay, east and south from the fort, is solidly built, but the streets are narrow and dirty. The population, as at Mangalore, is very mixed; but there is here a large proportion of Mohammedans—a peculiar tribe of Mapilas, the chief men of which are merchants, claiming princely authority. Up till this time Cannanore had been looked after by brethren from the Basle mission stationed at

Tellicherry, who paid monthly visits; but no great result had followed, and matters had fallen into confusion, when Hebich began duty in it. At first he was commissioned only for a few months to set things in order; but, seeing that a great work had been begun, all connected with the missions agreed that it would be well for him to stay. Very soon he had drawn converts from various classes. His apt replies, his affability, his unwearying endeavours, his original and quaint way of illustrating spiritual things, captivated the natives.

"One of the devices by which he sought to explain to them the incarnation of Christ, was to use a large copper coin and a silver rupee of the like size. He covered the silver coin with the copper one, and held it up to view. Naturally each one judged that it was copper only, of no great worth; but then he slipped the copper aside and showed what was underneath it—the silver, the Divine nature. The same coins served also to show the justification; the sinner's worthlessness being covered by the righteousness of Christ. Then the silver only could be seen, the great value of the Divine nature, though behind it ever was the old copper, the still sinful and worthless human nature. And he never rested till the poor obtuse Tamul women, full of notions of the law and of their own righteousness, began to see something of the mind and counsel of God."

In this way he wrought hard amongst the native population, not forgetting Portuguese and Indo-Britons, who, he declared, "need help, and whose influence on the people is not inconsiderable." He sought so to preach in the little Tamul church as that it should grow both in mind, power, and in members. He had not often the privilege of baptizing any of the Malayalas; yet, from that caste sprang a Nayer youth named Krishna, about eighteen years of age, who afterwards became his much-beloved Timotheus. Among the inmates of the poorhouse were many Malayalas, to whom he constantly preached, and some of whom were baptized. Of that work he records, "There is nothing there to please men." A Malayalim school, which was tried, was filled with one hundred children or more, and prepared the way for access to the people of the land.

One trace of his influence with the English residents we get in the following paragraph :—

" He strongly urged the importance of the women being taught to read as well as the men, and tried to make a beginning, but was soon brought to a stand. He found the people so filthy, that he had to give most of the women a garment in which they might decently appear at divine service. An English friend supplied the necessary funds for this. A chapel, at no great distance from the European barracks, was also given to him for the use of the mission. The chaplain added the gift of a small schoolhouse. It was arranged that, under the supervision of Mr. Gundert from Tellicherry, two catechists, who had been sent from Tinnevelly, would have the care of the church and school; but they were very inefficient, and had ultimately to take to other employments."

Hebich was therefore once more thrown on his own resources, without any efficient aid. But he did not fall down hopelessly because others failed in rendering the assistance he had expected of them. He visited the bazaars, preached in the streets, had preaching-stations in the bullock-lines among the artillerymen. "Poor fellows, weary of the service of sin," he says, "came in ever-increasing numbers to the chapel, which was so invitingly near to the barracks."

Many came at first to the services out of sheer curiosity and idleness, and indulged in a good laugh at the strange pronunciation and unusual manner of the preacher. But yet many also found an attraction in him—found that they could learn from him and be interested in him. His biographer tell us that—

"A Scotchwoman, a soldier's wife, declared that she had never understood any one so well since she left Scotland. Men hitherto known as drunkards and debauchees were converted, and became changed characters; and soon Hebich's name was in all mouths. . . . The English soldiers once asked him to preach at their anniversary temperance meeting. He thought this marked out his duty, to forego the use of beer and wine. It must be remembered that he often had to do with drunkards; and he found that in their case total abstinence was the only way to keep them from backsliding. He also strongly recommended his 'children,' whether officers or privates, not to hesitate about giving the only example that could be easily understood in this matter. He kept to this so long as he remained in India, and found the advantage of it."

One of the pleasures of his life was to pay a visit to the brethren at Tellicherry. "When Hebich felt some burden heavy upon him he would often ride over, sometimes even in the night, to talk matters over. More frequently he sent over boys and girls who had come under his influence, for the advantage of the Tellicherry educational establishments. At first he had not been careful to add schools or any means for regular instruction to his own station." And he adopted very politic and effective measures to stop the fatal impurity that prevailed both among Europeans and natives. He had been so successful in training natives to assist him in the work that we find him, in 1843, writing to the Home Committee, that "not only were he and his native helpers equal to maintain this peculiarly constituted station, but that he could even extend his line of work—and was he not even doing so at that moment in the direction of the fishery village of Tai? In so confined a field a second missionary would find it hard to work by his side. For his part he was now so bound in spirit to these dear souls, that he could no longer undertake distant journeys. Should he die at his post, one of the older brethren should take his place. A novice would never get on in work among the mob of this place."

But in spite of this, before another year, he was earnestly engaged in the establishment of out-stations, into which he went with all his wonted vigour, making deep impressions, and having conversions to record in many places; then he devoted himself to a course of visitations of the heathen temples at the times of festival; he instituted a mission at Angerakandi, and another at Palghat, where he was when the mutiny arose. Indeed, as the direct results of his labours, a great revival broke out in one section of his district, of which much might be said.

The following extracts will give an idea of Hebich's trials during these visitations—

"At a place called Cherukunu, near the high road to Mangalore, a steep hill, crowned by a temple dedicated to Kali, rises out of an extensive plain. On the 15th of April 1846—that is, just in the hot season—Hebich, having sent on his servants to pitch his tent during the night, arrived there. He was suffering much from boils at the time. The early devotions of the little Christian band were disturbed by angry shouts. A man came, and angrily declared that Hebich had no business to pitch his tent on the sandy spot which had been chosen for the purpose; it was his property. The head man of the village was sent for to settle this dispute, but he could nowhere be found. It was with difficulty that the peace was kept till mid-day. Afterwards, when Hebich, standing under a tree, began to preach, the youth of the place tried to drown his voice with their yells. They next began to pelt him with sand; then, suddenly the whole crowd rushed at the tent, cut the ropes, and tried to trample it and the Christians it sheltered in the dust. With difficulty the tent-pole was held upright, while the crowd without were shoving and striking it. This combat around the tent lasted for two hours. At six o'clock the tom-tom sounded, and some guns were fired, calling to the great sacrificial procession. An elephant took fright and shied at the tent, and the crowd went off after him. But Hebich had had enough of it. No sooner thus left to himself than he packed up hastily, and made the best of his way home to Cannanore, where he arrived at eleven o'clock at night. He truly rejoiced in bearing the cross. Though, as he called himself, 'a dull and unskilful and sinful scholar in the school of Christ,' he counted it all joy to be allowed to suffer shame for the Holy One. However, he never again visited this 'devil's place.'

"Once in 1847, while Hebich was praying, preparatory to preaching during a minor festival at Cherikal, the people attempted to drive the village cattle violently against him; but they failed in their effort, the cattle running off in all directions. The collector of Malabar, at that time, was a noble-minded man, anxious to prepare the way of the Gospel; though also, and naturally, anxious to do so with all caution. Hebich spoke to him about all these interruptions, saying that should he even be killed during his ministry he did not personally wish that any one should be held responsible for it; that none of the collector's police could prevent this, unless God Himself restrained the people. All that he desired was that the ringleaders should be sharply cautioned; for, in all these cases it was invariably one or two rascals who, exciting the mob, were really to blame. This the collector consented to do, and, thanks to a few private hints to the lower officials, things went on much more quietly at the principal festivals."

Hebich, after a time, had had so often to lament the languidness of the native catechists that we are not surprised to meet with this record in 1845: "I must confess that even the best catechists do very little. They have not as yet sufficient courage or *push* to go boldly among the heathen, or even to visit them in their houses. The natives have a rough manner, as though they would devour the catechist; and will not listen to him, and he is at once silenced. Yet, keen and unscrupulous as the natives are in the things of this world, no sooner are they converted than they stand as frightened, helpless sheep. It is only the actual presence of the missionary that gives a native catechist any courage."

Mögling, in order to meet the difficulties that had arisen from this cause, had set himself to inaugurate a system of European training which should have the effect of instilling more of independence into the native converts. This idea seems to have suggested to Hebich the possibility of making use of some of his European converts, more especially those in the several regiments that had visited Cannanore. He would so far as he could transform them into natives, and thus have an order of genuine assistants with European persistency, but with native habits and modes of thought, to preach and to itinerate. It was a bold idea, but not in every respect a prudent one. It is surprising that it turned out so well as it did. "If he," said Hebich, referring to that plan of Mögling's, "is about to turn an able native into a European, why should not I seek out Europeans of a suitable spirit and turn them into natives?" He had already, as he thought, the proper material: two soldiers, who had recently been converted, and who had devoted themselves, body and soul, to the service of the German Evangelical mission. These he now made to bind themselves even in case of sickness, not to return to England, or to go elsewhere, but to die where God had placed them; never to aspire to be aught but a Christian catechist; to marry, if they did marry, from among the native sisters; and to live in every respect as natives in food, dress, &c.

The discharges of these two—an Englishman, Joseph Searle, and an Irishman, George O'Brien—were accordingly bought, and they were set apart for this work, and others by and by were added to their number.

Some of these failed and went back—as, in midst of so many temptations, was to be almost expected—but O'Brien was firm and true. For years he worked in Palghat and obtained great influence. We read that, on one of his visits there—

"Hebich was pleased to notice that this warmhearted and somewhat impulsive Irishman of his was able to find admission without reserve into all circles. With nice tact he attended scrupulously to the minutiæ of Malayalim etiquette; using in his addresses to the higher classes those titles to which each rank considered itself entitled. O'Brien worked the station well. He was indefatigable, travelling about from market-town to market-town, to preach to the inhabitants. He was, however, not sufficiently careful about his own health. During the first year of his stay in Palghat, he had to be invalided at Coimbatore hospital for liver complaint. His desire was so strong to be out among the thousands who were still ignorant of Christ, that he was slow to adopt the necessary precautions against an Indian climate. As the congregation consisted largely of Tamul domestic servants, he learned that language from his brother-in-law, to be able the better to minister among them. He quite won the affections of the drummers and musicians of the regiment. One of the officers tried to counteract this by getting up a cricket-club; but this had only a very partial success. He even gained access among the Roman Catholics. From his childhood he had been familiar with Romanism; but meeting one day a procession carrying an image of St. Sebastian, to avert an outbreak of cholera, he was stirred to protest vehemently against the undisguised idolatry of Romanism in India. Of course, the priests warned their flocks against associating with the heretic; yet not a few from their fold appreciated the better pastures to be found in the interdicted pages of the New Testament."

Another of these soldier-catechists was Stocking. He had served in the 94th Foot, and was settled in Taliparambu; and prosecuted with considerable result many tours in the regions round about. A savage tribe, known as Mavilars, was especially taken in charge by him. To him, in a large degree, was due the marked change which by and by appeared in Taliparambu, and justified Hebich's strong conviction that "the richest harvest among the Malayalim people would be gathered in here!" The heathen soon began to feel and to acknowledge that ground was being gained. "One day," we are told, "a Brahman, after standing awhile watching the progress of the new building, exclaimed to the catechist, 'Well, we have stirred up everything to oppose your padre, but he has conquered. But now if you come to live here among us we will meet you on friendly terms, and deal fairly by you, but you must not tell us to become Christians.'"

But of all the European converts undoubtedly the most notable was Gompertz, a young officer of the 10th

Regiment, which came to Cannanore in 1850. Gompertz, who was of Jewish parentage, heard Hebich preach, and good impressions that had been left on hearing Bishop Dealtry were confirmed, and his resolution strengthened for the Christian life. After that, his whole heart was with the mission—he devoted all his spare time to aid it. Hebich's biographer may well head the chapter describing him as "a worthy son," for he was devoted to Hebich, and was prepared to sacrifice time, comfort, and money for his sake. The chapter on Gompertz reads like a passage from some religious story.

"To that of his words he added the testimony of a happy, simple, childlike walk — not, however, lacking manly firmness. Even unwilling observers were taken with it. His comrades would say, almost peevishly, 'We should like well enough to be like you, but it is not so easy for us. With you, you have but to will, and all goes smoothly.' Yet how little did even those who saw most of him really know him. What knew they of the battles won in the secret of his inmost heart? of the yearning desire ever to stand faithful and pure before his God, that he might ever present himself as a reasonable sacrifice to his God? To such as were truly in his confidence, he often confessed how pained he was at his own inconsistent walk: 'Though the world may not perceive it,' said he, 'I see it every minute that I live.'

He carefully avoided intruding upon what appeared to him only appropriate work for those regularly in the recognised ministry of the Church. It was only in his later years, and when circumstances seemed specially to point it out to him, that he would hold meetings for edification. He preferred confining himself to simple reading of the Word and prayer. In familiar conversation, all flowed from him so simply, freshly, and affectionately, that no one could accuse him of sermonising. If others had so much to say about horses and dogs, about military manœuvres, about politics, why should he have nothing to say about that one subject which was of the greatest importance to himself and to his hearers? He seemed by a special instinct to find those who were groping towards the truth, and would encourage them onward and upward. Many a one will thank him through eternity that he so patiently and perseveringly cared for his soul. An officer, who began his military career in Cannanore, writes, 'I can truly say that I never met an officer who maintained so holy and consistent a walk, none who so adorned in all things the doctrine of God his Saviour, as dear Gompertz. Under God, he was the means of bringing me to a saving knowledge of Jesus. I have cause to thank God, as long as I live, that I ever met with him.'"

At Maliapooram Hebich made so many converts amongst the officers and men of the 39th Madras Native Infantry, that the regiment came to be called "Hebich's

Own." Colonel Budd, Captain Sweet, and Captains Kerr and Hart, are names that particularly figure in the accounts we have of the work. In reviewing the year, Hebich writes—

"This year, 1853, has been especially fruitful in the conversion of officers and ladies, and perhaps it has been the most remarkable in this way of any year of my ministry. Some were won to the Lord only on their passage through the place, as, for instance, a lady passenger in the ship 'Owen Glendower,' while the ship lay at anchor in our roads. Then a lady (Mrs. S.) was, with her daughters, awakened by the sudden death of her husband. The reports, too, from 'French Rocks' sound well. During a visitation of cholera the brethren engaged one of our people to preach constantly in their own chapel and in the streets, so as to take advantage of the solemnising impression while it lasted. Counting the drummers, there are thirty-eight of them, and all in the fervour of their first love."

We are told further that when Bishop Dealtry visited French Rocks about this time he was agreeably surprised at the life and activity he found prevailing in the school. "He had imbibed no little prejudice against Hebich and his doings. He had been told that Hebich called the Church of England a 'Devil's Church.' (This originated in Hebich's manner of characterising as 'the Church Devil,' that spirit which he found in so many, which, under cover of a certain churchiness, resisted the simple following of Christ.) Invited to the mess dinner, the bishop found that, spontaneously and quite naturally, the conversation took a religious turn. Even those officers who were unconverted, respectfully gave in to the prevailing tone. At the close of the evening, a Bible was laid before the bishop, with the request that he would read the Scriptures and pray with them. He asked whether this was always done, and was surprised to learn that it was the regular custom. With a beaming face, he exclaimed, 'This is indeed something quite new in any part of India.'"

At length, Hebich found Cannanore in such a condition that he felt free to devote himself to itinerating. Travelling from place to place he found to be exactly the work for him. All the rest thought the same, and Mögling wrote a very touching letter, expressing his delight that Hebich had yielded himself completely to this mode of evangelistic labour. In 1856, when he took a retrospect of his work, this he records as his own conviction. But he had to acknowledge at the same time that he had no longer the ability to be constantly on the move. He now felt often weary and unstrung; so that after each journey, rest seemed the more welcome. He continued to persevere, however; and year after year making more unmistakable upon him the tokens of age and weakness.

In 1860 he had to acknowledge that he was waxing too weak for work in India, and reluctantly returned to

Europe. He was employed for some time preaching to the Germans at various famous watering-places, and was in London on that work during the Exhibition in May 1862. Before long, he found that even this told too severely upon him; he elected instead to receive a small pension, and to be free to preach or not as he might feel equal to it. But after this we find him now at Stuttgart, now in the Rhine provinces, and again in Switzerland, where he never grew weary of proclaiming Christ; and whenever opportunity offered, he would urge the claims of his scheme for an establishment for training itinerant preachers for India and Africa, collecting considerable sums by this means. So he went on, ripening day by day, like a shock of corn, till in May 1868, having been seized with pain in the liver, he passed peacefully away. As his mind wandered the night before he died, he fancied himself still preaching to the Hindus.

We have aimed less at giving an exhaustive and detailed account of his labours—which indeed was impossible in our space—than at conveying to the reader some idea of the spirit which actuated him. In this we hope we have so far succeeded. He was bold, zealous, single-minded in the service of the Master. Well did the "Madras Times" speak of him even in 1844 as "that indefatigable man, who by his affability makes substantial progress," for his great idea was to be as one of the people to win some. Like William Burns, and one or two other great missionary pioneers, he liked to work alone rather than in association, and did not always give to those associated with him the impression of running smoothly in harness with them; but he struggled bravely to overcome this defect. And, as has been said, it must not be supposed that he was cold and ascetic in temperament. He was the very reverse; but he had subdued all passions and impulses to one aim. He had foregone marriage, not because he had never loved, or was incapable of passionate attachment—for his early love-story is striking in that respect —but because he felt that *for him and for his work* the celibate life was best. Others were blessed and cheered with the thought of loved ones to follow them, and he never looked sourly on such hopes—nay, when the hopes had become realities, he accorded to the wives of his fellow-workers the kindest consideration and often tender aid. But for him, he was wedded to one service —to preach the Gospel was the one duty and the one call of life; and his biography is memorable because it shows how consistently he struggled, and how near he came to realise his ideal.

WILLIAM ELMSLIE AND KASHMIR.

IN the year 1840, a little boy of eight might have been seen running along a London street, with tears in his eyes, and now and then stopping eagerly to ask a passer-by a question. His Scotch tongue does not help him. But he is resolute in what seems a hopeless quest, and does not give over because of one or two rebuffs. At length one man listens to him patiently, and questions him with care; the joyful result being that he is directed to the place of which he is in search. It is a doctor's house. Both father and mother—who had only recently come to the great city from Aberdeen, and are consequently strangers—have fallen ill of fever; the one servant girl has run off in terror, and the boy is seeking to find the doctor who had been at the house before, though he does not so much as know his name. He returns successfully, however; and the parents are prescribed for. But the boy himself is next taken ill, and, only after terrible trials, do the little family, minus the savings they had taken Londonward with them, return to their native place. This incident of the search for the doctor indicates a great amount of seriousness and resolution in a mere child, and no doubt the recollection of it had also its own effect. At all events, his after life was so wholly in keeping with it—so full of quiet self-help, self-consecration, and high regard for the good of others—that we are quite sure our readers will agree that, though Dr. Elmslie died ere half the tale of his years, he deserves to rank among model missionaries.

His father was a shoemaker, and, on his return to Aberdeen from London after that unfortunate fever, seems to have so wholly lost heart, that, instead of endeavouring to put the boy to school, he insisted on his being set down beside him, while still only nine, to learn his trade. The mother, however, saw in her boy some promise of talent, and encouraged him so far as she could in his aspirations after learning. "She often read aloud to him, and got others to read, and in the evenings young friends frequently gave him a share of what they were picking up at school." But he was determined that he would not disappoint his father's hopes, and soon became so expert at his craft that "he was able to turn out a greater quantity of first-rate work, in a given time, than almost any competitor." Gradually he thus secured not only a little leisure, but a little money, wherewith to purchase books or to borrow them; and the more he read, the more strengthened he became in the resolve to get through a course at college. In 1848 he was successful in being entered as a pupil at the Grammar School of Aberdeen under that Arnold of the North, Dr. Melvin, of whom, like so many others, he never ceased to think save with gratitude and reverence. Here he attended for four sessions, all the time helping his father in his work. "He used to fix his book in the 'clambs' (an instrument employed for holding the leather), and placing these conveniently in front of him, he learned to pick up right quickly a sentence from Zumpt, or a line from Homer, or any other book, and thus he stitched and studied for long weary years."

In November 1853 he became a student of King's College, Aberdeen. But it must not be supposed he was yet free from arduous labour for bread. His father grew feebler, and the more responsibility fell on him to provide for the household. A companion of these days tells us—

"William's work was harder than mine, for his father's failing health and eyesight made him now more and more dependent on his son's exertions. On this account he undertook an engagement to teach in a school in Aberdeen, and he had also several private pupils. We were students of the same year, and I shared the room with him in his parents' house. We both worked hard. It was no unusual thing for us to restrict ourselves to five hours' sleep. We engaged a watchman to waken us at three o'clock every morning, and we took it in turns to rise first, kindle the fire and boil the coffee, which Mrs. Elmslie had made ready the night before."

In spite of the varied drawbacks of the position and attacks of ill health brought on by severe application, he was so successful in his studies that "before he had reached the end of his Arts' course he had gained five prizes in various classes." Aspiration and a sense of duty seem reconciled in this young worker; he will mark out a course for himself, but without doing despite to the claims of those near to him. Perhaps this would not have been possible if, along with all, there had not gone the elevating and hallowing influences of religion. Each morning the young, toilsome students knelt down together, and besought God's blessing on the day and its work; and though, in moments of illness, doubts sometimes visited Elmslie, they never long abode with him.

Having taken his degree in arts, William Elmslie went to Italy as a tutor, and thus saw a little of the world, taking now and then the English service for those with whom he had become friendly in the course of his travels. His intention up till this time had been to study for the ministry, and on his return he competed for and won a bursary, which enabled him to enter the Free Church Divinity College. But during this first session there his attention was drawn to the mission-field, and a consideration of the place which healing had held in the planting of Christianity, led him to resolve to become a medical missionary. This seemed merely courting difficulties, and so some of his best friends viewed it.

"To face four years of study, *with winter and summer courses*, besides the heavy expense of a medical education, seemed madness to his friends, and they vehemently opposed him in his resolution; but hitherto the Lord had helped him, and to be a workman thoroughly furnished for the Master's service seemed to him worth any amount of effort and self-denial. Accordingly he braced himself up to his work. Again he taught in the Academy, received private pupils, stitched the '*uppers*' of boots and shoes, and pored over his books. Sixteen hours of work daily was the rule in those busy years, study was a relaxation rather than anything else. Long-continued custom had begotten a love for it, and obstacles seemed to add a certain zest to his pursuit of knowledge. But during this preparation period there were seasons when the cares of poverty pressed heavily; and faith, hope, and patience required to be in fullest exercise."

Thus, in face of difficulties which would have prostrated most men, he managed to get to the last year of his medical course, and the Medical Missionary Society of Edinburgh, having already relaxed its rule and given him, though studying in another city, a grant-in-aid of £15, he came south to be an inmate of their Home in the Dispensary in 1862. The present writer has cause to look gratefully back to that old Dispensary in the

Cowgate. Dim and dingy, and far from brilliant in itself, yet light went out from it, and often transfigured the moral gloom that reigned around. He had friends among the students of certain years there, and has accompanied them sometimes in their rounds up the long, dark, winding stone stairs, where aforetime gay feet only trod, but now trodden only by the most mean and miserable. At these times he has seen instances of tender devotion and quiet and homely heroism, such as in his mind atone for nearly all the recklessness and vice charged against medical students as a class. In a school like this such an one as William Elmslie could not but profit, and we can well believe that in the "household visitation of his patients he soon became a great favourite," no less than with the class of boys whom he had gathered round him from the lowest quarters for religious instruction, and whom at first he found rather unruly. Various circumstances led to his remaining an extra year in Edinburgh, but in August 1864 he successfully took his medical degrees there; and soon afterwards, notwithstanding that he was a Presbyterian, he was appointed a lay agent of the Church Missionary Society at Kashmir. He sailed for India in the ship "Poonah" in September 1864, and landed at Calcutta on the 28th October, having got a glimpse of Egypt and of Malta *en voyage;* but what is yet better, having ministered spiritual comfort to his fellow-passengers, especially to a young Dutch lady, left at Malta too ill to go farther.

After a short time spent at Calcutta with Mr. Vaughan, of the Church Missionary Society, and Dr. Robson, Free Church medical missionary, he proceeded to Lahore, where it was arranged he should remain some time before proceeding to Kashmir. This was advisable, both on account of the study of the language, and the fact that, for a certain portion of the year, the missionaries could not remain in Kashmir. He immediately took a class in Mr. Forman's school, and busied himself in other Christian works. He writes home to his mother—

"How I long to see hills! This country of India is just a dead level—as smooth as the table of your best room. When journeying from Calcutta, I saw some hills, though diminutive ones; my heart was gladdened within me, they reminded me so much of Deeside. . . . I shall soon see higher mountains than you or I have ever yet beheld—the great Himalayas, in the midst of which lies cradled my future home, or perhaps I should say my field of work. The books which I find give one the most interesting information are Jacquemont's Travels, Moorcroft's, and Vigne's ditto. If God spare me, I purpose writing a book more comprehensive than any of them, as I shall have valuable opportunities for gathering information if spared to remain for a sufficient time in the valley. . . . You would laugh many a time, dear mother, at the significant looks and smiles of my little brown-faced charge at the mission school, when I attempt to launch out, and make blunders in the language in so doing. I never mind, but hold on my way, for some direct mission-work I must do, however feebly. When I go to Kashmir I shall have a new language to learn, and it will be much more difficult to acquire, because there are no grammars or dictionaries in Kashmiri. Those I must make for myself, and I have already done something towards this work."

It was proposed that he should go to Kashmir along with the Bishop of Calcutta, who was to spend a month in the valley for the benefit of his health, but he was afraid that were he to reach his destination in company with one on whom the natives looked as a high public functionary, this might lead to their regarding him also as a servant of the Government. He therefore set forth alone. The romantic ideas we might associate with the name of Kashmir somewhat vanish on contact with the people. The country, a succession of vales opening out from a greater vale into each other, and ever unfolding new attractions, is a panorama of beauty; but the people are miserable, chiefly through the excessive exaction and tyranny of the native rulers, to whom it was turned over by England at the time of the Sikh war. "At one swoop half of every man's produce goes into the Government treasury. Half of everything, not merely of his grain, but even of the produce of his cattle, or whatever he has; so that from each cow he must give every second year a calf to Government, and from every half dozen of his chickens three to the all-devouring Sirkar. More than this even, his very fruit-trees are watched by Government, and half taken for the Maharajah."

Mr. Grant Duff, in his account of a tour in Kashmir, thus sketches the beauty of the country:—"Jummoo is, as you know, the winter capital of the Maharajah, whose territory extends over some 25,000 square miles—is, therefore, about the size of Scotland, less the counties of Perth and Inverness. The famous shawls are chiefly made in the neighbourhood of his summer capital Srinigar, the chief town of the vale of Kashmir, which is separated from Jummoo by about 125 miles of mountain. We dined, of course, by ourselves, but from time to time the Maharajah sent us native dishes, some of which were excellent. Then we had fireworks. The night was perfectly still and very propitious to them. Seven fire balloons floated high in the air, and got exactly into the position of the Great Bear and the Polestar. I called the attention of one of my companions to this, who, pointing it out to the Maharajah, said, 'It is only your Highness who can add to the number of the constellations.' When the fireworks were over, we took our leave, and very picturesque was the ride home under the crescent moon, through the dark silent streets, with our attendants clamouring in front to drive the sacred bulls and camels out of the way. This morning we started soon after sunrise, accompanied by the son of Kirpa Ram and others. Just as we came in sight, through the city gate, of the woodland which I described yesterday, the troops presented arms, and the band struck up 'God save the Queen.' Then we slowly descended the steep declivity on which Jummoo is built. As we were crossing the river, General B—— called out to me, 'It would take a fine reach of the Rhine to beat this,' and so it would. Some half an hour passed, however, before we saw the full glories of Jummoo. We had crossed most of the woodland, and had descended from our elephants, when we reached a point where, in the clearer morning, the mountains stood out in all their beauty. On the left stretched the mighty snowy chain of the Pir Punjal—rising, I suppose, to about 17,000 or 18,000 feet. Then, in the middle of the background, came an outer range, not snowy, somewhat lower than Taygetus, and rather like it; lastly, far to the right, another snowy range on the borders of Thibet. Between us and the mountains lay Jummoo, with its white pyramidal temples shining in the sun, and surrounded by a near landscape which wanted nothing to make it perfect. It was the most beautiful land view I ever beheld. The Maharajah is a lucky man, with heaven for his winter and the seventh heaven for his summer capital."

But here, as in many other of nature's most favoured spots, the poet's words come to the mind, "Man alone is vile." The Maharajah may be a good host, as Mr. Grant Duff would seem to have found him; but he is hardly a good ruler. Not only are the poor people overburdened by the heavy taxation, but large sections of the industrial population are little less than slaves. Laws have been passed which prohibit them from moving from place to place; and the sanitary conditions of the towns are of the very worst. We read in a good authority: "The shawl-weavers get miserable wages, and are allowed neither to leave Kashmir nor change their employment, so that they are nearly in the position of slaves; and their average wage is only about three-halfpence a-day."

It is only to be expected that, among such a community there should be much ignorance and vice and suffering. Of the four hundred thousand Kashmiris, five-sixths are Mussulmans, and the other sixth Hindus. Diseases of various kinds are rife, some of them arising from the exceedingly filthy habits of the people. Very little had been done for them prior to Dr. Elmslie's arrival. The Rev. W. Smith of Benares, and the Rev. R. Clark, of Peshawur, had visited Kashmir in the spring of 1863; but Mr. Smith returned to his own station, and Mr. Clark, after a brave attempt to remain over the winter, and after his wife had established a dispensary, was compelled by the authorities to leave. Dr. Elmslie took with him from Lahore two promising boys from the missionary orphanage there, and a

Kashmiri catechist, Qadir Bakhsh. At each town or village on the way, intimation was made that a doctor had come who would be happy to see and treat all the sick people; and when they were gathered together Qadir read the Scriptures to them, and addressed them simply and suitably before the examination was begun. So by Chikote and Uri our missionary journeys on, catching sight of Srinigar, the summer capital, on the 4th of May. He finds a suitable bungalow after some difficulty, and, losing no time, on the 9th opens his dispensary; then he institutes the Saturday itineration among the neighbouring villages, and begins a system of visiting and tract-distributing in the city. On the 16th he has as many as thirty patients, mostly Sepoys, which makes him fear the Kashmiris will thus be kept away. On the 24th the British Resident calls and plainly tells Dr. Elmslie not to ask or to expect any support from him. On the 30th the patients have increased to fifty-three, seventeen of them being women. False reports that Qadir, in his addresses, had spoken evil of the Maharajah, leads the British Resident to request that Dr. Elmslie desist from itinerating; but he will not do more than promise not for a season to return to Hazrat Bal, whence the false report had come. On the 31st of May a small hospital, with five beds, is opened, and has ere long some cases; persons of influence and in official position begin to take advantage of the missionary's skill, and the feeling begins to grow among the Kashmiris that the medical mission is a great boon and blessing, though as yet there is no token whatever of spiritual good. Especially are his surgical cases successful, though "in operating my difficulties are legion, having no one to assist me." In midst of this it must have been very disheartening to learn that the Sepoys and people had been prohibited from coming to him, and that a watch had actually been set upon his movements. So, amid mingled joy and pain, he got through his first season, the circumstances of which we have already spoken making it needful for him to remove to Amritsar, where he worked as hard, opening classes in chemistry, &c., and staying from October 1865 till April 1866.

His second year's work in Kashmir was marked by great progress—the number of patients largely increased, and in a few cases there were hopes of religious impressions having been made. Even the Maharajah now began to send his Sepoys suffering from diseases which required surgical operations. An offer was actually made to Dr. Elmslie of a thousand rupees a month if he would enter the Maharajah's service, and give up the mission element in his work. To this, of course, he would not listen ! and, in chagrin, the Maharajah again placed Sepoys at the different avenues leading to his house to prevent the people from coming. About this time, the mission lost the little it had through the failure of the Agra Bank; but Sir John [later Lord] Lawrence, the Governor-General, sent two hundred rupees, and assistance came from other quarters. Dr. Elmslie writes—

"You will be happy to hear that, in a medical point of view, at least, my work in Kashmir is prospering. In spite of opposition on the part of the local authorities, the work continues to progress. A few days ago I had as many as one hundred and eighty-three patients, and at this moment a fine-looking, elderly Mussulman of rank, from the east end of the valley, has called to ask my advice. Many of my patients come from a great distance; and never a day passes without one or two surgical operations. The result is, that I am becoming more and more expert in this department. *At present three men are living in my tent who were totally blind, but now they see.* As to spiritual fruit, I wish I had something more definite to say."

The Rajah of Chamba—a territory lying to the south-east of Kashmir—having made an offer of two hundred rupees a month, free house, dispensary, and hospital buildings, Dr. Elmslie resolved to go there during the ensuing cold season. Here a great work was also begun and successfully carried on, notwithstanding that difficulties arose with respect to the complete freedom of operation that had been promised by the Rajah. At the close of the season Dr. Elmslie writes—

"The Rajah is most favourably disposed towards the mission, so that my stay here has been extremely pleasant, although not free from difficulty. I have had some of the most serious operations to perform, and God, up to this time, has made all things go well with me in this respect. Two men who have been attending the dispensary for some time, called on me to-day privately to speak about the wonderful story of the cross. I have great hope of them."

The work of the third year went on in face of unusual opposition, and was ominously varied by an outbreak of cholera both among the civil community and the troops, and though Dr. Elmslie's offers of service were at first declined, he ultimately found ways of being useful and of extending his influence. At last it was deemed needful to draw a *cordon sanataire* round the European quarters, and, as the dispensary was situated there, it put a stop to the work. "When it was intimated to the suffering and sick that they were not to return to the dispensary until they should receive intimation to do so, the scene can be more easily fancied than described. It would have melted a heart of stone." This only set the doctor free to visit among the cholera-stricken and others.

On the approach of cold weather Dr. Elmslie paid a visit to Calcutta; but in the beginning of January 1868, we find him back in Amritsar, working hard in the dispensary there. Then, at the wonted season, he is once more in Srinigar, where the common people throng to him in greater numbers than ever; no opposition is now offered him, and no fewer than two thousand patients are treated in two months, and the fifth year fitly continued the work. In the early part of 1870, Dr. Elmslie returned home for a brief furlough, but his heart was bound up in Kashmir. He worked so laboriously at the compiling of a Kashmir vocabulary, as to bring on an illness, from which he never completely rallied. He returned to India along with his newly-wedded wife in 1872, and resumed his work full of hope. But his old disease ere long returned to him, and, though he stuck to his post bravely, he was compelled at length to start for Madras. It is said that the Maharajah had never forgiven him for some strictures on the Government procedure during that cholera epidemic, and was not sorry to see him go. Mr. Andrew Wilson even hints that his grudge against the missionary took more active shape. He writes thus—

"Dr. Elmslie was a devoted medical missionary, who did an immense amount of good in Kashmir, and had published a valuable vocabulary of the Kashmiri language; but he had also published letters complaining of the carelessness of the Government in regard to a visitation of cholera which had carried off large numbers of the people, and pointing out that sanitary measures might save the lives of thousands every year from smallpox and other diseases. The Srinigar rumour was that his servants had been offered so much to poison him within the Kashmir territory, and so much more if they would do so after he got beyond. Unfortunately Dr. Elmslie, like Lieutenant Thorpe, died rather suddenly shortly after he had got beyond the Kashmir borders, and, it seems, also of heart disease."

However it may be with respect to the attitude of the Maharajah at the last, Dr. Elmslie passed away at the early age of forty, on the 18th of November 1872.

His patience, prudence, and tact—formed as they had been among early trials of no ordinary kind— combined with his independent judgment, engaging manners, and his depth of sincerity, made him a missionary of a high order. In the course of his biography, we get many hints of his capacity to take broad and comprehensive views, as witness his remarks on the training of native medical missionaries, and on the desirability of the medical missionary not receiving wages from a heathen prince, as, among a heathen people, the credit of what he does will then go to heathenism and not to Christianity. Altogether a brave and beautiful character, that under such difficulties as in most cases would only embitter and harden, grew more pure, sensitive, and self-denying, William Elmslie may be said to have died for Kashmir as he lived for it; so that there will be a peculiar fitness in the "Elmslie Hospital and Dispensary" at Srinigar,

L

the shape which the Lord Bishop of Calcutta suggested that the memorial proposed by a conference of missionaries in the Punjaub should most fitly take. " The name of William Elmslie, endeared as it is to the present generation of Kashmiris, may thus be permanently associated with the great work which he has been instrumental in beginning."

Master Missionaries.   p. 163.

GEORGE WASHINGTON WALKER AND THE CONVICTS.

I.

VOLTAIRE'S visit to the country residence of Andrew Pitt, a retired Quaker merchant of London, is a notable incident in the life of a remarkable man, and in the history of a remarkable sect. Its object was to satisfy the curiosity by which the keenest intellect of the age had become possessed as to the nature of the Quaker religion. Its result was that Cowper's "brilliant Frenchman" was almost persuaded to be a Quaker, and that Howard's "favourite sect" was for once described from without, almost as if by the pen of a Christian.

"My dear sir, are you baptized?" was the first question which Friend Pitt was expected to answer—it was the question which good Catholics were accustomed to put to the Huguenots. His reply was, of course, negative. "What? morbleu!" Voltaire asked, "are you not Christians then?" "My friend," answered Andrew, "swear not; we are Christians, but we don't think that Christianity consists in throwing water and a little salt on an infant's head." "Have you forgotten that Christ was baptized?" inquired Voltaire. "Christ," replied Andrew, "received baptism from John, but He never administered baptism. We are not disciples of John, but of Christ." "How about the Sacraments?" was the next article of the sceptic's catechism. "We have none," was the Quaker's response; and on this head he referred to Barclay's "Apology" for the sect, which he declared was one of the best books that ever came from the hand of man, and was shown to be excellent by the fact that their enemies agreed that it was dangerous. An allusion to Barclay naturally led Andrew to offer his own apology for the Friends. He excused himself from responding to his polite visitor's bows and compliments without taking off his broad brim. He explained the literal and spiritual significance of the Quaker use of the second personal pronoun singular. He had some remarks to make about Quaker dress. He expounded the objections of the Friends to the use of oaths and their opposition to war, being careful to state that this latter peculiarity was not due to any deficiency of courage, but to a becoming recollection of the fact, "We are neither wolves, nor tigers, nor dogs, but men, but Christians."

After attending a First Day meeting of the Friends at their "church" near the Monument, Voltaire had some more questions to propound, in reply to which he obtained information as to the peculiar forms of worship approved by the sect, as to their rejection of " new presbyter and old priest," and as to their doctrine of the inward light—a doctrine of which it seemed to him that he had heard before, and with reference to which he exclaimed, "Voilà le père Malebranche tout pur."

Thus interrogated in the person of Andrew Pitt before a friendly inquisition, the Society of Friends gave an account of itself in which all its well-known characteristics are to be seen at a glance. One thing only was overlooked, but that was more important than everything else, viz., the fact that among Christian sects the sect of the Quakers is eminently Christian, at any rate in its practice. It did not occur to Voltaire that there was anything to be gained by pursuing the line of inquiry which was started in the question, "Are you not Christians, then?" and thus, whilst it did not escape his notice that Andrew Pitt's pocket-flaps were superfluously ample, he missed the discovery in regard to the Quaker's religion, that its genius, according to the testimony of history, is displayed rather in the clothing of the naked than in wearing of phylacteries.

No sect has ever identified itself with purely philanthropic causes in the way in which the Quakers have been associated with Anti-Slavery, Abolition of Wars, Prison Reform, Treatment of the Insane. It is alleged that the Society has seen its best days; that it now shows signs of decrepitude and decay, at any rate, in England. Some years ago prizes were offered for an essay on the subject of the numerical decline of the Friends, and it would seem probable that the competitors for those prizes might have assumed it to be a fact that the prosperity of the sect is on the wane in this country. If this be so, the whole history of the fraternity, its rise and progress, and now its decline and fall, may, perhaps, be justly said to turn upon the peculiarity of the Quaker religion, which escaped the notice of Voltaire, and which made Quakers "the favourite sect" of John Howard. Verily, the latter end of the peacemakers is peace. The Quakers have now no enemies, unless possibly it be among themselves. If the Quaker society is doomed, the reason is not, perhaps, so much that a great deal of its earlier testimony is now growing antiquated, as that its one great testimony, that which it has borne to the truth, that Christianity means peace on earth, good-will among men, has been superannuated by being generally accepted. If it be true that it is time now for the Society to which Elizabeth Fry belonged to chant its "Nunc dimittis," it is because it has seen the salvation of God arrive in the form of all Christian sects learning to make some profession of that philanthropy which was long the glory of one. History will probably record, with regard to the Society of Friends, almost alone among Christians sects, not that it outlived its influence and then died hard, but that it lived till the principles for which it contended ceased to be those of a sect or a party, and then, at peace with the world which it had conquered and blessed, gave up the ghost.

The Quakers, in the course of a unique career of beneficence, have had much to do with convicts. Those meekest of the meek of the Christian world who, when they are smitten by an enemy on the one cheek, turn to him the other also, have been more intimately associated than all other Christians with burglars, horse-stealers, highwaymen, wife-beaters, and murderers. Since long before the days of Elizabeth Fry, the amelioration of the state of criminals has been one of the things with which the Society of Friends has most persistently occupied its philanthropic energies. They were called Quakers, as everybody knows, by a judge who was only too happy to give their founder, George Fox, a taste both of the prison and the lash. Their refusal to take oaths in courts of justice, as well as the stiffness of their general nonconformity, and their preaching of the Gospel of peace in an aggressive manner, gave thousands of them an acquaintance with the interior of prisons, and with jail-life, which could not be entirely without effect upon the traditions and tendencies of the sect. But be this as it may, it will not be denied that the cause of the prisoner (at least till a comparatively recent period) has been almost made exclusively their own by the disciples of George Fox, that cheerful culprit, who, as Voltaire puts it, when he had received his proper share of the lash, begged for a "double dose" for the good of his soul.

George Washington Walker, of whose life and labours it is proposed to give a brief account in these pages, was an excellent specimen of the Quaker fraternity, both on the score of its general philanthropy, and its special devotion to the cause of the prisoner. His name, though revered in the Society, and not forgotten in the colony in which he spent his later years, is all too little known in England; and for this reason a slight sketch of his career may have an interest for some readers, such as could not be easily imparted to the biography even of more celebrated ornaments of the sect. Like many of his brethren, with all his taking of Scripture literally where it would have been easier to take it otherwise, he took in that way its philanthropy, and especially the precept, "Let not your left hand know what your right hand doeth." He was one of those friends of humanity, perhaps exceptionally numerous among Quakers, who do good by stealth, and who do not take the same pains, or, it may be, enjoy the same facilities, as those of other and more powerful sects in the way of keeping the outside world informed as to what they have done and are going to do for its benefit.

George Washington Walker's fame has suffered in this way. It has suffered still more, perhaps, from what is rather an accident to which good men of all sects are posthumously liable than a rule of their Society, which bears heavily on the best of deceased Quakers. His life has been written in one of those bulky volumes in which the memory of the just is destined to perish. Any chance that there was of his renown extending beyond the bounds of the Society, and of its being perpetuated to a distant age, was abolished by its being entombed in a large octavo, published by the Society. So that if "Ne quid nimis" is a rule which ought to be strictly applied in biography as in other literature, our good Quaker's memory has suffered from the breach of that rule in more ways than one; as, according to their custom, there was most likely too little said of him by the Friends while he lived, so by an exceptional conformity to the customs of an evil world, they have had too much to say of him since his death to admit of his being known as he ought to have been.

A great part of the Society's bulky life of him is occupied by his journals and letters, written during the period of his travels in Australia and in Africa. Though written with Quaker gravity and simplicity and stiffness, and though relating to countries which have been visited by troops of missionaries since his day, these journals and letters are by no means dull reading. It is especially amusing as well as edifying to note in them how extremes of human character meet, and in their meeting display towards each other a courteous behaviour—the benefactor of his kind, purist even in his speech and in his dress, conversing amicably in the penal settlements of Australia with compatriots who had left their country for their country's good, thouing and theeing scoundrels converted by inhuman punishment into fiends, and at least in one case receiving from them what would thus seem to be a possibility of any conceivable state of sinners—a complimentary address: " We, the prisoners of the Crown, embracing the tenets of the Protestant faith," &c.

Walker was born in London in 1800, the son of Unitarian parents, of whom one died when he was very young, and the other, when he was five years old, removed to Paris, leaving him to the charge of his grandmother at Newcastle-on-Tyne. At the age of fourteen, after having been baptized by a Unitarian minister and confirmed by the bishop of the diocese, he was apprenticed to "a professor of religion," who was, nevertheless, "a very inconsiderate man, at whose death, his apprenticeship not having expired, he was transferred to the drapery establishment of Hawden Bragg," an upright and consistent member of the Society of Friends. After Hawden's death, his widow asked James Backhouse, of York, a leading member of the Society, and not one of its least brilliant ornaments, to assist her in the valuation of the stock. On this occasion Backhouse and Walker met for the first time, and their meeting at the stock-taking in a Newcastle draper's shop was the commencement of a friendship which was cemented by much travel, and by much co-operation of another than the commercial sort. The immediate result of this acquaintance was the conversion of young Walker from the faith of his fathers to that of Mary Bragg and James Backhouse. He began to attend the meetings for worship of the Friends, and in 1827 was formally received into the Society.

During his residence with the Braggs, an attachment sprang up between him and their daughter Mary, to which a melancholy end was put by her death. This episode in a life devoted to the sternest duties of philanthropy is not without a touch of poetic beauty. Poor Mary Bragg, for a year or two before her death, was afflicted with blindness, and in reference to this calamity her Quaker lover writes to her in a strain which would throw the audience in a law court on certain occasions into fits of laughter, but which here, perhaps, may be read not without a sigh. "I have thought much of the declaration of Ruth to Naomi, and with my whole heart and soul I can address thee in the same manner. No language of my own can convey a more genuine transcript of my heart as it relates to thee than the sixteenth and seventeenth verses of the first chapter of Ruth, *which thy dear mother will read to thee.*"

Mary's death was followed by a memorable crisis in his life. His friend Backhouse "had for many years had an impression on his mind that it would be required of him to pay a religious visit to some parts of the southern hemisphere; and in this impression he was confirmed by the judgment of the Society, which took the matter into consideration at its regular monthly, quarterly, and yearly meetings. After settling his affairs and leaving York, Backhouse waited in London for some weeks in the hope of a companion turning up. While he waited he prayed, and one evening, having as usual petitioned that a travelling companion might be assigned to him, he retired to rest, with the feeling strong in his mind that any doubts as to his mission which still lingered about him would be set at rest if that supplication were successful. "Towards morning," he says, "before I was thoroughly awake, I was considering who there were in various places who might be suitable for such a service, when the words, *Now look northward*, were distinctly and powerfully impressed upon my mind, and in a moment Newcastle and my friend G. W. Walker were set before me."

When this fact was communicated to Walker, he was brought "under close exercise of mind." He had not anticipated any call from being behind the counter in Newcastle to "ministerial duty" in the southern hemisphere. The oracular form in which it came to him did not, irrespective of the inward light, settle the question whether he should accept it. After much hesitation he did accept it, judging, in the first place, with characteristic sagacity and modesty, that the way to overcome tendencies to evil, of which he was conscious, was to avail himself of the opportunity to do good ; and also that some indication of his duty had been given him in the fact that he was not hindered by domestic and social ties from devoting himself to the service of humanity.

Accredited to "the southern hemisphere" by a circular epistle from the Newcastle meeting of Friends, Walker and his companion sailed from London for Tasmania in 1831. Some Chelsea pensioners, who had "commuted their life pensions for an advance of four years' payment," were their fellow-voyagers, and with these drunken and disorderly steerage passengers the Friends had much to do on the side of peace and of the captain. In the course of the voyage, Walker became impressed with the belief that he had a commission to preach the Gospel as well as his companion, who was frequently moved to address the ship's company. His courage, however, failed him; "through fear and human weakness" the few remarks which occurred to him were suppressed, and he turned again to the lighter and less formidable duties of separating pensioners who were fighting with each other, and of supporting J. B. and the captain in their efforts to suppress mutinies always breaking out afresh, either in the steerage or in the forecastle, on the subject of the daily dispensation of grog. How far the influence of goodness may extend, even when that influence is circumscribed by the fear and human weakness which suppress the tendency to preaching, was seen on this voyage on several occasions in Walker's case; and more especially when, on his interposing in a quarrel in which blows were going, one of the bystanders clasped him round the waist, and entreated him to let others mediate in a case in which there was so much risk of personal injury.

The ship having touched at the Cape, the Quakers visited the jail at Cape Town, thus beginning work in South Africa, in which they were destined some years afterwards to earn for themselves and for the Society an honourable name. In one of the condemned cells there was a prisoner whose case deeply stirred their sympathies. He was under sentence of death, having been convicted of murdering his wife in a fit of drunkenness. A Hottentot and a Mohammedan, he had since his confinement been converted to Christianity, by the efforts of Dr. Philip, of the London Missionary Society, who, it was reported, finally gained his object by suggesting to the prisoner that he should ask the Mohammedan "priest" who visited him whether any provision was made in his religion for the pardon of sin—a question at which, so to speak, the Moslem theologian was obliged to surrender at discretion. At the same time, however, that he noted this triumph of the Christian divine over the priest of the false prophet, our Quaker missionary, with characteristic fairness, records a fact, on the strength of which the defeated Mohammedan might perhaps, if he had chosen, have prolonged the contest with his adversary, viz., that the prisoner's brother, also a Hottentot and a Mohammedan, had subjected himself to confinement in order to be near him, and was converted along with him. Before they left Cape Town, a prayer meeting was held in the Mission Chapel, under the presidency of Dr. Philip, which the Friends "believed it right to attend," and they heard there what pleased them much, of the unity that prevails among spiritually-minded Christians " in essentials."

The Quakers, on their arrival in Tasmania, stayed three months in the capital, Hobart Town, which was then about a third of its present size, having a population of a little over eight thousand. During this time they arranged their plans for carrying out their mission, which, as described in a letter of Lord Goderich, the Secretary of State, introducing them to the Governor, Colonel Arthur, was "to promote the moral and religious welfare of the colony, especially of the convicts." More particularly defined, their object was to preach the Gospel everywhere, among prisoners and colonists; to inquire into the state of the aborigines; to inspect penal settlements, jails, schools, and public institutions; and lastly, to oppose the rampant evil of intemperance. Governor Arthur, no red-tapist, though something of a martinet, was ready to second their efforts, and his patronage was of course an invaluable help to philanthropists whose hat-brims were over the regulation breadth, and whose commission was only from Newcastle Friends to all whom it might concern.

In regard to the aborigines, the Quakers found that

their mission was as nearly as possible not to the quick but to the dead. Before their arrival, most of the few remaining Tasmanians had been benevolently decoyed by George Augustus Robinson into a convenient corner of the country, from which they were transported to Flinders Island, in Bass's Straits, with the view of being civilised. The experiment failed. A tardy effort to improve the race was not attended with the success that had crowned earlier endeavours to exterminate it, and since then the last of the Tasmanians, an old woman, has paid the debt of nature—paid it, or, perhaps, transferred it to the score of our national liabilities in relation to humanity.

George Augustus Robinson's story has been often told. The Quakers heard it from his own lips, and were much moved by it. It was, in fact, a story such as a Quaker might have loved to tell to Quakers. Robinson took up his abode with one of the tribes, or "mobs," as they were commonly called, on Bruni Island, and having established himself in their favour and confidence, he persuaded some of them to accompany him on a tour through the country in the capacity of interpreters. His hardships, and those of his black companions, were extreme. Such had been the effect of intimate acquaintance with the colonists and their convict servants on the minds of the natives, that every white man was to them an enemy. Most of the tribes were hostile to each other, and they were all at deadly feud with the Christians, free and bound. To approach a native encampment, therefore, in the character of peacemaker, was attended with the same consequences as to challenge it to fight; and from these consequences Robinson's interpreters were in the habit of running away, leaving him to encounter them the best way he could. In spite, however, of all difficulties and dangers, he succeeded in collecting about a hundred savages, and in inducing them to remove with him to Flinders Island, to be protected from Christians and to be civilised and Christianised.

Their interest in the aborigines, as well as their desire to till neglected spiritual ground, led the Quakers to court acquaintance with a party of sealers from one of the small islands in Bass's Straits who chanced to visit Hobart Town, and with regard to whom shocking rumours were in circulation as to their appropriation of native women and their treatment of their offspring. G. W. Walker and his friend, with the characteristic bent of Quakers towards practical philanthropy, understood that they had been sent as missionaries, not to convert the converted, but to save the lost, and here there seemed to be an excellent opening for their efforts. When the sealer party was brought before Governor Arthur to be subjected to a sort of patriarchal catechisation (with the cat-o'-nine-tails in the background), the Quakers who were present and all attention, expected to hear the most revolting evidence produced as to the ignorance in which the young sealers were allowed to grow up by their rude and lawless parents. They were agreeably disappointed to find themselves present at an examination in religious knowledge which would have elicited the approbation of a School Inspector. A sealer's so-called wife was asked if she had any children. The answer was, that she had two, both of them at the door, and ready to be called in for inspection. His Excellency had both introduced to him, and proceeded to catechise them. The elder, nine years of age, repeated the Lord's Prayer and the Creed, and in answer to the Governor's questions showed "that he had correct notions of a future state." The younger boy, little more than six years old, in spite of an impediment in his speech, acquitted himself under examination no less admirably than his brother. As their father had been represented to be one of the worst of a bad lot, G. W. Walker's reflection on the occasion was to the effect, "that care is requisite in listening to reports prejudicial to individuals or communities"—a remark the far-reaching justice of which may be taken as an excuse for its Quaker-like simplicity. He and his companion afterwards exhibited their sympathy for the sealer in his lonely life, and his supposed devotion to the care of his offspring, by cruising among the islands in Bass's Straits, at no small risk to their lives. In the meantime they were moved by pity for a calumniated class of men to be sectarian for once. In parting with three of the sealer friends they showed them, from the example of the Society, how worship might be maintained on Gun Carriage Island and other places, with a population of eighteen souls or thereabouts, without the presence of "a minister of human ordination."

If there was little to be done for the aborigines when the Quakers arrived in Tasmania, their mission to the convicts was not so ill-timed. As a home for prisoners Van Diemen's Land was then at the height of its dismal prosperity, and a better idea of Paradise colonised from its exact antipodes, could scarcely be got than from the pages of G. W. Walker's journal, descriptive of what he saw of the island. A few days after his arrival he went on board a ship which had just arrived in harbour with a cargo of two hundred and sixty male convicts, apparently a homogeneous load, but in reality miscellaneous, as was shown by the fact that the "magistrates were engaged in taking down a description of each as to character," &c. It was necessary, or at any rate useful, to take note of shades of reputation, though none of the very finest were to be looked for, inasmuch as the system of assigning prisoners as servants to the colonists was then in full vogue; and this cargo of villany, like many a previous shipload of the same sort, was destined for distribution over the colony, and among people of various tastes in the matter of character. Some colonists wanting a servant might prefer a burglar to a poacher; others might prefer a bigamous tailor to a larcenous shoemaker. Mr. Prinsep, a colonist, wrote to his friends, "In our small *ménage* our cook has committed murder, our footman burglary, and the housemaid bigamy." Mr. Prinsep's neighbour perhaps chose to have his establishment differently furnished in respect of moral character. Different tastes had to be suited on the part of colonists, and accordingly the first thing done with a cargo of convicts was to classify them according to their quality as regards breaches of the ten commandments. After being thus classified they were informed (sometimes by his Excellency himself, who was a capital preacher as well as a genuine statesman) of their prospects in the land of their probation. They were told that being assigned as servants to respectable colonists they would get food, clothing, and bedding, in return for their whole labour; that, as the result of good conduct, ticket-of-leave, conditional pardon, and even free pardon, were within their reach; that if they relapsed into crime there was first the watchhouse before them, then the prison or the chain-gang, then the scaffold, or, as a worse alternative, transportation to a penal settlement like Macquarie Harbour.

G. W. Walker and his companion began their labours among their countrymen, to whom a new start in life was thus offered on the part of the Government, by a visit to a party whose prospects had been exceptionally bad from the first, or had been marred by a relapse into old habits. This was a chain-gang, consisting of one hundred and fifty men, employed on the construction of a road across the Derwent by means of piers and a drawbridge. An undertaking of enormous magnitude and difficulty, this Bridgewater causeway, as the Quakers had probably heard before visiting it, had witnessed many strange and some terrible scenes, to which survivors of chain-gangs might be heard alluding in mysterious hints as to the material used being human agony and blood. The place, however, could scarcely have witnessed a stranger scene than was added to the memories connected with it by the visit of the Quakers. The prisoners, with their irons attached to the ankles, were drawn up in their barrack yard. A file of soldiers was stationed on an elevated position so as to hear, and perhaps also to see. In attendance upon the Quakers was a servant of the Governor in his livery. Backhouse read the eighth chapter of Matthew, in which it will be remembered there are several references to possession by devils and a solemn allusion to the last judgment, and, after a pause, expounded what he had read, urging "these poor criminals who had been condemned at the bar of an earthly tribunal," to prepare for a greater assize so as to be in no danger of condemnation. Very remarkable scenes indeed must have been witnessed at Bridgewater, if this was not one of the most memorable ever transacted in its neighbourhood. Never surely were missionaries farther from home than were Walker and his companion, thus preaching the Gospel at the antipodes to those who even there, as belonging to the chain-gang, were far off. Nor was the genius of Christianity as a missionary, as a universal religion, ever perhaps so strikingly illustrated in the adventures of Christian emissaries in heathen lands among savages and wild beasts, as by the disciples of George Fox, offenders against law and usage only, if at all, by opposition to war and oaths and all manner of violence in word and deed, standing at the very ends of the earth, before the chain-gang, victims of double crime and accumulated punishment, and reasoning with them concerning temperance and righteousness and judgment to come.

II.

After preaching to the chain-gang in Van Diemen's Land, there was possibly just one step further which Christian philanthropy could carry the Quakers on their religious mission to the southern hemisphere, and that step was taken when they proceeded to call Macquarie Harbour and the other penal settlements in Australia to repentance. Convicts for whom the society of the chain-gang was too good, select criminals who had attained a bad eminence at home, or had earned distinction after being transported, were consigned to these settlements when it was not found advisable to hang them. It is not altogether irrelevantly that the gallows and the penal settlement are here mentioned together.

Between the two, at any rate according to the views of those principally concerned, there was very little to choose, and if any choice was possible, it was to be given, in their opinion, in favour of the former. It might be, as Sydney Smith suggested fifty years ago, that "a London thief, clothed in kangaroos' skins, lodged under the bark of the dwarf eucalyptus, and keeping sheep fourteen thousand miles from Piccadilly, with a crook bent into the shape of a picklock, was not an uninteresting picture," or a picture of an unenviable lot; but there was a counterpart to be found to such a view of the condition of convicts in Australia, which might have been made use of to calm the fears of people at home lest their condition should be made too agreeable and attractive; and the counterpart was the penal settlement like Macquarie Harbour, to escape from which the London thief would often break into "the bloody house of life," so as to make sure of being hanged.

If it were determined to establish a penal colony in the wilds of the Western Highlands of Scotland, or on the western coast of Ireland, in a situation contrived to make solitude horrible and escape impossible; if such a situation were discovered on a rock in the middle of a loch like Torridon or Ewe; if instead of being accessible from places along shore, or from the interior of the country, this island jail, a prison inside of prisons, were separated from the nearest abodes of men by a hundred miles or more of insuperable difficulty in the shape of mountain and forest and jungle and fordless river; if to this place of the doubly condemned there were conveyed a few hundreds of the most desperate criminals now in Portland or Dartmoor, and if everything were done by conscientious officers of her Majesty's service to maintain among its inmates an unbroken monotony of misery and despair, it would have some resemblance to Macquarie Harbour.

No nation, perhaps, which has yet obtained a conspicuous place in the world is in danger of losing its place through the sin of pride, unless while remembering its victories by sea and land it forgets its treatment of poor relations, especially the poorest of all, that large section of the criminal class who, as the result of imperious social conditions, are left morally naked, and are sent to the hulks for not being clothed. Any one who reads what our good Quakers have to say of our penal settlements in Australia, at the commencement of her Majesty's reign, must confess that England, as well as other nations, is not without cause for blushing in this respect. Nor is it only perhaps in recalling the past that occasion might be found for such a display of humility on the part of our victorious country. If it be true that even at the present day discharged prisoners, as a rule, leave jail (possibly after a term of years) penniless and friendless, and thus with the temptation to crime redoubled; and if it be true that in many cases they re-enter respectable society wearing a suit of clothes which in its excessive shoddiness is a lesson in rascality, and by its pattern is an advertisement of "Who's who," addressed to the police and to the public—if this be true, the treatment of our poor relations is still so little to our credit that even Waterloo should hardly serve to support our pride.

Macquarie Harbour, on the west (the uninhabited) coast of Tasmania, when it was visited by the Quakers, though shorn by that time of some of its atrocities, was a disgrace to civilisation and to Christianity, such as the world has rarely witnessed. If it had existed in his time, Dante might have drawn from it, for his Inferno, hints of some quaint and some tremendous horrors. Those who approached it by "Hell's Gates," an almost impossible bar at the entrance, forgot the profanity of the name in thinking of its truth. Sarah's Island, nearly thirty miles from these gates, and three miles from the mouth of a river called the Gordon, closely resembling the Styx in colour, and also in the character of its noxious exhalations, was the place chosen for the settlement by Governor Arthur's predecessor. Such was the settlement as to justify Mr. West, the historian of Tasmania, in saying of the island, "Nature concurred with the objects of its separation from the rest of the world to exhibit some notion of a perfect misery. There man lost the aspect and the heart of a man."

This insular Tartarus, a rock half a mile long by a quarter of a mile broad, accommodated from two to three hundred prisoners in wooden barracks, through which groans and oaths, the sound of the lash, and the clanking of chains reverberated with horrible effect; and in a jail the cells of which were narrow and dark, and noisome to a degree, calculated to brutalise any known variety of human disposition and character. Two neighbouring rocks completed the accommodation required for the settlement: the one was Halliday's Island, where the wicked who ceased from troubling found earth to cover them; and the other was Grummet's or Pilot Island, where the wicked who were too troublesome to be endured were consigned to an unheard of solitude. In the sides of this latter island there are caves, which have a tale to tell of former days that seems barely credible, but the truth of which is attested as if by the oaths of Quaker witnesses before a Quaker judge and jury. Into these caves men clambered up out of the surf when they were tossed out of the boat which had brought them and their oarsmen from Sarah's Island, and, thus provided with a lodging, were left for days or weeks "to add their yells to the scream of the sea-birds and the moan of the western wind."

The Quakers were philanthropists who, instead of preaching too much, kept accounts, and kept them accurately. With a view to practical results they were careful to note facts with draper-like precision. Walker spent much time over his journals "writing out at night, in a clear and beautiful hand," what he had seen during the day. Here at Macquarie Harbour, there was much to be done by him in that way.

What with crimes of violence and accidents occurring to gangs of labourers, which could only have happened to convicts under the charge of convict overseers, it was almost three to one at this Australian settlement that death should result from other than natural causes. Of eighty-five deaths, only thirty were in the course of nature. In three years two-thirds of the population had had distributed among them six thousand two hundred and eighty lashes, or about thirty per man. The difficulty, or rather the impossibility, of escape did not deter even craven spirits from attempting the desperate enterprise. In the course of ten years a hundred and sixty-nine men attempted to get away, of whom sixty or seventy perished in the woods, fifty-seven were recaptured, and only six lived to tell the tale of how difficult is the ascent from the under world. As for the rest their fate is doubtful, or if anything is certain with regard to their end, it is that they were murdered to be eaten. "It is a horrid but indubitable fact," as the Quakers report, "that on several occasions when a party of men had determined to take to the bush, some unsuspecting simple man was inveigled into the conspiracy, for the express purpose of furnishing food;" and as we need hardly have been told upon other authority almost as good as the Quakers', it is an equally undoubted fact that when such a man had to be chosen it was a point in favour of the guileless man if he happened to be neither too old nor too lean. Or if this should be deemed an incredible horror, its historical character may perhaps be supported by the fact that when escape through the bush failed or was considered impossible, even with the help of the guileless fat man, there was one exit which was taken advantage of by many. If one man was murdered, several were delivered, at least for a time, from Tartarus. The murdered man's release was instantaneous and complete. His murderer's was sure to come soon. The witnesses, if not also emancipated by the gallows as accomplices, were certain, at any rate, of a holiday in being taken to Hobart Town to give evidence. So something in lieu of a coin was often tossed up to decide by an appeal to the fates how a life was to be taken—who was to be murdered, who was to murder, and who were to have a holiday as witnesses. "The blow would be struck," says a historian of Marquarie Harbour; "one would be hanged, and two or three would exchange for a few weeks the pine shore of one prison for the stone floor of Hobart Town jail."

Such was the field of work and observation into which the Quakers entered, taking that one step which it was possible for Christian philanthropy to take beyond the Australian chain-gang. They were here at the ends of the earth on their benign errand; the force of charity could no farther carry them away from home. They did not travel so far altogether in vain. Their visit to Macquarie Harbour and to other Australian penal settlements had undoubtedly the effect of helping to accelerate changes in the treatment of prisoners, which make it possible now, without looking beyond the bounds of the British empire, to look back upon forty or fifty years ago as a period of barbarism. They were amply rewarded, in their own opinion, for the dangers and privations which they incurred on this mission, by discovering that even among felons, to whom murder was a recreation, there were "human" hearts on which sympathy was not wasted, and by which religious conversation was properly and indeed intensely relished. It is the sobriety (as distinguished from stolidity) of Quaker Christianity, however, which is perhaps its most notable feature here at the ends of the earth. It appears as free from excitement at Macquarie Harbour as if the occasion and the place were a First Day meeting at Newcastle or York. Under circumstances to induce hysteria, it preserves its resemblance to common sense, adheres to its preference for "guarded expression," notes deficiencies in the scale of rations, at the same time that it points the way to heaven; and, while not refusing to credit marvellous instances of conversion among convicts of the worst class, recognises in regard to their history and their future the operation of the law of cause and effect—that law by which it is guaranteed to men and nations that whatsoever they sow that shall they also reap. Other missionaries may sometimes be carried away by a generous enthusiasm, so as to anticipate from a very small amount of Christian work enormous results, such for example as the civilisation of a continent like Africa in half a century, or the evangelisation of a populous South-Sea Island between one Christmas and another. Our good Quakers at Macquarie Harbour are of the number of those resolute and rational friends of humanity who anticipate no greater results from their greatest labours than to see the evil of to-day, which has existed for ages, a little lessened before to-morrow.

There was at least one Quaker to be found among convicts before our missionaries visited Van Diemen's Land. After their return from Macquarie Harbour to Hobart Town, a Quaker meeting was established, and convicts were among the first to become Quakers. Walker and his companion always and everywhere, in the most earnest manner that Friends are capable of assuming, disclaimed sectarian motives in their religious procedure. They prayed fervently to be strengthened against all temptations by which their human weakness was assailed and might be overcome on the side of sectarianism. And their sincerity was demonstrated when convicts were invited into Quaker fellowship— when the disciples of Fox showed themselves disciples of Him who sat at meat with publicans and sinners. Their meeting before long was joined by colonists like Robert Mather (destined to be Walker's father-in-law), whose presence would have done honour to any church in Christendom.

Walker's journals are worth reprinting. If they were reprinted they might be illustrated, and if illustrated it might be by the pencil of an artist alive to the touch of the humorous and the grotesque, which often accompanies the sublime and serves to heighten its effect. Such an artist would find scenes in almost every chapter to suit his taste. There is something which tickles the fancy, as well as something which moves the heart, in the idea of Quakers turning both cheeks to the smiter, and lifting up their testimony on that subject in presence of the bruisers and murderers of the chain-gang or of Macquarie Harbour. It is another sort of scene certainly than that of Faust and Mephistopheles in Auerbach's cellar at Leipzig, but it is perhaps not much less dramatic —our Quaker missionaries figuring on Flinders Island among the few remaining natives of Van Diemen's Land. Forty-four men, twenty-nine women, and five children had been here collected by G. A. Robinson— the last relics (except perhaps about as many still at large in the bush) of a race which was appointed to die. Many points of extremely great interest emerge in the Quakers' account of this now extinct variety of our genus, but it is impossible to glance even at the most interesting. Their sympathy for the "children ot nature" on this occasion cost Walker and his companion no little hardship, and exposed them more than once to serious danger, and yielded on the whole results which tended rather to melancholy than to philanthropic joy. They listened with pious satisfaction to stories illustrative of the goodness of the natural black man, and for what they heard of his occasional exhibitions of human frailty in the way of domestic peevishness and tyranny they had various grave and kindly apologies to offer. They were struck with the humane arrangements made for the dissolution of a species of the human race, so that its latter end should be as decent and comfortable as possible. But, on the other hand, they were undeceived as to their pious sealer friends in regard to their relations with native women, and any doubts they may have had as to the way in which the aborigines were treated before their removal to Flinders Island were dispersed by proofs that the worst stories ever told were but too true.

The Quakers were of opinion that the peculiar freedom or movement which they enjoyed as compared with most missionaries was in their favour, the free exercise of individual intelligence on the part of the friend of humanity being of more account in his work than any system or method of benevolence, however perfect. Be this as it may, their work as missionaries was done in a workmanlike manner in whatever field they entered. They had to return to the home of the aborigines in Bass's Straits, Flinders Island, a year after their first visit, and they were received with shouts of welcome from a black mob assembled to witness their landing. If their errand was known, the reflections of heathen minds on the subject must have been such as would have formed, had they been recorded, a curious epilogue to the history of a vanished race. Walker and his companion came this time, as before, in the capacity of peacemakers; but whereas formerly their authority was from heaven, and their errand was to the blacks, now they came from his Excellency the Governor, and their mission was to the whites. In a word, the commandant and the resident missionary were at war, and as a last effort in favour of peace the Governor had sent the disciples of Fox to deprecate the continuance of hostilities between English Christians and gentlemen in presence of black men.

During the period of their stay in Tasmania, which extended to nearly three years, the comprehensive plan of work which the Quakers had sketched for themselves on their landing in the colony was wonderfully accomplished. Apart from Hobart Town and Launceston, centres of population separated from each other by the whole length of the island, the inhabitants of Tasmania were thinly distributed over country, of which one mountainous district vied with another in forbidding travel except on urgent business. "No road, except on business," might have been seen notified east, west, north, and south, by travellers who were not disposed to incur fatigue or not impelled to run the risk of losing themselves in almost pathless forests. East, west, north, south, the Friends trudged forth on their benign and, to them, urgent business. It was of no use intimating, in the largest capitals, to such travellers, "No Thoroughfare." They were of the right sort of fighting Englishmen—those who fight difficulties for less than a shilling a day, and don't know when they are beaten. If no better accommodation could be found for weary limbs, they slept where they halted, with the sky for a canopy. Walker blistered his feet, and then only came to the conclusion that it was hardly practicable to go any farther. He and his companion were seen in places where no missionary had been heard of before, and left wholesome impressions of their sincerity, good sense, and goodness upon the minds of men who had considered themselves abandoned, alike of God and man, to solitude, and blasphemy, and drink. There were many colonists and many convicts (some of them possibly still alive) who for years afterwards dated all events with reference to the visit of the Quakers.

In a land containing 15,000 convicts they met with one solitary rebuff, and it came from a person with regard to whom they remark quaintly, that he seemed to be "one of those persons who are described by an inspired penman as 'fools that make a mock of sin.'"

In regard to the chief object of their mission they were indefatigable during those three years spent in Van Diemen's Land. Subsequently to their visit to Macquarie Harbour, and in compliance with his Excellency's request, they addressed a series of reports to the Governor respecting the condition of convicts, pointing out reforms which were urgently required, especially adverting to the evils of the system of assigned servants, and conclusively demonstrating that punishment was least efficacious where, as in the chain-gang and at Macquarie Harbour, it was most revolting and inhuman. It may be that they came to the colony with opinions on the subject already formed, but if so it was to have their convictions strengthened by much careful observation and much painful experience. Flagellation, the chain-gang, excessive doses of solitude and darkness, all the worst horrors of an antiquated penal system, they denounced to the Governor, with references to the law of Moses, which did not perhaps appear to his Excellency perfectly conclusive, and with appeals to reason and experience, which seem to have been not altogether fruitless either in the colony or at home. In reference to flagellation their protest was couched in terms of eloquent indignation. "It is calculated," they wrote to his Excellency, "to increase desperation of character; it is a part of that abstract system of vengeance which man is not authorised to inflict upon man."

Besides Macquarie Harbour they had visited Port Arthur, which was shortly to take the place of the former as the chief penal establishment of the island. They had inspected the jails of Hobart Town and Launceston; they had made acquaintance, in various places besides Bridgewater, with the chain-gang; they had had more than one meeting with Nottman's gang, consisting of one hundred and thirty select ruffians, with regard to whom the overseer informed them that as a rule they had no belief in a future state of rewards and punishments. It was not, therefore, without having been at pains to know the truth, if they fell into an error in protesting to Governor Arthur that to inflict "abstract" vengeance was a blunder worse than a crime.

On leaving Hobart Town the Quakers sailed for Botany Bay, to begin in New South Wales a course of labour like that which they had just finished in Van Diemen's Land. Their experience in the one colony was to a large extent a repetition of their career in the other, with perhaps some additional trial of their faith and patience in the form of miasmal fever, excessive heat, mosquitoes, and extended views of human degradation and misery. The oldest colony of the Australian group, though now best known by its capital, Sydney, and its harbour, more beautiful than the Bay of Naples, was in those days famous for a bay the name of which is Botany. In New South Wales then our Quaker missionaries, as far as their business was with convicts, had arrived at head-quarters. In coming from Tasmania to this colony the scale of their labours was altered from that of an island to that of a continent—from that of Ireland to that of a third of Europe. The penal settlement, the chain-gang, the system of assigned servants, flogging in large jails, suffocation in small lock-ups, were all in full swing here as in Van Diemen's Land, only on a larger plan and cumbering more ground called Christian.

Our Quakers began their labours with the penal settlement—one of the most remarkable and most famous establishments of the sort on which even an Australian sun has ever shone. Norfolk Island has been heard of on this side of the world, and is now known as the home of the Pitcairn islanders; but it is only in Australia, and among the survivors of a time when transportation was a crime committed to punish crime, that the name retains anything of the terrible significance which it once had. It is one of the loveliest of the lovely islands of the Pacific, a green and glorious Eden, the marvellous beauty of which could not fail to attract the attention of a government which, in transplanting crime, made a point of giving over to an ugly weed only the fairest scenes. Still more than in the case of Botany Bay or Van Diemen's Land, an island which combines rare grandeur and loveliness with the perfection of climate, what sin did when Norfolk Island was made a penal settlement, was to enter into Paradise and take possession of it in the name of the British Government. Norfolk Island had one thing besides its beauty to fit it for being the abode of crime and misery—escape from it was impossible. More than a thousand miles distant from the Australian shore, and surrounded by a reef in which there was but one opening, and that a narrow and dangerous one, it was the Macquarie Harbour of New South Wales in point of dread security as well as other terrible aspects. "It was Macquarie Harbour over again," so the Quakers tell us, "with an extra shade of darkness superadded."

Everything was done on Sarah's Island, Macquarie Harbour, to give to the life of the prisoner a dull, monotonous, depressing hue, like that of the sombre hills and forests by which he found himself surrounded. On Norfolk Island the art was understood and exercised of making the misery of man's evil days an effective contrast to the beauty, and glory, and luxuriance with which he was encompassed. "Where every prospect pleases, and only man is vile," had an application to Norfolk Island such as never presented itself to Heber's imagination, such as Ceylon with its "spicy breezes," or Africa with its "sunny fountains," never furnished. All vegetation was tropical; tropical, too, was the growth of the ugly weed sent over seas by the British Government to Botany Bay, and then transplanted afresh to the soil of this island. All that was good for food and pleasant to the eye abounded to excess; superabundant, too, was the profusion of all that is hateful and horrible in the form of sin and misery. It was found impossible to extirpate the orange-tree, though the attempt was made to deprive a harsh fate of the alleviation which its fruit afforded. It is impossible to allude to the fruits of that forbidden tree, whose mortal taste brought death into the world, which were here as plentiful as oranges. As had happened to them on their visit to Macquarie Harbour, so on their arrival at Norfolk Island the Quakers found that they were just too late to witness the last point to which inhuman severity could be carried out at a penal settlement. They were in time, however, to see and to hear enough of the island to be able to understand why, in spite of its spicy breezes, its name had become "infamous." Just before their visit, one of the colonial judges before whom prisoners came for sentence involving transportation to Norfolk Island, made this public declaration, "That it brought tears to his eyes when a Norfolk Island convict brought before him for sentence, said, 'Let a man be what he will, when he comes here he will soon be as bad as the rest; a man's heart is taken from him, and there is given him the heart of a beast.'"

"Evil, be thou my good," was the language of Norfolk Island, as of a place to which it might be supposed to bear only too close a resemblance. Evidence on this point was given before a committee of the House of Commons by Dr. Ullathorne, Roman Catholic priest of Sydney, which Walker was careful to preserve in his "clear and beautiful hand." Good men, whose conscience did not suffer them to conform to universal custom as regards the use of the second personal pronoun plural, the Quakers, heard at Norfolk Island of a perversion of language which argued an immeasurable depravity of mind. A convict, in Dr. Ullathorne's hearing, called another convict a good man. The priest was surprised, and asked a question, which elicited the information that in general, and according to the ethics of the island, a bad man was called good, and a man who was ready to perform his duty, or any part thereof, was called a bad man. "There was a whole vocabulary of terms of that kind, which seemed to have been invented to adapt themselves to the complete subversion of the human heart."

This was a fact which it was incumbent upon Friend Walker to record with care in his best style of penmanship. There was much of the same sort of information to be had with which to enrich the pages of his journal. Here, as at Macquarie Harbour, death in another than the Christian sense was gain; here, even more thoroughly than in the Tasmanian settlement, the ruffian whose crimes were monstrous was at one with the saints and heroes of Christian history in his longing to depart. The most horrible scene that the good priest, whose name has been mentioned, ever saw, was one which he witnessed on Norfolk Island, and it was a scene, so to speak, not of murder, but of deathbed resignation and departing ecstasy. Twenty-four men (perhaps because it was convenient to reckon by dozens) were sentenced to death as mutineers. The priest was sent from Sydney to administer the consolations of religion to thirteen of these, and to inform the rest that they were reprieved. As the names were read out, not the eleven who were reprieved, but the thirteen who were to die, dropped down, man by man, upon his knees and gave thanks to the Eternal Mercy that His salvation had visited them.

Down with this fact in thy journal, Friend Walker, and let it remain there for a testimony—against whom need not be said—but, at anyrate, against man's inhumanity to man.

It was at Norfolk Island, at the end of a visit of two months' duration, that the Quakers received the address to which allusion has been made, beginning, "We, the prisoners of the Crown embracing the tenets of the Protestant faith." Partly, perhaps, because with all their gravity they were not devoid of humour, the Friends would fain have been spared this testimony to the worth and success of their labours; but they were gentlemen, and lest they should seem to slight a kindness, which was all that Protestantism in reduced circumstances had to offer them, they accepted it. It had cost them a disagreeable voyage of three weeks' duration to reach the island. They had a narrow escape from drowning, as they swung in their boat on the edge of the reef which guarded the approach to an ocean prison, whose walls were inaccessible basaltic cliffs. Not without much fatigue and hardship, perhaps not without blistered feet, certainly not without aching hearts, they had followed the prisoners of the Crown embracing the Protestant faith into the depths of the narrow and sultry valleys winding among the mountains of which the island consists, and had noted how the vertical sun under which they worked had obliged them to dispense with clothes, and imparted to their skins a hue resembling that of negroes. They had seen the flower and crown of forest loveliness, the Norfolk Island pine, flourish along the ridges of hills the sides of which were covered with a jungle of fruit-trees, the orange, the lemon, the guava; and these features of a paradise in the Pacific had only served to deepen in their minds the sadness of the reflections which were suggested by the fact of Protestants not being allowed the use of knives and forks, and being restricted to the use of spoons, lest they should murder each other with any weapon except the regular hoe. Here, however, in this complimentary address from the almost negro-hued Protestantism of the island, was their reward; as much of a reward, perhaps, as the friends of humanity have any right to expect; a sign that possibly earnest and faithful work has not been altogether thrown away; a token that possibly the day is yet coming when the wilderness shall somehow blossom as the rose.

III.

Inclusive of their visit to Norfolk Island, the mission of the Quakers to New South Wales (of which Queensland and Victoria were then outlying portions) occupied them over two years. The thoroughness with which their work was done was not altered by the scale of their labours being changed from that of an island to that of a continent. Wandering not among the ruins of empire, but among the foundations of cities and commonwealths just rising above ground, they were known by their broad-brims and their zeal for human wellbeing as far north as Moreton Bay, as far south as that part of the bush which is now the city of Melbourne, and to almost every settlement, large and small, and nearly every lonely hut between these points. As in Tasmania so in New South Wales, their idea of visiting the colony was to enter not only into every town and village, but, as far as possible, into every house. They did not finally take leave of Sydney, which has now a population of one hundred thousand, and was then a considerable city, until they had gone from door to door giving notice of their meetings. Their object being to call the city and the colony to repentance, not to extend the influence of a sect, the primitive practice of a household visitation recommended itself to them as preferable to more sensational and less laborious methods of making their object known. To their credit, as well as not a little to the honour of the colonial clergy, when they entered into other men's labours, as was to a certain extent unavoidable in Sydney and other places, they did so without provoking any jealousy or wrath. As in other cases, so in the instance of G. W. Walker and his companion, it was noticeable that Quakers, whose differences with the rest of the Protestant world could be shown to be greater than those of any one part of it with any other, had no difficulty in establishing friendly relations with the representatives of sects between whom there was the bond of an almost identical creed, and the antipathy which too often accompanies that bond. Either as the reward of their having suffered much in past times for righteousness' sake, or as the result of their peculiar garb and speech being identified rather with prison reform and humane treatment of the insane, than with disputes about infant baptism or the eastward position of the celebrant, the Quakers would seem to have the privilege of differing with all churches, and, indeed, in a mild way, of excommunicating them all, and at the same time of being permitted peaceably to do what they can to benefit mankind. It is doubtful if there ever was in appearance a more provincial figure than that of the disciple of George Fox before the days of his conformity to the world—the Quaker of preceding generations, with his broad-brim, and his jargon more uncouth than his hat. Yet in virtue of his consistent and determined bearing as a friend of humanity, amenable in his conduct and activity to the rule of reason as well as that of the Scriptures, the old-fashioned Quaker, with his coat cut in the style of William Penn's and his pigeon English, would seem to be the most cosmopolitan character in religious history. Walker's journals, especially his entries relative to Sydney, suggest some such reflections as to the Friends and their relation to other Christians.

Old Samuel Marsden, the father of Church missions in Australia, famous for his labours and adventures and successes in New Zealand, still held his post of colonial chaplain, and still, it is to be presumed, retained those scruples about meeting convicts in society, for which he was mercilessly chastised by the wit of Sydney Smith. But even old Samuel Marsden, like the rest of the colonial clergy of all denominations, in spite of the connection, historical and actual, between Quakers and convicts, had a hearty welcome to give the Friends, and, indeed, did much to further their mission, especially by fostering the interest taken in it by his Excellency the Governor of New South Wales.

A serious and resolute attempt to conquer an empire rather than a province for pure and undefiled Christianity, for righteousness, temperance, and peace, the mission of the Friends in New South Wales is a fact the historical interest of which is in some respects unique. When the epoch of village politics, in which the question of dividing the village common is paramount, has come to an end in the Australian colonies, and when the laws that govern the intercourse of nations have superseded the legislative tricks and reprisals of parochially-minded parliaments, Australia will undoubtedly have to be reckoned among the great empires of the world. It will be curious then, no doubt, for the historian of Australia to recall to mind the fact that two unpaid missionaries in Quaker garb undertook the task of perambulating it, New Testament in hand, from north to south, and from east to west, and accomplished their undertaking. No Christian nation in the world, perhaps, can look back to a time when it was treated as a parish, and when every inhabitant of the parish was known to have been personally canvassed for his vote and influence in favour of peace on earth, good-will among men. Australia, when it attains the fulfilment of its destiny as the United States of the southern hemisphere, will be able to refer to such a period in its history. When that time comes, if the memory of James Backhouse and G. W. Walker is revived, as no doubt it will be, the fact, perhaps, will not be overlooked that their mission was, above all, to the outcasts from the Christian society of the Old World, the acknowledged failures of Christian civilisation in Europe ; and the remembrance of the fact may perhaps help to guide the course of civilisation and of Christianity under the southern cross. A new empire, in which the mission of Quakers to convicts is an important date, may possibly have an example to show to older Christian communities of how to treat criminals, and, it is to be hoped, may have something to teach them, in regard to crime, in the way of substituting prevention for punishment.

The year 1835, in which the Quakers began their labours in New South Wales, saw Batman, and after him J. P. Fawkner, arrive at Port Phillip from Tasmania, and unconsciously found the colony of Victoria and its splendid capital, Melbourne. With Batman, Walker and Backhouse had made acquaintance during their travels in Tasmania, and it was no doubt rather the interest which they took in the proceedings of a friend, than any anticipation of the future of Port Phillip and of Melbourne, which led them to record in their journals "the following rare example of justice in dealing with the aborgines":—"In the 'Sydney Herald' of the 6th inst. it is mentioned that J. Batman, with the assistance of three Sydney blacks, whom we saw at his house, has purchased from a native tribe in the vicinity of Port Phillip a tract of land of about five hundred thousand acres. The payment consisted, in part, of one hundred blankets, tomahawks, knives, flour, &c., and it was agreed that a certain quantity of food, clothing, and arms was to be paid each year to the amount of about £200 sterling. This novel example of equitable arrangement with the aboriginal possessors of the soil will be hailed with satisfaction by every friend of humanity." Perhaps the reader of this entry in the Quaker's journal may be pardoned for being less struck with the equity of the arrangement than with the fact that it was made only some forty years ago, and that since then the hunting-grounds of the aborigines of Port Phillip have become the Brightons and Folkestones of the wealthy citizens of Melbourne.

In the year 1835 there must have been, in the "sailor-king's" navy, ships sometime out of commission, from which it would not have been difficult to select one for a voyage to the Antipodes. There must have been in that year in England a great many officers of the army and navy on half pay, ex-diplomatists, sinecurists, non-resident clergy and bishops of small dioceses, of whom one or two might have been appointed to sail in that vessel, and to see how the experiment of calling a new world of criminals into existence to redress the balance of the old was going to succeed. But, as if to show how much room the noblest political organisations in the world, and the best ecclesiastical institutions, will always leave for the friend of humanity to occupy on his own account and at his own expense, it was left to Hawden Bragg's apprentice and his companion to discover in the southern hemisphere more than one Black Hole of Calcutta the property of his Most Gracious Majesty. "At Campbell Town, a village in the midst of beautiful English-like scenery," they came upon a jail such as it would be difficult to match among government properties in despotic or even barbarous countries. Walker had his yard-tape with him, measured the principal ward, and noted the dimensions in his journal, $20\frac{1}{2}$ feet by $12\frac{1}{2}$, height 8 feet. A wine-vault beneath the police-office or court-house had been converted into a prison which consisted of this dungeon and five solitary cells, lighted and ventilated only with a few small air-holes opening on the road, and only to be explored in the daytime with a lamp. Here as many as sixty persons being confined at one time, the effect on certain occasions, when the climate of Campbell Town was more than usually like that of Calcutta, was that the magistrates, sitting above, were driven away from the seats of justice, while the suffocated prisoners had to be carried out at intervals to have a chance of recovery, which it was almost a doubtful act of humanity to give them.

The huts of the chain-gang working on the road were surrounded with a wooden fence, and hence the name of stockade applied to a cluster of these huts. At Maitland the Quakers visited the Iron Gang stockade, Walker with his measure and note-book in hand. This roadside bastile consisted of huts set on wheels, and intended to accommodate twenty men each. Their measure was taken, and it was found to be $7\frac{1}{4}$ feet by 14, with 6 feet of height, thus allowing one foot and a half of space for each of the twenty inmates as they lay

o

side by side on wooden shelves. In the judgment of our unpaid inspectors of penal establishments, confinement in these cages from six in the evening till six in the morning, especially during hot Australian weather, must have entailed "a considerable amount of distress." Whether the amount of distress was in excess of the demands of justice was a matter which was not nicely calculated with regard to the stockade any more than with respect to the penal settlement. It was not dealt out by weight at either place like the daily rations. On the whole, Walker concluded that if there was excess it was greatest on the side of the stockade. "Were I a prisoner," he says, "and had my choice between a stockade and a penal settlement, I should decidedly prefer the latter;" which reflection, considering he had sailed through the Gates of evil name into Macquarie Harbour, and that he had seen Norfolk Island, may be taken to mean that it was time for the friend of humanity to appear at the Iron Gang stockade with his yard-tape and his note-book.

Among chain-gangs in New South Wales, one at Marulan held the place which was conceded to Nottman's in Tasmania—for incorrigible wickedness. The Quakers walked twenty-three miles one day in the month of February, probably a day too warm for the comfort of travellers, and found the men of this gang drawn up before the hut on religious parade. It was a " relieving season of labour " to Walker's mind, though the audience seemed almost as little hopeful as any he had seen. The lieutenant in command mentioned that in a gang consisting of seventy men two hundred and sixty cases of flagellation had occurred in the course of sixteen months, or about four weekly. One back had received nine hundred lashes. The Quakers were much impressed with what they heard, and still more with what they saw. They had noticed often before the malformation of the heads of prisoners. Here it was more marked than they had ever before seen it. And perhaps this helped to make the occasion of his visit a "relieving one" to the mind of a friend of humanity like G. W. Walker. Idiocy has no other pleasing effect, but it does serve to soften the harsh features of crime.

The Quakers, in fulfilling their mission to convicts, were struck with the resemblance between the heads of the criminals and those of idiots. Philanthropists, whose mission has been specially to the insane, have been impressed with the same family likeness. Sir Robert Officer, of Tasmania, to whom the Quakers refer in terms of grateful respect, will pardon an old friend for naming him as one of these philanthropists, one who, from his long official connection with the Colonial Hospital for the Insane, has been obliged to devote a keen intelligence to the study of the heads of madmen, and who has had rare opportunities in Van Diemen's Land of comparing the outward lineaments of idiocy and of crime. His testimony, given from the side of the hospital, is emphatic as to the truth of the testimony delivered by the Quakers from the interior of the jail. Neither science nor humanity has spoken its last word as to the connection between crime and insanity.

The patronage of the Governor of New South Wales was invaluable to the Quaker missionaries, especially as regards their journeys and voyages to the more remote districts of the colony. Moreton Bay, then a small penal settlement which was to grow into Brisbane, the capital of Queensland, was the limit of their travels northward. They were allowed a passage and rations on board the Government schooner going to the settlement, and the vessel, for their sole convenience, was ordered to call at Port Macquarie, another penal establishment on the way. On board the schooner the friend of humanity's measuring tape was once more found to be an indispensable part of his equipment. There were forty-one convicts on board, linked together by a long chain passing over the fetters of the ankles, and confined to a jail in the hold, in a nearly tropical climate, at the hottest season of the year, without water and almost without room to change their position. This floating Black Hole, carrying the meteor flag of England, was found to measure 18 feet by 16 feet. Walker, in recording the fact, ventures to express the opinion that "the debasing effect upon the mind" of confinement in such a place was not likely to be the smallest part of the mischief attending it.

About four hundred prisoners constituted the principal part of the population of the capital of Queensland, and the treadmill was the principal object of interest to visitors. Here again the Quaker inspectors of jails found that punishment was meted out to crime rather with profuse liberality than with nice discrimination. They found the climate outside the treadmill tropical, and learning that the chain-gang inside had to lift their feet three thousand eight hundred and forty times without change, they could not help considering that the sufferings of fat men must be excessive. Men of the type of Cassius might be the greatest villains on the wheel, but their punishment in sultry weather was light compared with that of corpulent felons, whose misdeeds were comparatively trivial.

One journey on which Walker and his companion had to endure much fatigue, was that which they made in the direction of Wellington Valley, two hundred miles north-west of Sydney, the seat of a mission to the natives. The former suffered severely on the road from cramps, which he had too much inward light or common sense to regard in any other way than as a gentle "rebuke" for breaking the laws of health by excessive exertion. Walker and his companion did not readily credit accounts of the total depravity of human nature. They saw reason, as they fancied, to distrust such accounts in the instance of the most hardened convicts. But what they heard and saw of the blacks at Wellington Valley convinced them that something very like utter depravity was possible. What has been the history of almost every attempt to civilise the natives of Australia repeated itself here, with perhaps some aggravations of disappointment to the philanthropist. A party of native youths would assemble at the mission house to be taught reading and instructed in the Christian faith. "They would eat voraciously of the provisions set before them, smoke as much tobacco as they could get," receive as little education as possible, and in a few days get tired of civilisation and Christianity, and find an excuse for decamping into the bush, either in a friend's illness or an important engagement, or, not unlikely, in the missionary's refusal to supply Billy or Bob with a new pipe.

Much more pleasing and satisfactory than the visit to Wellington Valley was that which the Quakers made to an outlandish place midway between the Green Hills and Newcastle. Their object on this occasion recalls the parable of the lost sheep in yet another form than any in which the story of their travels may already have brought it to mind. An elderly man who had once been a Quaker was here in the position of an assigned servant. This old convict paid a compliment to the Christianity of his brethren which not every form of Christianity has deserved by its treatment of the fallen, if he expected that any of them would leave the society of the ninety and nine respectable Quakers, who needed no salvation, and would come into the wilderness to see whether he could not be brought to repentance. But whether unexpectedly or not, the satisfaction of finding that he was not forgotten by the fellowship to which his career had been no credit, was in store for him. The missionaries had much friendly conversation with their erring brother, and at a meeting of assigned servants to which they preached the gospel of forgiveness and charity, he was moved to make "a feeling allusion to the solemnity of the occasion," and to signify to his fellow-servants that, in his opinion, it was good to refrain from evil. Walker's final entry with regard to him in his journal is not without pathos. "The wanderer above alluded to accompanied us some miles, and at parting we had a solemn season as we extended some counsel in a few words, under the renewed feeling of the love of our Heavenly Father, which would gather all into the garner of rest and peace." Perhaps, on one not untenable view of the meaning of the parable of the lost sheep, and of much of the primitive gospel, it might appear to have been worth while for the Newcastle Quaker to travel to the Antipodes, and into a desert place between Newcastle and the Green Hills, only in order to share this "solemn season" with a fallen brother.

Gross evils connected with the system of disposing of

convicts as assigned servants came under the notice of the Quakers in New South Wales, as formerly in Tasmania. Drunkenness and all manner of vice and crime were skilfully promoted by a regulation permitting masters to pay prisoner-servants a third of their wages in drink. In case the solitude of bush life should have any tendency to repress criminal instincts and to check criminal habits, convicts were required to attend a monthly muster, at which it was certain that drink and evil communications would have the result of providing fresh material for the chain-gang and the penal settlement. In the fewest instances were any pains taken by settlers to encourage prisoner-servants in well-doing. As a rule, the effect of families being served by ticket-of-leave was the rapid deterioration of character on both sides. Walker writes that the colonial youth whom he saw at more than one place were not of a hopeful aspect as regards physique, intelligence, or morals. He was disposed to attribute the fact partly to climate and much more to intercourse with a class of servants with regard to whom, as has been seen, "the malformation of the head" was a constant subject of remark on his part and on that of his companion.

With their experience of upwards of two years' travel in New South Wales, added to their intimate knowledge of convict life in Tasmania, the Friends were able to speak with an authority all their own in regard to transported felons. On that subject it may be safely asserted that no two men living were better qualified to give advice to the British Government than James Backhouse and George Washington Walker. Their advice was actually in due form imparted to Parliament, and was not, it may be assumed, without effect upon the course of legislation. Returning for a brief period to Tasmania, after once more and finally subjecting Sydney to household visitation in the interest of righteousness, temperance, and peace, they found a new governor in power in the colony, and, of course, a new private secretary attending the governor. The former was Sir John Franklin; the latter, Captain Maconochie, the prison reformer; and from both of these distinguished men the Quakers received a cordial welcome. Captain Maconochie, in drawing up the well-known report on the subject of convict discipline in the colonies, which was presented to the House of Commons, was indebted to the Quaker missionaries for valuable assistance, of which he made acknowledgment in these terms : " The well-known and highly-respected Quakers, James Backhouse and George Washington Walker, who have been above five years in the penal settlements, observing closely the operation of their existing constitution, not only cordially agree with the views which I have here attempted to explain regarding it, but also with those I entertain for its amelioration. They have accordingly given me a testimony to this effect, which I subjoin, and also placed their MS. journals and reports in my hands that I may select whatever passages I may find in them to my purpose. I feel extremely indebted for this kindness, and avail myself of it gladly."

A royal commission existing for the same number of years, travelling over the same ground, and performing the same work, would have cost England a good deal more than the rations on board a convict schooner with which the Friends were several times provided at the expense of the State. It would have cost more, done less, done it not so well, and yet perhaps would have received the thanks of both Houses. But the Quakers, serving another Master than that to which a commission would have looked for pay and praise, were well pleased that, as the reward of their five years' services, it was permitted to them to lift up their testimony in the British Parliament in favour of a more humane treatment of prisoners. Neither John Bright nor William E. Forster was then in the House, and though it was four years since Joseph Pease, upon his affirmation, had been admitted a member, probably he was the only Quaker, as he was the first, who had a seat within its walls. Did any member, except Joseph Pease, remember, on reading the report in which the testimony of the Quakers was quoted in favour of the humane treatment of convicts at the Antipodes, that one of the earliest public appearances of the Quaker fraternity was when they stated in Parliament, in 1659, that two thousand of their number had suffered imprisonment in Newgate, and when one hundred and sixty-four Friends in good health reported themselves by name to the Government as desirous of being imprisoned, in place of an equal number whose term of confinement illness threatened to cut short? If the report of 1837 did thus carry the mind of any M.P. back to 1659, he must have reflected that a long and intimate connection had existed between Quakers and convicts, to the advantage of the one, and not to the discredit of the other.

"On the third of the eleventh month," 1837, six years and two months after leaving home, Walker and Backhouse set sail from Tasmania for Melbourne. From this point, at which the main interest of their mission no longer lies among convicts, it is only possible to mark the direction which they took in their wanderings. All that lends to Walker's formal, unadorned record of their travels in Australia, Mauritius, and Africa, a deeper interest than belongs to all but a very few of the best stories ever told of missionary toil and adventure and observation, must be left in the bulky biographical sepulchre to which the memory of a good man has been consigned.

Melbourne was found by the Friends to consist of about one hundred weatherboard huts, helping the eucalyptus to shade ground gently sloping to the Yarra Yarra. Adelaide, to which they proceeded from Melbourne in the year one of both cities, supplied them rather with recollections of numerous ill-conditioned natives than of thriving English colonists, such as welcomed the Duke of Edinburgh in 1869. Excessive heat, mosquitoes, sand-flies—"bless you, a heart-breaking country" to look at—all the plagues which have made Western Australia a place of punishment to British soldiers and settlers as well as to convicts, did not deter the Quakers from completing the round of the colonies by a visit to Albany, Perth, and Freemantle. Sand and blight were in his thoughts as Walker made the last entries in his journal — the sand which was described as beautiful grass in advertisements relative to Western Australia; the blight which had been found to pervade all the colonies alike, and which was due, not to climate, but to drink.

Anxious to enter upon the field of work in South Africa, of which they had obtained a passing glimpse on touching at Cape Town, the Quakers spent only two months and a half in Mauritius—too short a period, as they felt, for making satisfactory acquaintance with the state of an island in which Quakers, as anti-slavery Christians, had much to observe. After seeing a good deal of a strangely mongrel population, and making the best possible use of their slender stock of French in the way of preaching the Gospel, they left the island, entertaining the modest hope that, "in connection with other sources of evidence," the knowledge which they had obtained might be made to subserve the general interests of humanity. The abolition of slavery was too recent an event, the prevalence of Parisian morals, not improved by exportation, was too palpable a fact, to admit of their indulging any more sanguine expectation. They were prevented by circumstances which they much regretted from seeing the grave of "Paul and Virginia;" but had they accomplished their purpose of visiting the spot, the web of reflection which would have been woven under their broad-brims would certainly have been of very mixed texture, and included something belonging to a French idyl, much appertaining to a Parisian Sunday, and something also connected with the prospect of a kingdom of God eternal upon earth. Their faith in this kingdom, apart from the results of their individual efforts on its behalf, and apart from the existence of the religious body to which they belonged, was characteristically firm ; it was only staggered for a moment, not shaken, by Macquarie Harbour, Norfolk Island, the Mauritius.

Their destination on leaving Mauritius was South Africa, where they spent two years and three months, and where their travels extended beyond the limits of Cape Colony, to within a few days' journey of Port Natal in the east, to Motito in the north, and across the Orange River into the Great Namaqualand on the west. Eighty mission stations at the time represented European Christianity in its beneficence and also its numerous divisions. The Friends paid a visit to every one of the eighty. Every town and village within the limits of the colony made acquaintance with their zeal for the promotion of temperance and righteousness and peace. In the course of their wanderings from south to north and from ocean to ocean, they travelled six thousand miles by waggon or on horseback. Starting from Cape Town, to follow the line of the East Coast, and afterwards to strike across country, they did not behold the Atlantic from the Great Namaqualand without having toiled and suffered in the service of humanity, under an African sun, as other missionaries in the same regions have toiled and suffered. Many of the best books of travel in existence relate to the ground over which Walker and his companion travelled on their errand of peace. Walker's journal will bear comparison with the best of them in point of interest and even entertainment. It is amusing as well as instructive to note in its pages the effect upon familiar African scenes and characters, of being looked at from under a broad brim and through Quaker spectacles, and of being set down, as much without exaggeration as without malice— described with the austere simplicity of the book of Genesis, yet not without the shrewdness of a Newcastle "canny" man. A special interest perhaps attaches for the moment to many passages in the Quaker's journal, referring to scenes in which the marks of the Kaffir War of 1836 were still fresh.

Sneers at Christian missions in Africa, which have been elaborated by wits at home, and which have received countenance from too credulous missionaries and too censorious travellers, have not been without effect upon the hopes of the Christian world in regard to the annexation of the countries of the Kaffir and the Hottentot. As an antidote to these sneers, nothing better than Walker's journal of his tour of inspection among Christian missions was ever published. The same faith in God as good, and in man as not altogether bad, which our Quaker missionaries found to be the strength of their hearts and the force of their sermons at Macquarie Harbour and Norfolk Island, enabled them with singular success to overcome the world where the world consisted of the dominion of rival Christian sects often at war, and of heathen tribes seldom at peace. They had to record at the end of their travels in Africa, that they had been received as friends and brothers, not only by persons of different religious persuasion and country, but of different colour and language. Quaker Christianity, consisting only of a very little of breadth of brim, and much of warmth of heart, was the best passport they could have carried with them on their journey. If their waggon, as it creaked upon its rude axle and jolted over stray boulders, in the Great Namaqualand, could have been pointed to as that which was conveying to the heathen the knowledge of a peculiar use of the personal pronoun, or of the importance of correct views respecting infant baptism, its approach might have been regarded with indifference, or have called forth hostility at some mission stations and at various native kraals. But wherever they went it was understood that their errand was peace and goodwill, and on that errand they were everywhere welcome.

Moshesh, the famous Bechuana chieftain, hearing what was done in the name of Christ in the territories of some of his neighbours, once set out from his kraal, with a thousand head of cattle driven before him, intending to buy a missionary. He would have been fortunate if chance had thrown in his way a missionary like G. W. Walker or James Backhouse. Wonderful might have been the results if Quaker Christianity, often persecuted in Europe, had been for once established by law in Africa. Problems of deep interest in Church and State, which perplex European statesmen, and are the gage of battle between European sects, might have been shown by the Bechuanas to be capable of solution. It is certain that if G. W. Walker, or his companion, or any missionary of the same spirit as theirs, had been intrusted with the direction of religious affairs in the dominions of Moshesh, the spectacle would have been exhibited there which has been rarely seen in England and in Europe, of a Christianity not too good for the world—not too studious of perfection in regard to its dress and ornaments to attend to the work of clothing the naked, and casting out devils, and turning spears into ploughshares, and swords into pruning-hooks.

On quitting Africa the Quaker missionaries parted,

after nine years of fellowship in toil and in the peace of God, never to meet again. Backhouse went home to York. Walker returned to Tasmania, married, and settled in that colony. In Tasmania he commenced business as a draper, and succeeded well enough to satisfy his modest ambition, though he rather restricted his trade by refusing to sell lace and other vanities for which his lady customers were in the habit of making anxious inquiries. Then he was appointed to a post in the savings bank, and in the occupancy of that office he died at a comparatively early age. It may well be supposed that such a missionary as we have made acquaintance with in him was not idle as a philanthropist after he took to trade. The colony owes Hawdon Bragg's apprentice as much gratitude, perhaps, as is due from it to any man that ever set foot upon its shores. Every good work proposed by anybody else was heartily seconded by him. Many a good work owed its commencement and its success to his almost unaided labour. His advocacy of temperance in particular, his warfare against drunkenness, was crowned, as it deserved to be, with splendid results. When he died it was not a class, or a sect, or a city, but a people, a colony of a hundred thousand English men and women, that lamented the loss of a brave, devoted, noble man. The lesson of his life does not need to be pointed out in these pages. It is that a good life, even if it begin in a draper's shop and end at a clerk's desk, may have imperial issues.

ROBERT MOFFAT AND SOUTH AFRICA.

LIKE some great citadel, the interior of Central Africa had for ages defied the endeavours of civilised man to make a breach and enter in. It was an unknown land,—some thought it a desert, others fancied it was a fruitful country. The Portuguese, full of adventure, and fired by the love of gain, had managed to find points of settlement on the outermost borders, both east and west, and as the outpost of an army will sometimes make exchanges of handy commodities with the enemy's outpost, they had contrived to enlist the tribes with which they came into contact in the most nefarious traffic. They set the one tribe to prey upon the other for the purpose of obtaining slaves. At other points, here and there, adventurous merchants had advanced so far as to enable them to barter the showy productions of European industry, for the ivory and the skins of the interior. But the great heart of the continent was still untrodden of the white man's foot : and it was reserved for a poor Scotch lad who, self-taught, had managed to

ROBERT MOFFAT.

Master Missionaries. p. 226.

scramble forward to a university, and to study medicine and theology whilst he lived almost on beggars' fare, to penetrate far into the interior and open up to the civilised world a new and most extraordinary region, likely at no very distant time to be the centre of a mighty commerce. Dr. Livingstone is the great explorer of Central Africa; but his way was, in a sense, prepared for him. The names of Moffat and Livingstone must hereafter be linked together in all future histories of missionary enterprise and exploration. Moffat was the first to put a foot forward, and the romance of Central African discovery may be said to begin with him. Before his settlement at Kuruman, the Dutch missions in Africa had been mere preparations. He connects the first great missionary enterprise in that region with the last one; and his recent home-coming makes a sketch of his work not unfitting at the present moment.

When Robert Moffat, with the consent of his pious Scotch parents, left his gardening and set sail for the Cape of Good Hope, on the last day of October 1816, he was only twenty years of age—a mere stripling. But he was a mature man in self-possession and in Christian faith; and these are the main qualities required in missionary enterprise. He had devoted himself to the cause without wavering, and he entered on his arduous work with self-reliant hope. His first battle was not with the heathen, however, but with the British Governor, who was loath to give his sanction to missionaries proceeding outside the Cape Colony, as it was feared that, through want of discretion, they would get the tribes of the interior into broils and misunderstandings. He was as firm in his representations and applications as the Governor was in his refusals; and, during the delay, he made good use of his time in getting instruction in Dutch from a pious Hollander with whom he had taken up his abode, so that he might be able to preach to the Boers and their servants. As a means of meeting his demands half-way, he was offered the post of Resident with one of the Kaffir chiefs; but he declined to mix up political duties with his preaching of the Gospel, and would either go untrammelled or not at all.

Permission at length was granted him, and he at once set out for the Orange River, to try to convert the notorious Africaner, who had made his name a terror by his maraudings and murders. On the way, Moffat preached to the Hottentots, wherever he could get opportunity. On all hands he was warned against approaching Africaner. One old motherly lady, wiping the tear from her eye, bade him farewell, saying, " Had you been an old man, it would have been nothing, for you would soon have died, whether or no; but you are *young*, and going to be eaten up by that monster !"

That Moffat was accompanied by the missionary Ebner, who had some time before been a resident at Africaner's kraal, was not much in his favour; for Ebner apparently had left on bad terms with the chief's brother. But the party went on—over desert plains, where sometimes the oxen would sink down in the sand from sheer fatigue, and where the want of water was a terrible infliction; and over rocky mountains, where the exposure to the scorching heat of the hot season was like to induce fever every moment.

Africaner's welcome was not warm; and the old misunderstanding between Ebner and the chief's brother soon issued in a quarrel. On this Ebner had to flee, and Moffat was left alone to deal with the remorseless chief and his bloodthirsty people as best he might. He dealt with them wisely, and won a victory which is memorable. If you look at Robert Moffat's portrait, what will most probably strike you at the first is the mixture of firmness, shrewdness, and tact that predominates in it. He was a born manager of men. You can see that in his eye. If it had not been that the grace of God soon took possession of his heart, he would no doubt have been a most successful man of business. But the grace of God does not kill man's natural faculties; it only consecrates them. Moffat *was* a successful man: he proved himself a wise master-gardener for God; he was prudent for the souls of men, as plants of rarest beauty and of untold value. So, in spite of the barrenness of the country, the want of water, and the thinness of the population, he began his work. "He commenced stated services, opened a school, and itinerated amongst the neighbouring 'werfs' or villages. His food was milk and meat. He would live for weeks together on one, and then, for a while, on both; but frequently he had recourse to the 'fasting girdle.' After a day's occupation, he would often, in the stillness of the evening, silently retire to the rocky boulders in the neighbourhood of the station, to commune in sorrow and joy with Him 'in whose service he had embarked; sometimes, too, to think over the past, and of the home and friends he had left behind, perhaps for ever; and occasionally to draw from his violin some favourite sacred melody, or the loved airs of his native country."*

So Moffat laboured for years. Often it seemed to him as though he was "beating the air;" and his heart sank. It was lucky for him that he had outward as well as inward resources. He could put his hand to anything; and that gained him respect from the Namaqua-men more than his learning. "My dear old mother," he tells us himself, "to keep me out of mischief in the long winter evenings, taught me to knit and to sew. When I would tell her I meant to be a man, she would say, 'Lad, ye dinna ken whaur your lot may be cast.' She was right; for I have often had occasion to use the needle since."

He was not unfrequently in sore straits for his daily food; but he only found himself the more disposed for

* "A Life's Labours in South Africa; being the Story of the Life-work of Robert Moffat, Apostle to the Bechuana Tribes." Published by John Snow & Company. A most interesting little work.

meditation. He wandered, and taught, and preached without faltering; and at length the blessing came. Africaner himself was the first convert. The change that came over the chief was marvellous. The wild Namaqua warrior was gentle as a child. And he was very solicitous for the temporal welfare of his friend—intently watchful that the missionary should want for nothing that he or his people could give him. The man who hitherto had only had one ambition—to lead his people to war and plunder—now directed them to build a house for the missionary, made him a present of cows, regularly attended the services, was assiduous in the study of the Scriptures, and sincerely mourned over his past life. His love for Moffat was deep and abiding. He nursed the missionary through the delirium of a bilious fever; and when his friend and teacher was compelled by circumstances to visit Cape Town, nothing would content Africaner but to be allowed to accompany him thither, even at great risk, for a price had years before been set upon his head. His appearance with Moffat in Cape Colony produced a very deep impression, as may be conceived. Whilst there it was proposed that Moffat should not return to Namaqualand; but should proceed to the Bechuana country, which lies to the north-east of Namaqualand, and found a mission there. To this Africaner consented, as he had some hopes of removing, with his people, to a district not far distant from where Moffat now proposed to settle. So went to Griqua-town for assistance against the common enemy. The Mantatees were now mercilessly slaughtered by the Bechuanas; so that Moffat had to ride into the field and intercede for the women; who, seeing mercy was shown them, would bare their bosoms, exclaiming, "I am a woman! I am a woman!" The self-sacrificing conduct of the missionaries so moved the chief, that he aided them in the laying out of the new station at Kuruman, which was for so long Mr. Moffat's head-quarters.

From Kuruman Moffat made many journeys. He visited Makaba, king of the Bauangketsi, some two hundred miles further north, and was received with favour, though at first the king was not disposed to converse on religious matters. But a favourable impression was then made on some of the courtiers. On returning from this visit to Makaba, he nearly fell into the hands of the Mantatees, who had surged onward in their devastating course into the interior. Vague reports of danger reached Mrs. Moffat, who remained in a fever of suspense with her two children. Moffat, however, reached home safely, though he had been much delayed and in great danger.

It was not till the year 1828—seven years after their arrival—that the Moffats began to see some signs of the fruit of their labours. A church and schoolhouse were erected; the morals of the people rapidly improved; for the greasy skins, decent raiment was now substituted.

Some knowledge of the arts of civilised life took the place of savage ignorance. Moffat was able now to pursue his work of translating the Scriptures into the Sechuana tongue; and he was day by day busy at the printing-press. The natives would watch the sheets go into the press white, and come out a moment after covered with black characters, to their unspeakable wonder.

News of the great work of the missionaries at Kuruman was soon carried far into the interior. A very notable event was the appearance of two messengers from the Matabele king, Moselekatze, who wished to know more of the work of the white men. This potentate ruled a large portion of the territory now known as the Transvaal Republic, was a great warrior, and a terror to all the surrounding tribes. Moffat received these ambassadors with great kindness, and showed them as much of civilised appliances as he could. Owing to some risk they ran from the tribe through whose territory they must pass on their return home, he himself accompanied them on their way. Having gone so far with them, they urged that he should go on and see the king. And so, at last, he agreed to do. Moselekatze took kindly to the missionary, and showed himself capable of gratitude. Placing his hand on the missionary's shoulder one day, he addressed him by the title of "Father," saying: "You have made my heart as white as milk. I cease not to wonder at the love of a stranger. You never saw me before, but you love me more than my own people." Moffat did not leave until he had got the king's consent that a mission should be established there. A party from the American Missionary Society were sent. But the missionaries were very unfortunate. They were much tried with fever, and one of their wives died soon after reaching the station. And then the Matabele were set upon by another tribe and had to flee, and all that the missionaries could do was to throw themselves on the mercy of the victors.

In 1832 Moffat had completed his translation into Sechuana of the Gospel of Luke. He went to the Cape, and got liberty to use the official press; but who was to supply him with compositors? He had simply to set to work himself, under the direction of the official printer. He "set up" the matter with his own hands, and was soon able to return in triumph to the station with copies of Luke's Gospel and his own hymns, together with the press, which Dr. Philip had presented to him, and some other gifts. By 1840 the translation of the New Testament was completed, and before 1843 thousands of copies had been distributed, Moffat having superintended the printing in London during a short visit home.

And at this point Moffat's story gets interlaced with that of Livingstone, who went out with him at this time, together with some other missionaries. While

Livingstone was wandering among the Bakwains, in retirement at Lepeloli, or labouring at Kolobeng, Moffat was pushing on with his translation of the Old Testament, amid ill-health and much loss of power. He worked without pause; for the cause of the Gospel was prospering, and each fresh proof of its power was with him only a new incentive to effort.

The attacks of the Transvaal farmers on Livingstone's station at Kolobeng forced him to think of setting out to try and find a new field for his people further to the north. In God's good providence this was the beginning of Livingstone's missionary explorations. He saw so much, and was tempted further and further on until, as the result, the famous journey across the continent of Africa was undertaken. And that the reports of Moffat's good work had already travelled far into the unknown countries, was proved by the fact that, while Livingstone was on the Zambesi, he learned from the natives there that the English had come to Moselekatze and told him that it was wrong to fight and kill; and that since the English had come he had sent out his men not to kill and plunder, but to collect tribute of cloth and money. There can be no doubt that this rumour, spreading further and further inland, prepared the way for Livingstone's extraordinary journeys.

And whilst Livingstone was thus engaged, Moffat

was planning how to help him. His health had suffered from the close application, continued now through years, to the translation of the Scriptures. He was urged to go home for a time. Instead, he resolved to recruit himself by a trip to the Limpopo district, several days' journey to the north of Kolobeng, where Moselekatze and his people had settled when they were driven from their old quarters. Moffat's visit was of singular interest. He was kindly received by the king, now grievously ill of dropsy, and, after some time, obtained permission to preach to the people. He also prescribed for the king's ailment, and secured his interest in Livingstone's travels, getting him to forward men with letters and supplies to Linyanti, on the Chobe river, two or three hundred miles further to the north, which letters and supplies, as we know, were received by Livingstone from the Makololo people, who had taken them in charge, nearly a year afterwards. As for Moselekatze, he was loath to let Moffat leave him, pleading that he had not yet shown him sufficient kindness. And as for Moffat, he returned greatly restored in health, and full of hope that very soon Christianity would be regularly introduced among these people.

Livingstone's visit to England in 1856 had the effect of wondrously reviving the interest in African missions, the London Society resolving to establish missions among the Matabele and Makololo. Naturally Moffat was overjoyed at receiving this news. It was what he had for forty years been working for. His translation of the Scriptures into the Sechuana tongue—dialects of which, not varying much from each other, are spoken over almost the whole of South Africa as far as the equator—could now be cast abroad to do its work. The undertaking had been a very trying one in the circumstances, and Moffat's health had suffered from the close application which for many years had been required from him. But now the task was finished—a task which of itself would have been enough to give Moffat a place among the greatest of human benefactors, even had he not been the adventurous missionary he was. "No evidence," writes the learned Seiler, "can be produced that the whole of the Scriptures was, by any one person, rendered into Saxon. Even Wickliffe had the help of many persons; much more Coverdale. Bede was translating the Gospel of John at the time of his decease. But Robert Moffat, who began with the Gospel of Luke, has lived to translate the whole Bible into the barbarous dialect of South Africa, and will, we trust, live to see it circulating among the natives, who both speak and in many instances can read it."

Moffat himself has given a very remarkable instance of the power of the Scriptures over the heathen mind—an instance which forms quite a romantic episode. "In one of my early journeys with some of my companions, we came to a heathen village on the banks of the Orange River, between Namaqualand and the Griqua country. We had travelled far, and were hungry, thirsty, and fatigued. From the fear of being exposed to lions, we preferred remaining at the village to proceeding during the night. The people at the village rather roughly directed us to halt at a distance. We asked water, but they would not supply it. I offered the three or four buttons which still remained on my jacket for a little milk; this also was refused. We had the prospect of another hungry night at a distance from water, though within sight of a river. We found it difficult to reconcile ourselves to our lot; for, in addition to repeated rebuffs, the manner of the villagers excited suspicion. When twilight drew on, a woman approached from the height beyond which the village lay. She bore on her head a bundle of wood, and had a vessel of milk in her hand. The latter, without opening her lips, she handed to us, laid down the wood, and returned to the village. A second time she approached, with a cooking vessel on her head, and a leg of mutton in one hand, and water in the other. She sat down without saying a word, prepared the fire, and put on the meat. We asked her again and again who she was. She remained silent till affectionately entreated to give us a reason for such unlooked-for kindness to strangers. The solitary tear stole down her sable cheek when she replied, 'I love Him whose servants ye are; and surely it is my duty to give you a cup of cold water in His name. My heart is full; therefore I cannot speak the joy I feel to see you in this out-of-the-way place.'" She was a lonely disciple indeed, and her only means of keeping the spiritual life awake within her was a copy of the Dutch New Testament which she had got from Mr. Helm when in his school years before, previous to removing with her relatives far up-country.

And so, realising the great opportunity that was now given to spread the knowledge of the Gospel, and to distribute the Word of God, in the interior, Moffat declined to seek the rest he so much needed in retirement, or in a trip to England, as he had been recommended to do. In spite of the risks of African travel and his advanced years, he resolved to visit his old friend Moselekatze again, in order to further the proposed settlement of missionaries. When there on a former occasion, Moffat had set forth to the king the simple principles of Gospel truth, and urged upon him to receive Christian teachers. But the king would not hear of any "teachers" coming unless Moffat would come with them. Moffat was this time received with great enthusiasm both by king and people; they had been longing for another visit from him. The king was willing to receive the teachers, if Moffat would only stay with them. "You must come too," the king urged. "How shall I get on with people I don't know, if you are not with me?" But after awhile he said enthusiastically,

"By all means bring teachers. You are wise; you are able to judge what is good for me and my people better than I do. The land is yours; you must do for it what you think is good." And so the king agreed to give the missionaries a spot of ground on which to settle, Moffat having made him understand clearly that they were not to trade, nor to look to him for their food, as they would themselves dig, and plant, and sow, and purchase whatever they required. Moffat, however, urged on the king to do all that he could to open up a trade with the tribes on the Zambesi.

It was during this visit that Moffat's influence with Moselekatze was so clearly shown by his obtaining the release of Macheng, the son of the late king of the Bamangwatos. Macheng's father had been killed in an engagement, and the child had been taken prisoner some time afterwards, when he was under the care of a Bechuana chief, Sechele. He had been so kept for several years. Moffat accompanied him to his own country. There were great rejoicings over the deliverance of the young chief. "Is it not through the love of God that Macheng is among us to-day?" said Sechele. "A stranger, one of a nation—who of you knows its distance from us?—he makes himself one of us, enters the lion's abode, and brings out to us our own blood." One of the Matabele, who had accompanied Moffat and Macheng, now assured the assembled multitude that Moselekatze desired nothing but to live in amity with them. Sechele and his people were overjoyed to hear such words from the representative of a tribe which, though distant from them, had been till now a terror to them both by night and by day.

Moffat now proceeded to Cape Town to meet Livingstone, who was on his way to the Zambesi. They had not seen each other for six years. The joy of the meeting may be imagined. There would be much to speak of and discuss. But Livingstone's halt was short. He proceeded on his great expedition; and in a few months more Moffat was once again at Cape Town, welcoming the new missionaries, among whom was his own son, John Moffat. At Kuruman they divided into two bands. One party went under charge of Mr. Helmore, who had been for many years stationed at Likatlong, northwards to the land of Makololo; the other went forward, in the care of Mr. Moffat, to Moselekatze's country. Here they were not only received kindly, but met with a sort of triumphal reception. An epidemic had broken out among the missionaries' oxen. Moffat advised the king respecting it, but he was willing to run the risk. The missionary, however, had more consideration for the vast herds of the Matabele, and still hung back. The king, therefore, sent word to return the oxen, and men were despatched to drag the waggons to their destination, which in spite of many obstacles was accomplished. Thus auspiciously the missionaries reached the settlement of the Matabele.

This mission has been very successful. Moselekatze died some years after the settlement; but his successor, Lobengole, was as favourably disposed towards the missionaries as he was. The Makololo mission, however, did not fare so well. A series of misfortunes awaited it, whose story has been told very graphically, though with full details, by the Rev. John Mackenzie in his volume, "Ten Years North of the Orange River." We must turn to him and his companions for a little space.

It had been one of the inducements to the establishment of these missions that the chief of the Makololo had agreed with Dr. Livingstone to shift from the swamps of Linyanti to the north bank of the Zambesi, on missionaries being settled amongst them; whilst, at the same time, it was believed that Mr. Moffat's influence with Moselekatze was so strong as to be trusted to induce him to desist from any kind of armed interference with the Makololo. The missionaries, Mr. Helmore, Mr. Price, and Mr. Mackenzie, of course, anticipated difficulty in the accomplishment of the plan (for the removal of a tribe is a hard matter, even though the chief has promised), just as they looked forward to many sufferings in their journey; and, indeed, it is doubtful whether they would have been brave enough to have set out at all, had it not been that Dr. Livingstone had promised to meet them at Linyanti, and to make them known to the people.

The journey proved trying beyond all their expectations. They had due share of disappointments and hindrances between Cape Town and Kuruman; but the last stage was little short of being only a succession of misfortunes. Owing to sickness, it was found necessary that Mr. Helmore and Mr. Price should at once go forward, in case they should miss Dr. Livingstone at Linyanti, and that Mr. Mackenzie should follow them in a few months. Durings these months at Kuruman, Mr. Mackenzie devoted himself to the study of Sechuana, and by mixing as much as possible with the people, was soon able to preach in their language. His spare time was given to the study of medicine. In May 1860, he started in the wake of Messrs. Helmore and Price, with supplies which a native had failed to take on, as he had agreed to do. When they had gone forward through the desert, so as to get news of Mr. Helmore's party, they found that they had suffered much from want of water in passing through it. Mrs. Helmore wrote: " I felt anxious at the thought of spending another day like the past; and was looking out in distress, when I saw in the bright moonlight a figure at a distance coming along the road. At first I could not make it out, it looked so tall; but on coming nearer, who should it prove to be but my servant girl Kionecoe, eighteen years of age, carrying on her head an immense calabash of water. On hearing of our distress she volunteered to aid us. She had walked four hours. Another servant had set out with her; but as he had driven the sheep the day before a great distance, without either food or water, he became so exhausted that he lay down under a bush to rest, and on the girl came, in the dead of night, in a strange country infested with lions, bearing her precious burden. Oh, how grateful I felt to her! Surely woman is the same all the world over! She had only lived with me since June, was but an indifferent servant, and had never shown any particular attachment to the children; but this kind act revealed her heart, and seemed to draw us more closely together, for her conduct since has been excellent. I made a bed for her beside me in the fore part of the waggon, the children having slaked their thirst in the deliciously cool water. We all slept till six o'clock. I made coffee, and offered some to Kionecoe and her companion, who had now come up. At first they declined it, saying the water was for me and the children. I had now the happiness of seeing the children enjoy a meal of tea and biscuits; and then once more filling up my two bottles, I sent the calabash, with the remainder of its contents, to my husband, who by this time stood greatly in need of it. The distance was about twelve miles. I afterwards found that we were about the same from the water."

Through Bushmanland, where on more than one occasion the track was lost, they proceeded slowly; now waiting for guides, now in terror of lions, now delayed by the breaking of waggon-wheels, the sinking of the waggons in the sand, or the want of water. "A missionary," as Robert Moffat says, "must be able to put his hand to anything." "I had to exercise my skill as a waggon-mender," says Mr. Mackenzie. "I had to put in a false nave in one of the wheels, which, with my materials, was a most difficult undertaking. A shoemaker or a cabinetmaker making and inserting a set of false teeth would be in a position somewhat analogous to mine."

Now and then, owing to the fact that in some districts in the hot season there may be no water for hundreds of miles, the party had frequently to take very indirect roads. "One does not mind a roundabout road," said good old Mebalwe when a new route was proposed, "provided we have water on it." This expresses the whole character of travel in the African interior. Often there were difficulties with the guides. They would disappear in search of water for themselves at the most critical points, and all that was then left for the party was simply to unyoke the oxen and take such rest as they could. In a little time the defaulters would come back; and, on being asked the reason of their sudden disappearance, they would say that "the sun had killed them, and they had gone on to drink." Nevertheless, the guides were on the whole faithful, and disinterestedly considered in most cases what was best for all the party. Instead of recriminating on them when they returned, Mr. Mackenzie acknowledges that the party were always deeply relieved to see them again.

When they reached the Zouga, they were warned against proceeding towards Linyanti because of the tsetse, whose bite is so fatal to the oxen; and they were told that all the teachers who had gone last year to Makololo were dead save one. Not believing these reports, they went on; and while moving along the banks of the Zouga they were met by Mr. Price returning, who confirmed the report they had heard. Dr. Livingstone had not come forward to introduce them to the people, having been detained on the lower parts of the Zambesi. The chief had compelled the missionaries to live with him, and would not consent to their going to seek out a healthy place of settlement for themselves.

" He refused to remove to the highlands of Tabacheu, and objected to the missionaries going to reside in Shesheke, insisting that, as they had come to teach them, they should live where he lived. The missionaries soon saw that whatever influence Dr. Livingstone on his arrival might be able to exert upon Sekeletu and the Makololo, in his absence there was no hope of removing to the highlands north of the Zambesi." But the missionaries began to preach and to teach, crowds coming to hear them, till, unfortunately, fever broke out amongst them. The children went first, then Mrs. Helmore fell asleep, and in a few days Mr. Helmore followed her. The people did not seem to care whether they died or lived. The property of the mission was openly stolen whilst Mr. Price lay prostrated with fever. When he recovered, the same rapacity was practised, and it was evidently encouraged by the chief. In fact, he came to Mr. Price's quarters himself, and carried away several things, guns and ammunition amongst others. Mr. Price was not allowed to go away till he was completely robbed. He urged that if they did not let him go away soon they would have to bury him beside the others. The reply was, that he might just as well die there as anywhere else. After a good deal of talk and representation he was allowed to proceed. "Already," he says, "they had taken all my bed-clothing with the exception of what was just sufficient for one bed. But before my oxen could cross the Chobe, I had to deliver up one blanket. Every grain of corn which I had for food for the men they had taken; and I did not get even a goat for slaughtering on the road. These were my prospects for a journey of upwards of a thousand miles to Kuruman."

Mr. Price had suspicion of foul play and of poison having been given—a suspicion which Mr. Mackenzie does not countenance, preferring to believe charitably. But there can be little doubt, we imagine, that the Mambari, or half-caste Portuguese, who were in the habit of trading with the Makololo for ivory and for slaves, would use every means in their power to poison the minds of the Makololo against the new missionaries and Dr. Livingstone. Their interest lay in doing so; and such wretches as these will always act for their own interest. Mr. Price thus summed up his personal experiences at Linyanti:—

"If suffering in mission work is doing anything, then I have done something; if not, then I have done but little."

There was now, therefore, nothing for it but that the missionaries should turn their backs on Linyanti. They preached in various Makoba villages on their way, some of which had been before visited by missionaries; Lechulatebe, the chief of the Batowana, urging that a "teacher" should be sent among his people, as he had before gladly heard the truth, though it had now almost died away from the memories of him and his people. After some trials from fever, Kuruman was reached on the 14th of February, and Messrs. Mackenzie and Price were glad to find themselves once more in a Christian home under the roof of Mr. Ashton, Mr. Moffat's able and trusted coadjutor.

Just when another journey to Makololo-land was being meditated by Mr. Mackenzie, on account of Sekeletu having solemnly promised to remove to Tabacheu on his arrival, the news reached Kuruman of that chief's death. There was a contest for the chieftainship, and much bloodshed followed. The tribe was so decimated by internecine strife, that it soon became a prey to the weaker neighbours, who had formerly been periodically despoiled by it, and who now united to put an end to the existence of the common enemy. Mr. Mackenzie then settled at Shoshong, the capital of the Bamangwatos country, on the borders of the Kalihari desert. Here he was very successful. He then undertook a journey to the Matabele, and remained there for five months. Notwithstanding the liking Moselekatze had had for the white man, it was clear that it is, above all things, difficult to do away with heathen practices in a warlike tribe, trained as they had been, and to subdue their greed and bloodthirstiness. Mr. Mackenzie was offered a site for a mission and the same freedom as Mr. John Moffat and the rest had at Inyate; but Mr. Mackenzie fancied he was bound to remain at Shoshong, and told the chief that he could not decide till he had consulted his superiors. This elicited the commendations of the chief: "This is how the white men prevail; by the obedience which they render to superiors," said he.

"When I last saw Moselekatze he was very ill, unable to lift the cup to his lips," writes Mr. Mackenzie. "I was heartily sorry for him, and was glad to be able to say that his own missionaries would be able to help him as to medicines, as they had done before. To show the respect entertained by the chief for missionaries, and something akin to the dignity attaching to his own character, I may mention that, as we entered the yard previous to my final interview, we were informed by an attendant that 'we must not be offended, the chief's heart was white towards us, but there would be no shaking of hands that day.' We soon saw the reason; the chief had not power to move his arms from where he lay."

The ingrained military habit of the Matabele people

has been much against their thorough acceptance of Christianity; but a great change has been already effected, which is, no doubt, only the evidence and pledge of a still greater change. The missionaries have always been regarded with favour; and in one of their more recent battles under Lobengole, the successor of Moselekatze, the missionaries were allowed to attend to the enemy's wounded along with their own.

Mr. Mackenzie returned again to Shoshong, where he laboured, with much good result, till his return to England in 1870; doing, little by little, much for the cause of truth in the interior of South Africa. The work at Shoshong was left in the hands of a native teacher—Khamane—in whom Mr. Mackenzie has great confidence. He informs us that at the date of the publication of his work he had had two letters from Khamane, written by himself in his own language, in which he states that all the recognised members of the congregation continue to attend the weekly services; but that the members of the "outer circle" have fallen off during Mr. Mackenzie's absence. But Mr. Mackenzie can add these hopeful words:—"I am persuaded, however, that the new religion has taken such root at Shoshong as that, with a supply of Christian literature, it would not readily disappear, even if left to itself." He has since returned to his field of labour.

As for Mr. Moffat, Kuruman was with him henceforth but a centre for many and varied journeys to points of interest. His son, Mr. John Moffat, who came to Kuruman to act as his father's assistant in preaching and printing when Mr. Ashton left, tells how that his father, though then threescore and ten, shared with him the labour of riding to distant villages to preach or hold prayer-meetings. But the untiring energy of the old man could not hold out always; and in 1870, he and Mrs. Moffat returned to England, after he had served in the most trying portions of the missionary field for upwards of fifty years. Looking back on his life, it seems a very marvellous one. He himself is able unconsciously to summarise the result of his labours thus: —" Christianity has already accomplished much. When first I went to Kuruman scarcely an individual could go beyond. Now they travel in safety as far as the Zambesi. Then we were strangers, and they could not understand us. We were treated with indignity as the outcasts of society, who, driven from among our own race, took refuge with them. But, bearing in remembrance what our Saviour underwent, we persevered, and much success has rewarded our efforts. Now it is safe to traverse any part of the country, and traders travel far beyond Kuruman without fear of molestation. Formerly men of one native tribe could not travel through another's territory, and wars were frequent. Where one station was scarcely tolerated, there are several. The Moravians have their missionaries; the Berlin Society, theirs. Others, too, are occupied in the good work, besides many native gospel preachers. Very prosperous is our advanced station at Matabele, who, I quite expect, will one day become a great nation. They sternly obey their own laws; and I have noticed that when men of fixed principles become convinced of the truth of Christianity, they hold firmly to the faith and are not lightly shaken."

In these few words we have Robert Moffat's biography in essence and spirit. And what more needs to be said? Nothing; save to express the hope that to the aged servant of God there may yet be allotted many years to see fruit growing up from the seed which he himself in long-past days cheerfully planted in much faith and hope. He is the centre of the missionary history of South Africa—the connecting-link between its various apparently disconnected parts; and when Science and Trade shall have carried their lamps through the length and breadth of the vast continent, discovering all its outs and inns, they will yet be compelled to cast a generous and grateful glance back at Moffat as having done more than any other man to make their many triumphs possible.

DR. JAMES STEWART AND LOVEDALE.

WHEN the proposal was being discussed, to establish a monument to Dr. Livingstone in the shape of a missionary settlement on the south-western shore of Lake Nyassa, to be called after him Livingstonia, the name of Lovedale was very frequently introduced. The new mission-station, indeed, was to be formed after the model of Lovedale; and, not unnaturally, we wished to know about Lovedale, its origin, its mode of management, the work it has done, and is doing. So we have gratified ourselves by putting together all the information we could get; and believe that our readers will not be disinclined to receive an epitome of it at our hands.

They may remember, then, that in the most interesting papers, which were contributed to the pages of the "Sunday Magazine" by Dr. James Stewart, on "Dr. Livingstone and the Zambesi," he tells us that his object in joining Dr. Livingstone was to see for himself the possibility of establishing a mission in Central Africa. For this purpose he explored a large section of the Zambesi and the Shire river. The members of the English Universities' Mission, in spite of the sad loss of their lamented head, were still striving to establish themselves in the neighbourhood of the Lake Shirwa, on the mountain heights to the east of the Shire. But their work looked only too likely to collapse; and when Dr. Stewart returned from his adventurous expedition, the fate of that mission was taken as a warning by those most interested. Dr. Stewart himself was unshaken in his conviction of the possibility of such an enterprise; but, as decisive action at that time—now over thirteen years ago—seemed hopeless, he accepted Dr. Duff's advice to proceed to Lovedale, to strengthen the mission seminary there. "I can testify," says Dr. Duff, "that one of his difficulties was the possible diversion from his favourite scheme of invading Central Africa, which his acceding to such a course might entail. On the contrary, I took it upon me to assure him, that his going to Lovedale, and helping to raise the institution there to a position which might command the respect and confidence of the Cape Colony abroad and the Church at home, would be one of the surest means of enabling him to realise his long and fondly cherished design."

And so it has proved. Dr. Stewart may be regarded as the original proposer of the Nyassa Mission, and his practical experience gained at Lovedale must greatly aid him in making effective efforts for Livingstonia.

"Our intended position at Nyassa," says Dr. Duff, in

a graphic account of all the arrangements, "would be closely linked, in many ways, to Lovedale—receiving much help from it, and contributing something to it in return—so that the two missions would be made beneficially to act and react on each other. If the proposed settlement on Lake Nyassa, by God's blessing, succeeded, it was already Dr. Stewart's purpose, when he went there about a year hence (*i.e.*, about the present time), to take fifty or sixty young natives with him to Lovedale, train them there in industrial habits, useful knowledge, and, above all, the truths of the Christian faith, send them back as propagandists of the useful arts and true religion, and continue to carry on this reciprocal process until Livingstonia should not only have its primary and secondary schools, but its own higher gymnasium and collegiate institution too."

Though Livingstonia was planned originally by Scottish Free-Churchmen, it has been cordially supported by the Reformed Presbyterian Church, while the United Presbyterian and other Churches have shown the fullest sympathy, and indeed supplied some of the mission staff. A mission at another point on Lake Nyassa, founded by the Established Church of Scotland, is in friendly relationship and indeed in constant communication with it; boats and other things being held as common property. Livingstonia is thus in the best and highest sense non-sectarian; Dr. Stewart having, as we shall see, learned by experience that it would be disastrous to introduce the home divisions among Africans; and it is certain that by this feature of its character also it will be the better and more expressive monument of the manly, sympathetic Christianity of him after whom it is rightly named. In devoting himself to Lovedale, we thus see that Dr. Stewart, after all, took the shortest and most effective way to work, when the proper time arrived, on an ever-widening circle, in the interior, thus realising the old truth, that "Providence is the best preparer." While we leave him on his way to Lake Nyassa, let us glance for a little at the history of Lovedale.

Lovedale, named after the Rev. Dr. John Love, who was for a long period energetic Secretary to the Glasgow Missionary Society, is situated on the west bank of the Chumie, about six hundred and fifty miles in a south-eastern direction from Capetown. It is not, however, the original settlement of that name; the first mission buildings having been destroyed in the war of 1834. On returning to resume their work after peace had been declared, the missionaries fancied they could make a better choice. This they seem to have been successful in doing, since Mrs. Dalziel in 1870 describes the Lovedale Buildings as "prettily nestled among the grassy hills, reminding us of Moffat."* The later developments, which have made Lovedale more especially

---

* Quoted by the Rev. Robert Hunter in his "History of Free Church Missions in India and Africa," p. 349. T. Nelson & Sons.

interesting, were not for several years thought of. It was simply an ordinary mission-station, where earnest and fearless men week by week proclaimed the truth to a handful of converts—the number in 1831 was only eleven—and were ever making expeditions on this side or that, among the native tribes around them; founding new preaching stations wherever circumstances would permit. In 1841, the Rev. William Govan, who had been home on furlough, was sent out to establish a seminary, as it was felt that the education hitherto given to the children was too elementary. Natives and Europeans were to be associated on an equal footing in school, and taught to regard each other with mutual respect. It was hoped that, as in India, native teachers and preachers would thus be raised up. One peculiar fact was noted by Mr. Govan, and has been often verified since: "So long as the representatives of the two races remained boys, they were almost equal in mental power, as was shown by the fact that the prizes gained by the members of each race were almost exactly proportioned to the members of that race then in the class; but subsequently it was ascertained that when the boys grew up to manhood, the superiority of the Europeans became very marked."

In 1844 the stations of the Glasgow Missionary Society were transferred to the Free Church of Scotland, and amid changes and adversities of many kinds, the work was pushed forward, so that in 1847 there were thirty-seven communicants of various nations, and about one hundred and sixty pupils—boys and girls. In 1849, the Government, recognising the value of the institution, gave it practical support, and promised to increase it. The great Kaffir war by and by came on, and very much impeded the work; but in 1854, we read that the membership at Lovedale had risen to one hundred and sixty. In 1855, Sir George Grey, who was then the Governor of Cape Colony, and appreciated highly the work that was being done at Lovedale, suggested that an industrial department should be added. Sufficient money for this was soon forthcoming, and four trade-masters were brought from England—a carpenter, a mason, a waggon-maker, and a blacksmith. Suitable workshops were built, and apprentices assigned to each. The Government paid the masters—not interfering otherwise with the direction of the seminary. This plan would have wrought well, but after Sir George Grey had returned home, the Government support was not continued.

The industrial department was not allowed to drop, however. It was sustained with unflagging energy and patience. The converts had now reached that point, when they were able to give out of their small store. They subscribed to build their own churches; and education began to be so appreciated that it became evident they might by and by be able to pay to have their children taught. In 1863, the number of communicants in the Lovedale district was three hundred and forty-five, and the average attendance nine hundred and sixty-five. The whole sum contributed to the mission during the seven years prior to 1863 was £2000, and of that no less than £1750 by the people themselves. So matters went on, till changes occurred in the staff of the institution, and Dr. James Stewart, as we have said, joined it in 1865, soon to become its Principal. He at once set himself to work to improve the domestic condition of the people in the district; managing to induce some of them to try the experiment of "squaring the circle," *i.e.*, building their houses or huts square instead of round; and he added to the number of the trades in the institution, introducing printing. He also added largely to a library, which had been formed, and which he reorganised, so as to make it more easily available for the public from fifty to eighty miles round Lovedale as well as for the institution. The most notable change, however, that has taken place since Dr. Stewart's advent, is the reorganisation and extension of the girls' schools—the funds for this purpose having been collected by the Ladies' Society for Female Education in India and Africa. The great success of this school, first under Miss Waterston and then under Miss MacRitchie, rendered necessary the enlargement of the premises, and a commodious building for the girls' schools has been the result. But to get a clear idea of the work done, we must make abstract of a few figures gleaned from recent reports.

progress. There are also literary societies, senior and junior, well attended.

In the girls' department industrial work is combined with teaching, as in the boys, and the total receipts for work done during one year for sewing, washing, dressing, &c., was £60.

Of the various industrial departments we have not left ourselves room to speak particularly. They seem to vie with each other in attaining good results; only of the printing we must say that the specimens we have before us of the "Kaffir Express"—a newspaper started in 1871, and half in English, half in Kaffir—show not only good "composition," but really careful presswork; amply justifying Dr. Stewart's appeal to his fellow-missionaries for any printing work they may have to give. We are inclined to think that great wisdom was shown by Dr. Stewart in the introduction of telegraphy some years ago, before it had yet been thought of in many institutions in the home-country. Several of the natives are now adepts in manipulation, and others are being trained. This is likely to prove a most advantageous industry, as it has been found at home. We do not know if a small class in photography would succeed there as it has done at home in several instances. The natives, we learn, are imitative and neat-handed, and might turn out good photographers; and such skilled craftsmen, we presume, must be wanted already at Capetown, as they will by and by no doubt be in other parts of South Africa.

We regret to observe that loss is sometimes sustained in the farm work, there as elsewhere. But the loss in one direction is so far counterbalanced by gain in others; and we are glad to observe that Dr. Stewart can offer a good investment to capitalists at home.

"The loss of sheep and goats from the rains in 1874 was great—three hundred; but this result must be ascribed to the necessity of farming without capital, with which sheds might be erected. The want of capital need be no mystery to those who compare our income with our necessary expenditure, and probably a single glance into the dining-hall at the dinner hour will satisfy any one as to what the latter must be; but we must either stop the work or get on in the best way possible. Christian philanthropy might find a favourable investment in the purchase of farm implements and other plant for Lovedale. The annual return, for the good of so many African young men, would not be less than twenty-five per cent."

The mixing of European with native youths in the classes, &c., has been found to have a very good effect. On this point the Report for 1874 speaks well :—

"Some among our Europeans here are young men of superior talent and great promise, and we would be glad to have more of this higher class. They have an excellent influence on the native youths. The two races are separated entirely in boarding. They meet in the classes and on the grounds. There is here not the tithe of the danger which European youths may incur at their own homes from contact with their father's servants. The annual examination ought to show whether there is not a healthy rivalry between the different races in study. With the same sets of paper, the printed lists, which give the percentage of marks, show Europeans and natives mixed without any rule. Five of these lists are headed by natives, who write the papers in to them a foreign language. Europeans have a good opportunity here of learning the Kaffir language. Probably nothing so effectually prevents Europeans from having any influence over the Kaffirs as ignorance of their language."

The following paragraph will give a fair idea of the daily life at Lovedale :—

"The first or lowest year begins with the junior reader and simple rules in arithmetic, and they proceed onwards during the two succeeding years to British history, student's Hume, geography, grammar, and arithmetic to square and cube root. The earliest classes begin at seven o'clock in the morning, for the purpose of translation from English into Kaffir and Dutch under native assistant masters. There are three of these classes in Kaffir, and one in Dutch. Pupils attend these classes for two years, as, after first entering the institution, it has been found that without a knowledge of English their subsequent progress is exceedingly slow. At eight o'clock these classes are dismissed, and all assemble for worship and breakfast from the educational and work departments. At nine o'clock all the classes in the institution begin regular work. With the exception of the classes in the college department, the first half-hour in each class is given for religious instruction, based on the historical books of the Old Testament, the Gospels, or the Acts of the Apostles. From half-past nine A.M. till one P.M. the classes in the various years go on with the work mentioned above. At a quarter-past one they assemble for dinner. At two o'clock, or three in summer, all those not engaged in trades meet for two hours for work in the fields or in the grounds about the institution. With the exception of a few married men, and one or two head men, who have come to the institution under considerable disadvantages from having had to leave their families or their employments, all the native pupils are engaged in some kind of work."

When, four years ago, fees were introduced, it was feared that the numbers would fall off. This, however, has not been the case, the numbers having steadily increased. At that time Dr. Stewart wrote—

"Education can never be greatly extended till the natives themselves assist in the work, and therefore we levy fees in Lovedale, and we should be glad to see all similar places doing the same. It is not to press heavily on the native that we propose this, but because the benefit of education cannot be widely diffused till the natives themselves assist; because a fair proportion of them are able to pay; and because there is abundance of employment in the country for those who are willing to work."

Dr. Stewart at one place wisely remarks, "Our experience of 'civilising apart from Christianising the native,' leads us to expect but small results from the former alone." He is only verifying an experience common to India, Africa, and the South Pacific, when he writes as he does in this passage :—

"The class we find the most troublesome and the least promising, are those whose views of things and general mental attainment are as yet uninfluenced by the habits and opinions of civilised life. There are some who absorb the contents of school-books very rapidly, and who are yet in all their sympathies, likings, and beliefs little different from those who have had no such advantages. We observe that it takes a good many years before the influences and modes of civilised thought come to be adopted by many who come here. When the information contained in these books is only received into the mind without influencing the views of the individual in favour of Christianity and civilisation, the result is generally a large amount of pride and self-conceit, which renders many comparatively useless, and effectually stops all further mental and moral growth."

With all drawbacks, however, it does speak highly for the Kaffirs that they have shown so much self-denial and self-help. And certainly Dr. Stewart is well justified in claiming credit for them, as he does here:—

"During 1873, the Fingoes, Kaffirs, and other natives have paid £800 for education. For the new Industrial and Educational Institution in the Transkei, £1500. Total native payments during 1873, £2300. It is doubtful if any facts similar to these have occurred in connection with any single institution in the mission field in any part of the world during the past year."

The story of that Transkei institution deserves to be made widely known, because it shows better than almost anything else, the decision and hopefulness of the people.

"Some short time ago the natives of a district known as the Transkei, beyond the frontier of the Cape Colony, asked that a branch of Lovedale Missionary institution might be erected within their territory. Dr. Stewart visited them, and at a meeting with their head-men, said, 'Probably that would be done if they would raise at least £1000 as a proof that they were in earnest.' He recommended them to take the matter back to their villages, and discuss the subject thoroughly among themselves, and give their answer to Captain Blyth, the British resident in the Transkei. In a fortnight a large meeting was held, at which more than a thousand natives were present, and they agreed to undertake the work. Five months afterwards Captain Blyth wrote to Dr. Stewart,—' Come up; the money is ready.' A second meeting was then held, also in the open air. On a small table were placed the contributions of the people, in the shape of a heap of silver and gold—but mostly the former—amounting to £1484, increased to £1500 before the close of the day. The proceedings were short and business-like. The meeting did not last more than an hour. The native speeches might all be condensed into an expression used by one head-man. Pointing to the heap of money, he said, 'Now, there are the stones, go on and build."

Mr. Trollope, in his "South Africa," when treating of Kaffir schools, gives a very good account of Lovedale, presenting in a summary the facts we have given. He is a witness not at all likely to err on the side of sentimental admiration of such an institution, unless its conduct is associated with elements not too frequently met with in such work. He says:—

"Lovedale is a place which has had, and is having, very great success. It has been established under Presbyterian auspices, but is in truth altogether undenominational in the tuition which it gives. I do not say that religion is neglected, but religious teaching does not strike the visitors as the one great object of the institution. The schools are conducted very much like English schools, with this exception, that no classes are held after the one o'clock dinner. There are various masters for the different classes, some classical, some mathematical, and some devoted to English literature.

When I was there, there were eight teachers, independent of Mr. W. Buchanan, who was the acting head or president of the institution. Dr. Stewart, who is the permanent head, was absent in Central Africa. At Lovedale, both the boys and girls, black and white, are mixed when in school without any respect to colour. Lovedale at present owns a flock numbering 2000. The native lads are called in to work two hours each afternoon; they cut dams and make roads and take care of the garden. Added to the school are workshops in which young Kaffirs are apprenticed. The carpenter's department is by far the most popular, and certainly the most useful. There they make much of the furniture used about the place, and repair the breakages. The waggon-makers come next to the carpenters in number; and then, at a long interval, the blacksmiths. Two other trades are also represented—printing, namely, and bookbinding.

"This direction of practical work seems to be the best such an institution can take. I asked what became of these apprentices, and was told that many among them established themselves in their own country as master tradesmen in a small way, and could make a good living among their Kaffir neighbours. But I was told also that they could not often find employment in the workshops in the country, unless the employers used nothing but Kaffir labour. The white man will not work along with the Kaffir on equal terms. . . . .

"I do not imagine that a Kaffir printing-press will for many years be set up by Kaffir capital and conducted by Kaffir enterprise. It will come, probably, but the Kaffir tables and chairs, and the Kaffir waggons should come first. At present there is a 'Lovedale News' published about thrice a month. 'It is issued,' says the Lovedale printed Report, 'for circulation at Lovedale, and chiefly about Lovedale matters.' The design of this publication was to create a taste for reading among the native pupils. 'It has been carried on through twelve numbers,' says the Report, 'with a fair prospect of success, and rather more than a fair share of difficulties.' . . . .

"To see a lot of Kaffir lads and lasses at school, is of course more interesting than to inspect a seminary of white pupils. It is something as though one should visit a lion-tamer with a group of young lions around him. The Kaffir has been regarded at home as a bitter and almost terrible enemy, who, since we first became acquainted with him in South Africa, has worked us infinite woe. The Kaffir warrior with his assegai, and his red clay, and his courageous hatred, was a terrible fellow to see. And he is still much more of a savage than the ordinary negro to whom we have become accustomed in other parts of the world. It was very interesting to see him with a slate and pencil, wearing his coarse clothing with a jaunty happy air, and doing a sum in subtraction."

The "Lovedale News," of which Mr. Trollope speaks, is probably the "Kaffir Express," which has now gone on for several years; and is really a very noteworthy sheet, both in respect to the attractive reading it supplies, and as being in its practical aspect wholly the product of Kaffir hands. It is as well printed as some of our English weekly papers.

As to spiritual results, the reports and papers we have read give many pleasing tokens. We cannot pause to dwell upon them. The greatest anxiety of those at the head of the institution is to see those in their charge exhibiting the practical fruits of a Christian life. All else is secondary to this; and we can say that a manly, healthy Christian influence pervades all. When Lovedales are multiplied a hundredfold over Africa, the day of full deliverance will not be far off.

DR. WILLIAM BLACK AND LIVINGSTONIA.

THE ashes of Livingstone sleep in Westminster, and over them the sculptured stone speaks of how he sought unswervingly, in sickness and in health, to heal "the open sore of the world;" but a still more eloquent memorial of his life and labours is to be found in the East Central African Mission Station, Livingstonia, which the enkindled enterprise of his countrymen has planted. Public feeling being deeply moved by the untimely death of the great missionary, at the suggestion of the Rev. Dr. James Stewart, of Lovedale, Livingstone's old yoke-fellow, it was determined in May 1874 to enter in and possess the wide and effectual door of work which his labours had mainly set open. The Church of Scotland and the Free Church, with unanimous voice, embraced the idea, and chose the great lake Nyassa as the site of the proposed mission. Money — a sure pulse by which to test the true from the spurious enthusiasm—flowed in quickly. and now the treasuries of the two Churches

DR. WILLIAM BLACK.

Master Missionaries. p. 274.

for this special object have received about £20,000. Other Churches, caught by the same wave of enthusiasm, have followed this example, and have selected other parts of East Central Africa as fields of evangelisation. The Church Missionary Society, with a starting-fund of £12,000, has chosen as its sphere the shores of the Victoria Nyanza; while at Lake Tanganika, intermediate between the two preceding stations, the London Missionary Society, also with a commencing-fund of £12,000, has organised a third new and distinct mission; so that it would seem as if the death of Livingstone has been as powerful as his life to help mission work—the cause he at once represented and advocated as the hope of Africa.

In May 1875, the first or pioneer band of missionaries was sent out by the Free Church to Lake Nyassa. It was guided by Mr. E. D. Young, R.N., and Dr. Robert Laws. They started on the latter half of the journey from Port Elizabeth on 6th July; and, putting together the pieces of their little steamer, the *Ilala*, at the mouth of the Zambesi, they steamed up that noble river and its tributary, the Shiré, into the great lake, the only interruption to their steady progress being the formidable Murchison Cataracts. They entered Nyassa on the morning of the 12th October at sunrise, and joyfully hailed the sudden flood of glory as a propitious emblem of the advent of the Sun of Righteousness upon its sin-clouded and slave-peopled shores.

From that day to this an unexampled prosperity has been vouchsafed them. By friendly arrangement with the neighbouring chief, Mapunda, a sandy bay with adjacent territory has been secured upon Cape Maclear as a permanent site, "having a western exposure, while sheltered on the east by tree-clad mountains, and on the south by three islands." Here a rough harbour has been formed, a general building plan laid out, and a native population has begun to settle under the sheltering wing of their "fathers, the English." A large reinforcement reached the station on 21st October 1876, headed by Dr. Stewart, of Lovedale, and Dr. Black, a young and promising missionary, upon whom the leadership was meant to fall after the withdrawal of Dr. Stewart. This second party had been accompanied as far as the Murchison Rapids by another band of mission-workers, headed by Dr. Macklin and Mr. Henderson, and sent out by the Church of Scotland. They selected a site near Magomero, and called it "Blantyre," after the birth-place of Livingstone.

At both these stations schools have been opened, and scholars are now coming in plentifully, while religious services on Sabbath and week-days are regularly held. For this work the native volunteers trained at Lovedale are of great assistance. Side by side with the teaching, preaching, and healing of the sick, training in husbandry, carpentry, masonry, weaving, and blacksmith-work is being carried on by competent tradesmen from home attached to both stations. Cattle, too, have been introduced as beasts of burden, and, ultimately, it is hoped, as a meat supply. But it is feared that the dreaded *tsetse* may be in the district, and upon the absence of this pestiferous fly may be said to depend all possibility of agriculture on a large scale; and, what is almost as important, all possibility of bullock-travelling when roads shall be made. So the health of the cows and the calves is daily as anxiously looked after as that of so many human beings threatened with the plague.

The moral effect of the British flag upon the local slave-trade has been most wholesome. Before the mission was planted it was estimated that across the ferries of the lake and along its southern shores slaves were carried to the number of twenty thousand per annum. This has now been very largely decreased, and could be entirely checked if a small armed party were kept cruising about on the lake. Charged with the duty of considering the desirability of this, and with the survey of a new route to the coast from the north end of the lake, it is cheering to know that her Majesty's consul for Mozambique, Captain Elton, and three others, are now probably at Nyassa, having passed Mazaro on the Zambesi on 18th July last.

Already the possibility of opening up trade with these rich island districts has had considerable attention. The existing route is, as we have seen, chiefly by river, with Port Elizabeth as a basis. The Murchison Cataracts form, however, a huge break in the line of communication. Everything going up or down must be at that point unshipped and undergo porterage for sixty miles over a rough broken pathway. Besides this drawback, the Portuguese Government have advanced claims to the exclusive right of steam navigation of the Zambesi, on account of their settlements upon it, and during the last two years they have exacted high duties upon certain merchandise. How far their right on both points has a solid foundation, may well be questioned. But a friendly settlement of differences seems to be near; and quite recently the Lisbon Government have, we learn, reduced their tariff upon duty-charged goods to a uniform rate of two and a half per cent. This route, therefore, as at once the easiest and least liable to interruption, is now being perfected with a view to developing trade. A new porterage-road at the Cataracts, connecting the upper and lower Shiré, and passing through Blantyre, has just been surveyed, and its construction begun. The defrayment of the expense entailed will be solicited from the International African Exploration Society, inaugurated by the King of the Belgians. Mr. James Stewart, C.E., of the Punjab, has most generously given up a year of his furlough to undertake this and other road surveys in connection with the new station.

An entirely new route to the settlement is, however, now in process of being opened up. It is meant to start from Kilwa, about latitude 9°, in Zanzibar territory, and strike the north end of the lake near the Mazitu settlement of Ironga. The needful survey is, as we have already said, being now undertaken by Captain Elton and his party, who will work their way eastwards, *viâ* Mesule and Lukose, to the sea-board terminus. Kilwa has been chosen on account of its good harbourage, a serious deficiency both at Quillimane and Zanzibar. This route will be about three hundred and fifty miles in length, and would meet equally well the necessities of coast communication for Lake Tanganika, by a branch road of one hundred miles more. Such a highway would thus have command of about two thousand miles of coast upon both lakes, and, besides, would keep up communication with the vast territories beyond, towards the Lualabo. Some Glasgow merchants have sent out an experimental trading expedition to Nyassa, *viâ* Kilwa and Mesule. It is in charge of Messrs. J. and F. Moir, sons of a well-known physician in Edinburgh, and they are accompanied by Mr. Maze, an engineer of much practical experience. In all probability this expedition and that of Captain Elton will meet one another about half-way.

We have, in our wish to give a connected general view of the prospects of Livingstonia, kept purposely back any reference till now to the first black cloud cast over the promising sky of the young mission. By the loss of the mails of the "Cashmere," we are as yet without the full details of the sad calamity. But the facts that have been received are briefly these. In the beginning of May, Dr. Black was prostrated by an eighth or ninth attack of fever, which rapidly increased in intensity of effect, and was accompanied by stupor and delirium, from which he never rallied, in spite of every attention lavished on him, and on Monday, the seventh of the month, he "fell asleep in Jesus."

Thus ended, half a year after his arrival at the lake, and in the thirty-first year of his age, the brief career of a most devoted missionary, to whom the Church had committed a great trust, because he had given promise of great things.

The story of William Black's life is replete with interest. Permeated as it was by one grand overmastering emotion, which governed implicitly every energy and faculty, its simplest events, to those in sympathy with him, attract and command notice.

He was the first-born of his parents, and, like the infant Samuel, was, before his birth, consecrated by his mother's prayers to the Lord's service. His early life, 1846 to 1866, was spent at his birthplace, Dunbog, a sparsely-peopled rural parish, prettily placed under the shadow of Norman's Law, in the north-east district of Fifeshire. Here he grew up a stirring, daring boy, whose heart was much more in his play than his lessons. His fishing-rod, his rabbits, and his pigeons sadly preoccupied his mind, when it should have been centred upon sums in proportion, and dates in history. And this strong bias, which neither advising nor flogging was able to alter, obstinately clung to him, as if in the blood. Nature, not books, was his delight, and every farmer for five miles round knew the bright-eyed, handsome face of the schoolmaster's son, and generally connived at his oft-repeated raids upon the trout, the peewit's eggs, and the hawks' nests. The Saturdays were to him elysium, for books could then be lawfully shelved, and long excursions indulged in without fear of consequences.

Such a life developed in him great self-reliance, decision, and fearlessness, so that soon no errand was thought too difficult for him to execute. In illustration of this, when about ten years of age his mother was taken suddenly ill, and the nearest help from relatives was at Letham, a place six miles over the hills, and towards which there was only an imperfect sheep-track. But to this place, in the murk of midnight, Willie was the appointed and ready messenger, passing dauntlessly in his way a spot which, in local superstition, was haunted by the ghost of a murderess. There are few men, not to speak of boys, would have cared for such a walk, weirdsome with the shuddering scream of the curlew, and the noiseless spectre-flit of the heron suddenly beclouding the path as you proceed.

When about thirteen, his father, anxious for his more

thorough education, entered him as a pupil in Cupar Academy, and there the larger number of advanced scholars of his own age roused him somewhat to emulate their application, and he upon the whole made more satisfactory progress in book-learning. His old love, however, of deeds of daring still clung to him, and on one occasion nearly caused him permanent bodily injury. A narrow ledge on the second floor of the academy runs externally from window to window, and along this, in mere bravado, he was progressing one day, when he fell heavily to the ground, where he lay for a while bruised and stunned. But as no bones were broken, the accident but sufficed to sober him for a week.

When fifteen he became enamoured of the calling of an architect. His mother unceasingly hoped and sought for him some sphere as a worker for Christ, but he having as yet evidenced no change of heart, she allowed him to follow his own decision. So, as a training towards his aim, he engaged for a time in practical joiner-work. While thus employed, about the age of nineteen, he became deeply anxious about his religious condition. No special circumstances led to this anxiety other than a diligent use of his Bible, and his mother's earnest prayers. His distress was deep and prolonged. With strong crying and tears he sought for spiritual peace, but, for many months, he found it not. The Lord was thus, doubtless, leading him to deep heart-searching to humble him, but also to fit him for after usefulness in his service. A marked feature in his awakened state, at this time, was the fear of being spoken to by others on the subject of his personal interest in Christ. So that he seemed to be at one and the same time anxiously seeking, and yet dreading to find the light. It was, perhaps, the conviction of—" I ought to know and rejoice in the truth, but I don't, and am ashamed to say so." There was one whom he specially shunned, the family physician, Dr. John Lyell, a skilful and much-esteemed practitioner in Newburgh. He was so well known for speaking pointedly to others about their interest in the Saviour, that when William saw his gig approach he invariably went and hid himself.

Pursuing still his desire of being an architect, he in his twentieth year entered a suitable office in St. Andrews. It was in this ancient city, while thus occupied, in 1867, that he passed through the great crisis of his life, and lost his doubts and fears by a clear apprehension of the simplicity of salvation through faith in Jesus. As in the case of many more, led like him through prolonged darkness, the joy and comfort of assurance was such as compelled him to proclaim it to all around. It seemed to him that if he did not speak the very stones would cry out. So, "straightway he preached Christ" in the streets, and became very bold in his appeals to the consciences of the careless, insomuch that many reckoned him "a pestilent fellow." Shortly before he left for Livingstonia he had the great joy of coming on traces of the fruit of such work. He had been speaking at Stirling upon the subject of the mission, and at the close a young man came up and shook hands with him, saying, "I know you. You are the street-preacher of St. Andrews!" The truth then heard had impressed him, and it had at length led to his conversion. Strange to say, the same week he had a letter from another young man in Columbia, U.S., telling of the blessing he had got from his meetings in St. Andrews, and that he was now himself working for Christ in the backwoods.

From this time onwards the work of grace in his soul gradually deepened, and he began to long for a complete consecration of all his energies and time in direct work for the Saviour. The wish was at first but dimly shaped in his mind, as the barriers toward its realisation, in the shape of money and education, were apparently insuperable. But a mother's prayers had to be answered, and so the missionary spirit took deeper root in his heart, and the lions in the way lost their awe-inspiring appearance as he was led up to them.

With characteristic fortitude he began at once to revise and extend the studies that he had so slighted in former years. Burdensome beyond idea was the work he now went through, in rearing for himself a solid and permanent basis of exact scholarship. But with unshaken determination he sternly girt himself to the work, saying, "What has been done can be done, and why not by me?" But while these efforts were in time crowned by a moderate success, he never shut his eyes to the fact that many an aching head and sleepless night might have been saved him, and better work been done, if he only had, while a boy at school, been as diligent in study as he had been in play.

Meanwhile, Dr. Lyell, of Newburgh, the family doctor, had, in the providence of God, relinquished the ordinary practice of his profession and become superintendent of the Glasgow Medical Missionary Society. Knowing Mr. Black's missionary longings, he in 1870 offered him an assistantship in his dispensary. This was joyfully accepted, and the Christ-like work of the medical missionary, as there seen by him from day to day, decided him as to the branch of service for Jesus to which he ought to devote himself. His resolution was warmly approved of and forwarded by Dr. Lyell, and the same winter saw him enrolled as a medical student in Glasgow University. Thus the difficulties towards the accomplishment of his object vanished as he went forward.

For about three years he continued helping in the Medical Mission work, making the while steady progress in the systematic study of the art of healing. He was greatly liked by the poor, his generous and sympathetic nature readily begetting their confidence and gratitude. Not content with the opportunities of usefulness he enjoyed at the dispensary, he started cottage meetings in an out-of-the-way and remote corner of the city. His memory yet lingers in the place, and to this day the

Medical Mission receives more patients from that locality than from districts as destitute situated much nearer to its chief centre of work. In the college his religion was not hid, and his fellow-students soon knew that Black was a "revivalist." Occasionally they sought to make him the butt of their ridicule; but his *quid pro quo* was usually so pointed that his would-be castigators soon tired of their work. On one occasion his reply, perfectly justifiable in self-defence, so exasperated his tormentor that he lifted his hand to strike him. Black, with that quiet impressiveness which, when he lost self-consciousness, seemed his natural mood, placed his large and firm hand gently upon the shoulder of the passionate youth, and said, "Why, man, were I minded I could strike you down at a blow; but what's the use?" And with a few more words about the folly of quarrelling, the enemy of the one moment, before he quite understood how, became the friend of the next.

The Glasgow University Medical Students' Christian Association was started at this time, and, through the kindness of the Senate, the free use of one of the class-rooms was given it for its meetings. Mr. Black, prominent in its organisation, delighted greatly in its Saturday gatherings, and during the last winter of his studies became its president. These meetings still continue, and, while usually devotional, are varied about once a month by an address from some senior member of the profession.

In 1872 Mr. Black was selected as the Paterson Bursar (a bursary restricted to students in training for medical mission work), in itself a high testimony of the esteem in which he was deservedly held. In 1873, having resigned his assistantship at the Medical Mission, as the hours of duty prevented lecture attendance, he had the further honour of being chosen a district missionary to the Free Barony congregation, of which the Rev. James Wells was then minister. Into his direct duties in this office he threw himself with great zeal, besides identifying himself with and helping all departments of the Christian work of the Church. His Sabbath evening Bible-class was one of his most attractive and most useful works. The membership was of both sexes, and not uncommonly a hundred and fifty were under his instruction on such occasions. Over them he exercised a kind of magnetic power, securing their rapt attention, not by any novelty of style or matter, but by the golden bond of a perfect sympathy. He came so alongside of his hearers that he seemed to hold the hand and speak in the ear of each.

Having very largely the gift of organising, and that enthusiasm which begets enthusiasm, he had a wonderful power of getting others to work. A band of some thirty young men gave themselves up to his leadership, and his own earnest spirit was soon largely infused into them. Cottage meetings and district tract distributions were never before so extensively undertaken as through them. Influenced, too, by his example, a number of these are now working and studying towards various departments of mission work. One of them, indeed, has become the new Paterson Bursar, and will, in due time, doubtless walk in his steps and devote himself to the foreign field.

In this way the winter passed of 1873-74. In the succeeding one, he unfortunately decided to carry on simultaneously with his studies in medicine theological studies at the Free Church College. The Paterson Bursary enjoins on the acceptor that two years should be spent in such studies *before* or *after* graduation in medicine. He chose, and there can be no doubt imprudently chose, to begin those new studies before he had finished the others. So that at one and the same time he was a student of medicine, a student of theology, and a district missionary. This blunder was destined to bear its own punishment. His health, by the excessive tax such engagements made upon it, and by a reduction of the hours of rest, became in the course of the session seriously impaired, and he was thus compelled to abate his unceasing application. One, however, while grieving over his mistake and its disastrous result, cannot but envy and admire that perfervid zeal which seduced him from a sober judgment of his own powers of performance. A burning desire for present usefulness and early complete consecration to direct mission work consumed him. He said in deeds what others have in words, "better to wear out than to rust out;" forgetting, however, that undiminished continuity of force, in both religion and physics, is much more influential than momentary intensity.

The severe strain upon Mr. Black's strength was at this time such that often he could not get sleep but from the use of opiates. Nor need we wonder at it when we read from his own hand (in his " Opus Dei," an occasional diary) what he compressed within the compass of four-and-twenty hours. We give the last entry in the book, slightly abridged:—

"March 28, 1875. Sabbath. This has been a day of great work.

" 1. Among the young men at 8·30. Subject, 'The unpardonable Sin.'

" 2. Among the Kirk Street children, 11 o'clock. Some of the little darlings wept when I told them that this was presumably the last time I would be among them as chairman. Most of the monitors, too, were weeping. May God bless them all! I feel very sorry myself to part with them.

"3. Afternoon. Went with Mr. Russel as a deputation for the Students' Missionary Association to Free St. Matthew's. Both of us received great attention. Results, over £13 to the Livingstonia fund.

"4. My Bible Class at 5·30. A large attendance, and unusually attentive. Many cried, specially the young women, when I said that I should likely not meet them again as their teacher. I shook hands with all of them as they retired. May I meet them *all* in heaven. They wish to give me some present before I sail for Bombay, but I have no time to arrange a meeting. The question was put to me, 'But if you don't come back, what shall we do with the money?' I said, 'Give it to Jesus.'

"5. I took the evening meeting in the hall. It was crowded, and all the people were very attentive. My subject was 'Hid' (Col. iii. 3). Lord, make impressions for eternity."

The reference to Bombay made above refers to the medical advice which he had received, to take complete rest and a thorough change. He accordingly, a few days after the Sabbath's work just detailed, spent three months as surgeon of the steamship *Macedonia*, making, during that time, a voyage out to India and back. This seemed thoroughly to recruit his shattered health, and his worst symptoms, before he returned, seemed entirely removed.

During the preceding year he had been introduced to the Rev. Dr. Stewart, of Lovedale, the promoter of the Livingstonia Mission, as a suitable head for that new centre of evangelisation. And so greatly had his zeal and general ability impressed those who knew him that on their recommendation he was, before the completion of his studies, appointed to be the head of the mission under Dr. Stewart. This was an opening entirely after his own heart. He coveted pioneer work. Indeed his great love of nature from boyhood, and his trade experience in early life, in addition to his other acquirements, made him peculiarly suitable for the post.

His aim was in due time attained, and in the spring of 1876 he had the pleasure of graduating in Glasgow University as M.B. and C.M.; while a few weeks afterwards he was ordained, by the Glasgow Presbytery of the Free Church of Scotland, to the ministry, after an abridged theological course, by special authorisation of the Assembly. Numerous presentations, tokens of the sympathy and approval with which himself and his work were viewed, were showered upon him. So warm, indeed, was the "God speed you" expressed by all, that the young missionary felt that if the path to duty had been toilsome and laborious, his achieved position, as the Church's chosen herald, was worth it all; and he saw that he was being sent out strengthened and supported by her united prayers, and that no lukewarm interest would be taken in his future career. He had also the blessed consciousness of his mother's joy. The long-cherished and oft-repeated desire of her heart, that her first-born should be a worker for Christ, was thus, in His own time and way, heard and answered.

It will be remembered that early in 1875 the first Livingstonia Mission party left. A reinforcement to this first party now fell (May 1876) to be led by Dr. Black; and it was accompanied by another goodly band of pioneer missionaries, sent out by the Church of Scotland, under Dr. Macklin, who, as we have already seen, have occupied a new centre of operation at Blantyre, near the Cataracts. This large company, after being enthusiastically welcomed in Cape Colony, and receiving an important native contingent from Lovedale, started for Nyassa, accompanied by Dr. Stewart. The party, on the 21st of October, reached their destination without serious mishap; and Dr. Black, though prostrate from fever, managed to crawl on deck and join in the shout of triumph and psalm of thanksgiving that could not be restrained as their little steamer glided towards the mission settlement at Cape Maclear. Here, as we already know, after six months of unwearied toil, so joyfully endured, so heartily performed, was he summoned home, by a fresh attack of fever, to receive from his Master's loving hands the conqueror's palm; and from His gracious lips that welcome, more enviable than the loftiest niche in the temple of fame, "Well done, good and faithful servant, enter thou into the joy of thy Lord."

Our purpose is all but done. We have attempted to show what was the calling and the training of the missionary which the cause of Livingstonia has lost. His labours in that distant field we have indicated rather than traced, for, brief as they have been, are they not written in the chronicles of the Church? But over his boyhood and early years we have lingered more lengthily, and have tried to bring out that God's grace made him what he was—a noble type of just such a missionary as Africa needs; a man with a Christ-like spirit, an indomitable will, an unflagging zeal, and a consuming passion for the salvation of souls.

JOHN COLERIDGE PATTESON AND THE SOUTH PACIFIC.

THERE are some chosen lives which present a unity of aspiration and effort such as is generally to be found only in fiction. The life of John Coleridge Patteson belongs to this class. His lamented death, at the hands of the natives at Nukapu, filled England with sorrow; but it was wholly in keeping with the tenor of his labours and his aspirations. Had he himself been asked whether he would desire to die quietly in England at home among his own people, or among the dusky tribes he had gone forth to teach, and in such a manner as to witness most effectually, in after times, to the great cause he had at heart, he would assuredly have preferred the latter. Though he cherished the most affectionate remembrances of friends and of home, he had, in fact, ceased in much to regard himself as "being from home" amid the races of the South Pacific. His one purpose was to civilise and to Christianise them, hold them as friends and brothers, training up those who were most fit for helpers in his work, that he might send forth men of their own blood to extend the field. While still a mere youth, under the noble influence of his mother and the friendship of Bishop Selwyn, he had dedicated himself to this object, never knowing secondary calls; but he had, as we shall see, not a few defects and faults to contend against; and one great lesson of his life, therefore, may lie in tracing out the way in which he subdued them, and made them, in fact, become helps rather than hindrances to him in his great work. The outward results and the inner life, in this case, have a sustained harmony, which gives the Memoir a soft and subdued beauty that is only too seldom to be found in biography, even missionary biography, which ought most liberally to exhibit it.

John Coleridge Patteson was the eldest son of Sir John Patteson, who, after a short but successful course at the bar, was raised to the bench in 1830, and of Frances Duke Coleridge, daughter of Colonel Coleridge, elder brother of the poet, Samuel Taylor Coleridge. The Patteson family thus stood in close relationship to another family which has given judges of highest repute to the English bench; and the pathway to society and to eminence in various walks of life was in this way thrown open to any scion of the house. Coleridge, or "Coley" Patteson, as he was named by his family and friends in boyhood, was born in Bedford Square, London, in 1827. In his childhood he showed great thoughtfulness as well as quickness, being able to read by his fifth year—on his birthday receiving from his father the Bible which was used at his consecration as bishop twenty-seven years afterwards. We are told, "He read it eagerly, puzzled his brains as to what became of the fish during the Flood, and, when suddenly called to the nursery, begged to be allowed 'to finish the binding of Satan for a thousand years.'" Even from this early period the desire to be a clergyman was cherished. Saying the Absolution to people, he thought, must make them so happy. And the purpose, we learn, was fostered by his mother. "No thought of a family to be made, and of his being the eldest son, ever interfered for a moment. That he should be a good servant at God's altar was to her above all price." The mother made the religious instruction of the children her especial care, reading the Psalms and the Lessons for the Day with them every morning immediately after breakfast. "His old nurse (still his sister's valued servant) remembers the little seven-years-old boy, after saying his own prayers at her knee, standing opposite to his little brother, admonishing him to attention with, 'Think, Jemmy; think.' In fact, devoutness seems to have been natural to him."

When eight years old he was sent to school at Ottery St. Mary, in Devonshire, with which the name of Coleridge is so intimately associated; but in spite of the various interests of the place, the beauty of the surrounding country, and the quaint grandeur of St. Mary's Church, Coley longed for home. And this too, notwithstanding that his grandparents lived at Heath's Court, close by, and in the manor-house his uncle, Francis George Coleridge, whose boys were just of the age to be companions for him. His home-sickness was only relieved, indeed, by boy-like failings, of which he has once or twice to make confession. Probably this longing for home had something to do with the " uninterestedness" which his biograper tells us marked his school-life here; but youth is plastic, and easily learns to accommodate itself. There can be no doubt that the liking he at this time formed for outdoor games and sports had its own result in the way of developing a healthy nature, and modifying in many ways the self-conscious introspectiveness to which we soon detect some tendency. The companionship of his younger brother at school in the latter period of his stay at Ottery, furnished him with an interest, and fostered what was always a characteristic trait—kindness and consideration for others. But this consideration for others was accompanied even at this early period with that utter bravery and power of endurance, which is more often formed at a public school than elsewhere. We are told that, "While at Ottery, he silently bore the pain of a broken collar-bone for three weeks, and when the accident was brought to light by his mother's embrace, he only said that 'he did not like to make a fuss.'"

If he did not carry from Ottery the highest attainments in scholarship, he was a strong healthy lad when in 1838 he entered Eton, very soon to get glimpses of the young Queen Victoria, in the first year of her sovereignty, going to Salt Hill to make her youthful contribution to the poor scholars, according to the old custom. At Eton his career was not marked by any special success; he had to guard himself against the love of cricket, in which he continued to excel; but his affections and his spirit were already receiving the first signal determinations towards the course which he finally chose. He heard Dr. Selwyn, the newly-made bishop of New Zealand, preach at New Windsor Chapel, and wrote home :—

"It was beautiful when he talked of his going out to found a church, and then die neglected and forgotten. All the people burst out crying, he was so very much beloved by his parishioners. He spoke of his perils, and putting his trust in God; and then, when he had finished, I think I never heard anything like the sensation—a kind of feeling that if it had not been so sacred a spot all would have exclaimed, 'God bless him!'"

And then, as Providence would have it, the impression was deepened by an appeal, which, as often as it recurred to the memory of the lad, must have aroused in him new resolution and hunger for spiritual helping. Before the Selwyns left England, they paid a visit to the Patteson family, when there was much conversation respecting the prospects of the mission in the distant Pacific.

"Coley did not happen to be then at home, but when the Bishop took leave, half in earnest, half in playfulness, he said, 'Lady Patteson, will you give me Coley?' She started, but did not say no; and when, independently of this, her son told her that it was his greatest wish to go with the bishop, she replied that if he kept that wish when he grew up, he should have her blessing and consent."

We are therefore not surprised to find him ready to forego the pleasures of cricket rather than identify himself in any shape with what was coarse and degrading:—

"On the occasion of the dinner annually given by the eleven of cricket and the eight of the boats at the hotel at Slough, a custom had arisen among some of the boys of singing offensive songs on these occasions, and Coley, who, as second of the eleven, stood in the position of one of the entertainers, gave notice beforehand that he was not going to tolerate anything of the sort. One of the boys, however, began to sing something objectionable. Coley called out, 'If that does not stop, I shall leave the room,' and as no notice was taken, he actually went away with a few other brave lads. Afterwards he sent word that if an apology was not made he should leave the eleven, but the feeling of the better style of boys prevailed, and the apology was made."

Soon after Bishop Selwyn's farewell, he was confirmed,

and a further impulse to serious thought and self-consecration came that same year in the death of his mother, whose teaching and example had been so benign.

He entered Balliol College, Oxford, in 1845, and fell into an excellent circle, from which he derived much good. Here he lost any love for general society he might ever have had, and cultivated more and more the companionship that favours full and frank expression of deeper sentiments and convictions. A visit to Switzerland, Rome, and Venice in 1851 gave him much to think of; and in 1852 he obtained a fellowship at Merton College, and went into residence there; but in the long vacation of that year he proceeded to Germany, that he might study Hebrew and other languages more favourably and cheaply. His letters to his family and friends at this time breathe the most exquisite devotion. While at Oxford he had listened, fascinated, to the earnest appeals of Dr. Pusey, which were then stirring many earnest minds; but he still kept a questioning intellect at work on some of the points involved in the special doctrines presented—a trait which marked him to the very close of life, notwithstanding that all the influence of family tradition inclined to make him lean to implicit acceptance of these views. This is proved by the letters which he wrote to his father from Dresden, where he was busy on languages, but also on theology and points of Church policy

In languages he had real aptitude, and now he added

Arabic to his list, and soon was proficient in it. He varies his studies with such things as a description of Dresden fair, and long before the time of return home he begins to select presents, acknowledging himself "concerned about getting something for everybody." Returning to Merton College, he remained there till the long vacation of 1853, prosecuting his studies of theology and languages, and forming friendships which till his death remained unbroken. Mr. Roundell says that, by this time—"Self-cultivation had done much for him. Literature and art had opened his mind and enlarged his interests and sympathies. The moral and spiritual forces of the man were now vivified, refined, and strengthened by the awakening of his intellectual and æsthetic nature." And Principal Shairp thus succinctly indicates the elements that, now prominent in him, gave him such weight and practical influence:—

"It was character, more than special ability, which marked him out from others, and made him, wherever he was, whether in cricket, in which he excelled, or in graver things, a centre round which others gathered. The impressions he left on me were of quiet, gentle strength and entire purity—a heart that loved all things true and honest and pure, and that would always be found on the side of these. We did not know, probably he did not know himself, the fire of devotion that lay within him, but that was soon to kindle, and make him what he afterwards became."

And truly the flame soon leapt forth when the man came face to face with the practical duties for which he had been prepared. He served a rigorous apprenticeship to pastoral work under Mr. Gardiner, in the parish of Alfington, in Devonshire, before taking orders. He found the parish in a mournfully low condition; the morals of the people were such as would only have shocked and disgusted many a young man of high ambition and pure mind, and rendered him wholly helpless. But Patteson's practical foresight and tact soon made themselves felt, no less than a faculty for organisation such as even his nearest friends had not suspected to exist in him. And he took very decided measures when he had once estimated the real need of the people. The only efficient means he could light on as a first step towards improvement was the establishment of homes for boys and girls, where they could be preserved from the contamination. His first effort was for a boys' home, in which he had the support of all the more thoughtful people. He thus gives his sister his idea of the project :—

"I shall, of course, begin with only one or two boys —the thing may not answer at all; but every one, Gardiner, several farmers, and one or two others, quite poor, all say it must work well with God's blessing. I do not really wish to be scheming away, working a favourite hobby, &c., but I do believe this to be absolutely essential. The profligacy and impurity of the poor are beyond all belief. Every mother of a family answers (I mean every honest, respectable mother of a family) : ' Oh, sir, God will bless such a work ; and it is for want of this that so much misery and wretchedness abound.' I believe that for a year or so it will exhaust most of my money, but then it is one of the best uses to which I could apply it ; for my theory is, that help and assistance is wanted in this way, and I would wish to make most of these things self-supporting. Half an acre more of garden, thoroughly well worked, will yield an astonishing return, and I look to Mary as a person of really economical habits. It is a great relief to have poured all this out. It is no easy task that I am preparing for myself. I know that I fully expect to be very much disappointed, but I am determined to try it. I am determined to try and make the people see that I am not going to give way to everybody that asks ; but that I am going to set on foot and help on all industrial schemes of every kind, for people of every age. I am hard at work, studying spade husbandry, inspectors' reports of industrial schools, &c."

He remained and ministered as curate at Alfington after his ordination, winning the hearts of the people, so that they came to look upon him as peculiarly their own; the wrench of parting being, of course, all the more painful, when, on the arrival of Bishop Selwyn in England for a short furlough, all Patteson's aspirations for missionary life were revived. Opening his mind to

Bishop Selwyn on the matter, he proposed that he should not leave England while his father lived. The bishop answered, "You should not put off till you are on in life. It should be done with your full strength and vigour." His father's first exclamation on being told of his son's desire was, "I can't let him go!" but in a moment he added, "God forbid I should stop him!" The matter was discussed by Bishop Selwyn and Sir John, who, notwithstanding the comfort he felt in having his son near him, said, at length, "What right have I to stand in his way? I may not live another year." And when the conversation was ended the father said, "Mind, I give him wholly, not with any thought of seeing him again. I will not have him thinking he must come home to see me." When told of this, the young man said at once that he was ready to go now.

Seven months later he bade his family good-bye. His sisters stood at the door till he was out of sight; then going in, they found the old Judge sitting silent, his little Bible in his hand. Next day he wrote from London : "I am, thank God, calm and even cheerful. I stayed a few minutes in the churchyard after I left you, picked a few primrose buds from mamma's grave, and then walked on."

His family were not alone in feeling as though deprived of the near presence of a son and brother. The Alfington people mourned as they had hardly done before. "Ah, sir," was the schoolmistress's answer to some warm words from Mr. Justice Coleridge in praise of Bishop Selwyn, "he may be, no doubt he is, a very good man. I only wish he had kept his hands off Alfington!" And in this she spoke the feelings of the people, from the old and infirm, whom the curate had attended solicitously, down to the Sunday-school children, who wept when they heard he was about to leave them. "Our Mr. Patteson," the people called him to the last.

His uncle, Sir John Coleridge, writing of Coley's first sermon, had said: "I bless God that he is what he is, and that, at least for a time, if his life be spared, I have secured his services for my poor people at Alfington. Many years I can hardly expect to retain him there; but I feel sure that so long as he is there he will be a blessing to them."

On the 28th of March 1855 he sailed from England in the "Duke of Portland" emigrant ship. The voyage was not suffered to pass without its own profitable occupations. Of course, Bishop Selwyn and the young missionary were ready to minister in many ways to the wants of those on board, Mrs. Selwyn taking her share in the teaching of the young; but they had their mechanical pastimes too, carpentering being one of the many qualifications required in a missionary bishop. It has been said, that if you wish to know a person, go a long voyage with him. Many voyages went those two together; and, during this first one, Bishop Selwyn set down what he would have warmly endorsed years thereafter: "Coley Patteson is a treasure, which I humbly set down as a recompense for our own boys left at home at school. He is a good fellow, and the tone of his mind is one which I can thoroughly enjoy, content with the τὸ ἀεί present, yet always aiming at a brighter and better future."

They arrived at Auckland on the 5th of July, and, reaching the college some six miles distant, at once set to work. Bishop Selwyn's scheme had been to collect young lads from the distant islands of the South Pacific—from Tanna and Nengoné, from New Caledonia and Lifu, from the Solomon and Banks Islands and other accessible groups—and take them to New Zealand for a period of the year for training at the college, returning them again to their respective homes, in the mission ship, during the season when the climate of New Zealand, as it was found, was too trying for them. Of the college, Patteson says:—

"It is really all that is necessary for a thoroughly good and complete place of education : the hall all lined with Kauri pine-wood; a large, handsome room, collegiate, capable of holding two hundred persons; the schoolroom eighty feet long, with admirable arrangement for holding classes separately. There are two very cosy rooms, which belong to the Bishop and Mrs. Selwyn respectively, in one of which I am now sitting. . . . Our rooms are quite large enough, bigger than my room at Feniton, but no furniture, of course, beyond a bedstead, a table for writing, and an old book-case; but it is never cold enough to care about furniture. ... I clean, of course, my room in part, make my bed, help to clear away things after meals, &c., and am quite accustomed to do without servants for anything but cooking."

In fixing the limits of his field of operations, Bishop Selwyn had shown singular wisdom and breadth of character. He had resolved not to preach in any place already occupied by missions, so as not to confuse the heathen with the sight of variations among Christians. The properly Polynesian Isles had been all occupied by the London Missionary Society, and a few islands had been taken in hand by a Scottish Presbyterian mission; but the groups which seemed to form the third fringe round the north-eastern curve of Australia— the New Hebrides, Banks Islands, and Solomon Isles— were almost entirely open ground, and to these it was that Coley Patteson should especially devote himself.

Some years were spent in preliminary work with Bishop Selwyn, voyaging among the islands in the "Southern Cross" (which, sailing from England on the same day as the "Duke of Portland," had reached Auckland exactly a fortnight after her), making excursions into the bush; teaching the boys at St. John's College, and later at St. Andrew's, Kohimarama, and learning, practically, the thousand outs and ins of missionary life. A certain docility of mind and a happy temperament helped him vastly. He often thought of home, and father, and friends; but a second thought of God's covenant care sufficed to calm and strengthen him; and whilst it seemed that distance and absence only made him, if possible, more interested in all that concerned home, he was able to apply himself to his work with complete devotion and oneness of mind.

"I have very little time," he writes, "for indulging in fancies of any kind now—I begin to get an idea of what work is; but in my walks out at night (if I am awake) I think of dear mamma, of your dead father, and others who are gone before, with unmixed joy and comfort. You may be quite sure that I am not likely to forget anybody or anything connected with home. How I do watch and follow them through the hours of the day and night when we are both awake and at our work! I turn out at 6.45, and think of them at dinner or tea; at ten I think of them at evening prayers; and by my own bedtime they are in morning church or busied about their different occupations, and I fancy I can almost see them. So it goes on, and still I am calm and happy and very well, and I think I am in my place, and hope to be made of some use some day. I like the natives in the school very much. The regular wild, untamed fellow is not so pleasant at first—dirty, unclothed, always smoking, a mass of blanket, his wigwam sort of place filthy, his food ditto; but then he is probably intelligent, hospitable, and not insensible to the advantage of hearing about religion. It only wants a little practice to overcome one's English feelings about dress, civilisation, &c., and that will soon come."

All his hardships and trials but drew forth his kindliness the more thoroughly There have been men who have sacrificed themselves in such work as he undertook, who were after all devoted merely to ideas, and had but small power of attracting individuals. It was not so with Bishop Patteson. He soon came to like his New Zealanders and Melanesians as well or even better than he would "English boys, up to all sorts of mischief." "Savages," he said, "are all Fridays, if you know how to treat them;" and he soon came to see that the "menial offices," as they would be called, which he so cheerfully undertook, formed a practice such as could not be matched for working beneficial changes upon their habits. He would have confirmed the declaration of the Maori—"Gentleman-gentleman thought nothing that ought to be done too mean for him: pig-gentleman never worked." He would often write in this strain—

"Every missionary ought to be a carpenter, a mason, something of a butcher, and a good deal of a cook. Suppose yourself without a servant, and nothing for dinner to-morrow but some potatoes in the barn, and a fowl running about in the yard. That's the kind of thing for a young fellow going into a new country to imagine for himself. If a little knowledge of glazing could be added it would be a grand thing, just enough to fit in panes to window-frames, which last, of course, he ought to make himself. Much of this cannot be done for you. I can buy window-frames in Auckland, and glass, but can't carry a man a thousand miles in my pocket to put that glass into these frames, and if it is done in New Zealand, ten to one it gets broken on the voyage, whereas glass by itself will pack well. To know how to tinker a bit is a good thing, else your only saucepan or tea-kettle may be lying by you useless for months. In fact, if I had known all this before, I should just be ten times as useful as I am now. If any one you know thinks of emigrating, or becoming a missionary, just let him remember this."

And this from a man who had shown himself not only willing, but singularly ready and versatile—apt at making beds, and mending tea-kettles, and doing odds and ends of joinery, as well as learning languages as if by instinct, and with peculiar power of communicating knowledge to others. He was indeed a typical missionary, and, though what he says of training is true and valuable, his experience sufficiently shows that when the whole heart is in the work, everything yields to loving interest and self-sacrifice.

The peculiar change of habits, the attempting to do so many unaccustomed things, would have been found by many to divert the mind from study; but it was not so in Patteson's case. On the 17th of January, some six months after landing in New Zealand, he is able to compose and preach a Maori sermon, and soon thereafter he commits himself to extempore delivery; and though he has already made some progress with the tongues of the Pacific, his notes of books read are indeed surprising. In all this discipline, hard though it seemed, and though he sometimes confessed that his sensibilities rebelled, he had the judgment to see clearly that it was making him " something different from what I was—*more of a man ;* to say nothing of the higher and religious side of the question." Seeing this was the spirit he carried into his work, it is no wonder we find Bishop Selwyn saying, in a note to Sir John Patteson, in 1857—

" Coley is, as you say, the right man in the right place, mentally and physically ; the multiplicity of languages, which would try most men, is met by his peculiar gift ; the heat of the climate suits his constitution ; his mild and parental temper makes his black boys cling about him as their natural protector; his freedom from fastidiousness makes all parts of the work easy to him ; for when you have to teach boys how to wash themselves and to wear clothes for the first time, the romance of missionary work disappears as completely as a great man's heroism before his *valet de chambre.*"

Lady Martin, who had been absent from New Zealand for three years, and saw much of him on her return, thus gives her impressions :—

"It was very pleasant to see him among his boys. They all used to go off for a walk on Saturday with him, sometimes to town, and he was as full of fun with them as if they had been a party of Eton boys. He had none of the conventional talk, so fatal to all true influence, about degraded heathen. They were brethren, ignorant indeed, but capable of acquiring the highest wisdom. It was a joke amongst some of us that when asked the meaning of a Nengoné term of endearment, he answered naïvely, 'Oh, it means "old fellow."' He brought his fresh, happy, kindly feelings towards English lads and young men into constant play among Melanesians, and so they loved and trusted him."

But to make in any remote way clear the progress of the mission, it is needful that we give some attention to the efforts made, and the results of the work year by year. Before he had time to receive the first letters from home, he had found interesting work in classes, up-country, and in the hospital. This is how he replies to his sisters :—

"Your first letters upset me more than once as I re-read them, but I think of you all habitually with real joy and peace of mind. And I am really happy; not in the sense that happiness presents itself always, or exactly in the way that I used to feel it when with you all, or as I should feel it if I were walking up to the lodge with my whole heart swelling within me. It is much more quiet and subdued, and does not, perhaps, come and go quite as much; but yet, in the midst of all, I half doubt sometimes whether everything about and within me is real. I just move on like a man in a dream; but this again does not make me idle. I don't suppose I ever worked harder, on the whole, than I do now, and I have such anxious work at the hospital. *Such* cases, Fan! Only two hours ago I left a poor sailor, by whose side I had been kneeling near three-quarters of an hour, holding his sinking head and moistening his mouth with wine, the dews of death on his forehead, and his poor emaciated frame heaving like one great pulse at each breath. For four days that he has been there (brought in a dying state from the 'Merchantman') I have been with him, and yesterday I administered to him the Holy Communion. He had spoken earnestly of his real desire to testify the sincerity of his repentance and faith and love. I have been there daily for nine days, but I cannot always manage it, as it is nearly two miles off. The responsibility is great of dealing with such cases, but I trust that God will pardon all my sad mistakes. I cannot withhold the Bread of Life where I see indications of real sorrow for sin, and the simple readiness to obey the command of Christ, even though there is great ignorance and but little time to train a soul for heaven."

In October 1855 he set forth with the bishop in his first voyage in the "Southern Cross." How readily he could adapt himself to the sea, and to new circumstances, is seen in the easy way in which he slips into nautical language; his happy ways, both with the sailors and the natives; and his powers of swimming and walking, which astonished them. At Waitoki, in Queen Charlotte's Sound, he is left, while Bishop Selwyn goes inland. This is a description of dinner while on a pedestrian journey through wilds and forests :—

"At noon we dined—biscuit and a slice of bacon, which the two Maories cooked by sticking a piece of wood through the rasher, and putting it on the wood-embers. Like a great light of old, we ate our dinners first, and our plates afterwards, the plate being, of course, a biscuit. The bishop went on at 1 P.M., and I started back with a Maori guide, reaching the beach at 6.30. The people at Waitoki were rather surprised when they heard that I had been at Massacre Hill since seven, and it was a good walk. The wood was fine, some trees huge, the white pines especially. Small green parrots flying actually in coveys, eight at a time, and perching close to me; large red ones in numbers, pigeons innumerable, ducks, &c., not to forget the sandflies and mosquitoes, which, indeed, take good care not to be forgotten, though several of the crew are suffering more from them than I am, and I hope to be mosquito-proof some day."

The usual voyage to the Banks and Solomon groups had, in 1855, been intermitted, owing to the bishop's absence in England. Three months usually intervened between the short voyage which was undertaken for the purpose of returning these lads to their several homes, and the regular long missionary cruise which lasted from five to six, or even seven, months, and during which, of course, the college was directed by the bishop's assistants, who had been carefully trained to the work. This long voyage was always taken during the winter, for the sake of the cooler weather, and to avoid the dangerous hurricanes which often arise in the hotter season, and are frequently so violent as wholly to alter the appearance of the land.

The system of education at St. John's College combined agricultural labour and printing with study, and the authorities and the boys shared according to their strength in both, for there was nothing more prominent in the scheme than that the coloured man was not to be treated as a mere hewer of wood and drawer of water.

In 1856, Norfolk Island was visited, and Sydney harbour was touched at; then a landing was made at Pitcairn Island, and finding that Mr. Nobbs, who had been appointed pastor there, would be glad of help, Mrs. Selwyn remained a short time. When the bishop picked her up, he confirmed a large number of Pitcairners. Then they made for Anaiteum and the fatal Santa Cruz, where the people at first presented arrows, but afterwards became more friendly, and made presents of yams.

"The people," says Patteson, "came out in canoes with quantities of yams and taro, of which they knew the full value; but the numbers were so large that no 'quiet work' could be done, and there was little to be done but to admire their costume, armlets, necklaces, plates of mother-of-pearl, but no nose ornaments. They had strips of a kind of cloth, woven of reed, and elaborate varieties of head-gear, some plastering their hair white with coral lime, others yellow, others red; others had shaved half the head with no better implement than a sharp shell, and others had produced two lines of bristles, like hog manes, on a shaven crown."

These Santa Cruz people were, however, very suspicious and unmanageable, with a confirmed bitterness and dislike towards Europeans—the grim legacy handed down for the manner in which, generations before, the Spaniards had treated them. In spite of this, Mr. Whytehead, the second mate of the "Southern Cross," tells us, that Mr. Patteson was wont to say that he was sure he could reach their confidences if he could once induce one of them to spend six months with him.

Bellona was next touched at, and here it was that the bishop and Mr. Patteson had to take off their coats, and with hatchets and adzes, or other things in their hands, take a good header and swim ashore. But this never dulled his eye for the beauty of the scenery, which he ever describes with enthusiastic eloquence :—

"Oh, the beauty of the deep clefts in the coral reef, lined with coral, purple, blue, scarlet, green, and white!

the little blue fishes, the bright blue star-fish, the little land-crabs walking away with other people's shells. But nothing of this can be seen by you; the coral loses its colour, and who can show you the bright line of surf breaking the clear blue of this truly Pacific Ocean; the tropical sun piercing through masses of foliage which nothing less dazzling could penetrate? . . . I trod upon and broke flowering branches of coral that you would have wondered at."

But admiration of the beautiful scenery had to go along with some degree of wariness amid the pleasant exploits of swimming ashore in these regions. Sometimes groups of sharks, of half-a-dozen at least, would be seen, as at Rowa, one of the Banks group, making havoc among the leaping shoals of fish, large and small, in water about four or five feet deep.

Even here, too, the echoes of toils and strifes at home from time to time reach him : we have significant record of the manner in which they affected him in the following letter :—

"My dear father writes in great anxiety about the Denison case. Oh, dear! what a cause of thankfulness it is to be out of the din of controversy, and to find hundreds of thousands longing for crumbs which are shaken about so roughly in these angry disputes! It isn't High Church or Low or Broad Church, or any other special name, but the longing desire to forget all distinctions, and to return to a simpler state of things, that seems naturally to result from the very sight of heathen people."

To Miss Neill, who had been his governess, he shows the utmost regard and affection, writing to her often the most touching letters. It is characteristic that to her he speaks fully on some points on which he is silent towards his own sisters; but her keen interest in him, which never abated, is another proof of the power he had of attaching in closest bonds of affection all with whom he came in contact. He writes to her thus :—

"You ask me, dear Miss Neill, where I am *settled*. Why, settled, I suppose, I am never to be : I am a missionary, you know, not a 'stationary.' But, however, my home is the 'Southern Cross,' where I live always in harbour as well as at sea, highly compassionated by all my good friends here, from the governor downwards, and highly contented myself with the sole possession of a cosy little cabin, nicely furnished with table, lots of books, and my dear father's photograph, which is an invaluable treasure and comfort to me. . . . Of course, wherever the 'Southern Cross' goes, I go too, and am a most complete skipper. I feel as natural with my quadrant in my hand as of old with a cricket-bat. Then I do *rather* have good saltwater baths, and see glorious sunsets and sunrises, and starlight nights, and the great many-voiced ocean, the winds and waves chiming all night with a solemn sound, lapping against my ear as I lie in my canvass bed, six feet by two and a half, and fall sound asleep and dream of home. Oh! there is much that is really enjoyable in this kind of life; and if the cares of the vessel, management of men, &c., do harass me sometimes, it is very good for me—security from such troubles having been anxiously and selfishly pursued by me at home."

It is very surprising, and sometimes it is touching, to come on such confessions from such a man. But now, as in youth, his distaste for mental exertion was so great that only a sense of duty sustained him in any effort requiring continued concentration of mind.

In the voyage of 1857, he tells us "that they visited sixty-six islands, and landed eighty-one times, wading, swimming, &c. All were most friendly and delightful," he adds; "only two arrows have been shot at us, and only one coming near,—so much for *savages*. I wonder what people ought to call sandal-wood traders and slave-masters if they call my Melanesians savages," is the tone in which he closes the record. The Banks Islands, as usual, were the most hopeful, Santa Maria coming first. Canoes came round the vessel, and the honesty of the race showed itself, for one little boy, who had had a fishhook given him, wished to exchange it for calico, and having forgotten to restore the hook at the moment, swam back with it as soon as he remembered it.

This voyage of 1857 was further memorable for a landing at Guadalcanar, or Gera, which is thus described:—

"I slept on shore about three miles up the bay among a number of natives, twenty-five or twenty-six in the same room with me—at least, I lay down in my things, which, by the by, were drenched through with salt and rain water. They said I was the first white person that had been ashore there. They treated me very well. How, in the face of all this, could I run the risk of letting them think I was unwilling to trust them?"

The victory of this trustfulness had been proved in the landing at this very place, when the mission ship was, as if though providentially, saved from being stoved on a reef, and where, coming near to the natives, who were there in crowds, he had to choose between standing close in, or letting go a kedge, which might have made them feel "he does not trust us." He declares that, though perhaps the bishop, being an older hand, might think his action rash, the result had fully justified it. "The natives behaved very well. They gave me two pigs, about 500 or 600 cocoa-nuts, and upwards of a ton of yams, though I told them I had only two small hatchets, five or six adzes, a few gimlets, and empty bottles to give in exchange."

In missionary work, as in more secular affairs. it may therefore be said that bold adventure is a needful element to accompany firmness and caution. And still, in the midst of all this labour and excitement, his study of languages did not pause. Nengonese had become almost as familiar to him as Maori, and his Sundays on his return home in this year, 1857, were decidedly polyglot; since, besides a regular English service at Taranaki, he often took a Maori service and preached extempore in that tongue, feeling that the people's understanding went along with him; and there were also, in early morning and late evening, prayers, partly in Nengonese, partly in Bauro, at the college chapel, and a sermon, first in one language and then repeated in another.

Nor were the studies of the sacred text, or the results of later learning in England, wholly neglected. To none of these matters was he indifferent, as some enthusiasts have been. He was intent on being up to the time in regard to the critical knowledge of the Word of God, and all related questions. He plied his friends with requests for books of value in this kind, and often wrote such letters as the following :—

"Any really good book on the New Testament, especially dealing critically with the Greek text, I certainly wish to have. I feel that *the great neglect* of us clergy is the neglect of the continued study, most critically and closely, of the grammatical meaning of the Hebrew and Greek text. . . . I fear I shall never be a good Hebrew scholar; I can't make time for it; but a decent Greek

x

scholar I hope to be. I work away, but, alas! only by fits and starts."

In 1858 he writes to his sister :—

"Things go on in a kind of routine. Two voyages a year, five months in New Zealand, though certainly two-thirds of my flock are fresh every year. . . . And you know, Fan, I can't write for the world at large anecdotes of missionary life, and swell the number of the 'Gems' and other trashy books. . . . The school is the real work. Teaching adults to read a strange tongue is hard work; I have little doubt but that the bishop is right in saying they must be taught English, but it is so very difficult a language, not spelt a bit as pronounced; and their language is all vocalic, and so easy to put into writing.

"But if you like I will scatter anecdotes about—of how the bishop and his chaplain took headers, hand-in-hand, off the schooner and round-house; and how the bishop got knocked over at Leper's Island by a big wave; and how I borrowed a canoe at Terriko and paddled out yams as fast as the bishop brought them to our boat, &c. ; but this is rubbish."

The question of the advantage of forming a school on an island within the tropics was one which often suggested itself to the bishop and Mr. Patteson. The advantages and disadvantages were so nearly balanced, that it was difficult to fix on a decided course of action. First of all, there was the consideration of health—some of the lads were much tried by a residence of any length of time in the cold climate of New Zealand; but then, on the other hand, there was the consideration that in the midst of civilisation the general influence itself was educative. "I can hardly have quite the same control," says Mr. Patteson, "over lads brought to an island itself wholly unconverted, as I can have over them in New Zealand: but, as a rule, Melaneisans are very tractable."

At the same time, however, it was thought best to try the experiment, and Lifu was fixed upon in 1858. On June 16th, accordingly, Mr. Patteson was landed there, for residence, having with him twelve lads from the north-west islands — from seven islands, speaking no fewer than six languages. He and four boys slept in one of the corner rooms, the other eight lads in another, and the Rarotogan teacher, Tutoo, and his wife, in a third. The central room was parlour, school, and hall, and as it had four unglazed windows and two doors opposite each other, and the trade winds always blowing, the inconvenience may be conceived. Here Mr. Patteson in every respect shared the life of the natives—the main staple of food being yams, with only now and then a fowl or bit of pig for dinner; but, after due trial, in which patience did all that patience could do to overcome nature, it was found that English strength could not be kept up on an exclusive diet of yams. But the Loyalty Islands are not fruitful: "the soil is nothing, indeed, but rugged coral, upheaved, bare, and broken, and here and there with pits that have become filled with soil enough to grow yams and cocoa-nuts."

On August 2, 1858, he preached his first two Lifu sermons—"Rather nervous, but I knew I had command enough of the language to explain my meaning." Constant private teaching to individuals was carried on; 250 copies of the Lifu primer had been dispersed where thousands were wanted, and Mr. Patteson wrote a little book of some sixteen pages, containing a statement of the outlines of the faith, and of scripture history; but this had to be printed in New Zealand.

The many difficulties that had arisen—including those with respect to variety of diet—might have been overcome, had it not been that perplexities began to arise through the French Government occupying New Caledonia, and the nearness of the Loyalty group becoming tempting to them. More and more obstacles were placed in the way of the work. Mr. Patteson soon began to see that the station could not be continued at Lifu, but he wrought on till the time fixed for the appearance of the " Southern Cross." She was delayed, however, owing to an accident which had befallen her, and he thus wrote while waiting anxiously for her appearance :—

" The interest of the work is becoming more and

more absorbing, so that, much as there is indeed going on in your world to distract and grieve one, it comes to me so weakened by time and distance, that I don't sympathise as I ought with those who are suffering so dreadfully from the Indian Mutiny, or the commercial failure, or the great excitement and agitation of the country. You can understand how this can be, perhaps; for my actual present *work* leaves me small leisure for reflecting, and for placing myself in the position of others at a distance; and when I have a moment's time, surely it is right that I should be in heart at Feniton, with those dear ones, and especially my dear father, of whom I have not heard for five months, so that I am very anxious as to what account of him the 'Southern Cross' may bring."

The "Southern Cross" had run on a reef, and had to be re-coppered; and owing to this delay, and the bishop's arrangement to start on a confirmation tour among the New Zealanders in November, only a few of the seventy and odd islands could be visited; but they had no fewer than four Pitcairners and forty-seven Melanesians on board, of whom three were young married women, and two were babies—a very large number for the size of the ship; but all were kept in excellent health and order by Bishop Selwyn's arrangements for cleanliness, &c. Mr. Patteson thus describes the style of life during the voyage:—

"One gets so used to this sort of thing that I sleep

just as well as I used to do in my own room at home, and by 6.30 or 7 A.M. all vestiges of anything connected with sleeping arrangements have vanished, and the cabins look like what they are—large and roomy. We have, you know, no separate cabins filled with bunks, &c.—abominations specially contrived to conceal dirt and prevent ventilation. Light calico curtains answer all purposes of dividing off a cabin into compartments; but we agree to live together, and no one has found it unpleasant as yet. We turn a part of our cabin into a γυναικεῖο at night for the three women and two babies by means of a canvas screen. Bishop looks after them, washes the babies, tends the women when sick, &c., while I, by virtue of being a bachelor, shirk all the trouble. One of these women is now coming for the second time to the college; her name is Carry; Margaret Cho is on her second visit, and Hearore is the young bride of Kapua, now coming for his third time, and baptized last year."

During the summers of 1857-8 and 1858-9, the Loyalty Islanders mustered in great numbers at St. John's College. Mr. Patteson worked very hard these years at translations, and there was an immense enthusiasm about printing; the Lifuites and Nengonese striving each to get the most in their own language.

For the sake of the pupils from tropical islands, the college was in 1859 removed to St. Andrews, Kohimarama, a sheltered bay opposite the entrance to the harbour at Auckland, and Mr. Patteson devoted himself with fresh energy to their training and welfare. A settlement had likewise been made in the Banks group, on Mota, or Sugar-loaf Island, which lies opposite to Port Patteson—named, as it will be remembered, by Bishop Selwyn after Sir John Patteson—and the "first home in Melanesia" built here, "at least a hundred natives coming to help in the building, and pulling down materials from their own houses to make the roof."

Probably the considerations that more than any other determined this settlement were the comparative healthfulness and fruitfulness of the island—the bread-fruit growing profusely—combined with the fact that, whilst the Solomon Islanders were found to be the quickest and most brilliant, they were far less steady and trustworthy and attachable than were the Banks Islanders. But the three months' residence on Mota had its own disadvantages, for, during that long period, Mr. Patteson was entirely out of the reach of letters.

The days were laid out thus :—Morning school in the village, first with the regular scholars, then with any one who liked to come in; and then, when the weather permitted, a visit to some village, sometimes walking all round, a circuit of ten miles, but generally each of the two taking a separate village, talking to the people, teaching them from cards and encouraging interrogatories. Mr. Patteson always had such an attraction for them that they would throng round him wherever he went.

He tells us :—" We have seven Solomon Islanders—
five from a village at the north-west of San Cristoval,
and two from the south-east point of Guadalcanar or
Gera, a magnificent island about twenty-five or twenty
miles to the north-west of San Cristoval [*i.e.* Bauro].
From frequent intercourse they are almost bilingual, a
great 'lounge' for me, as one language does for both;
the structure of the two island tongues is the same, but
scarcely any words much alike." From Nengoné there
were four men and two women.

Here he found much of the rest and quiet of mind for
which he longed.

In 1859 he had written :—" With the languages of
four groups we are now fairly acquainted, besides some
of the distinguishing dialects, which differ very much
from one another; nevertheless, I think that by and by
we shall connect them all, if we live ; but as some dialects
may have dropped out altogether, we may want a few
links in the chain to demonstrate the connection fully to
people at a distance."

Every day, indeed, afforded illustration of his remarkable aptitude in following up difficulties in language ;
and had he been spared, there can be no doubt that he
would have made substantial contributions to philology.
As it is, he has done more than any other to compare
and co-ordinate the various tongues and dialects of the
South Pacific.

But amid all this his interest in home and his old

friends was, if possible, intensified by absence and distance. How he loves to snatch a half-hour to think of them and to write to them! Scarcely a chance was missed by him for sending a despatch home, and other friends were often pleasantly surprised to find they were remembered, by a note which was utterly unexpected. Near the close of his life—a time of peculiar perplexity— he wrote to Principal Shairp, thanking him for the teaching embodied in his "Religion and Culture," &c. His relations to his aged father were quite unique. He was the eldest son, but no consideration that was in the remotest alien to the work in which he was engaged was allowed to intrude for a moment. The mutual renunciations of father and son, for the sake of Melanesia, from first to last are indeed very beautiful to read of. How the ties of kindred and affection seemed to grow closer and closer the more that Mr. Patteson became engrossed in his work, affording him 'sweet relief' in brief moments of leisure or weariness! and how, on the other hand, the aged Judge became, if possible, more reconciled to his son's absence the more that nature would have urged the necessity of his having Coley beside him, to support him in the midst of growing infirmities! Thus the son writes in July 1859 :—

"Of course it is useless to speculate on the future, but I see nothing at all to make it likely that I shall ever revisit England. I can't very well conceive any such state of things as would make it a duty to gratify my constant inclination. And, my dear father, I don't scruple to say (for you will understand me) that I am happier here than I should be in England, where, even though I were absent only a few months, I should bear about with me the constant weight of knowing that Melanesia was not provided for. And, strange as it may seem, this has quite ceased to be a trial to me. The effort of subduing the longing desire to see you is no longer a great one; I feel I am cheerful, and bright, and light-hearted, and that I have really everything to make a man thankful and content. And if you could see the thankful look of the bishop, when he is again assured that there is no item of regret or desire to call me home on your part, you would feel, I know, that colonial work does require an unconditional, unreserved surrender of a man to whatever he may find to do."

And this was the tone in which, amid failing faculties, the old man was wont to write concerning his son; he is addressing Bishop Selwyn :—

"You write most kindly touching him, dear fellow, and truly I am to be envied, *qui natum haberem tali ingenio præditum.* Not for a moment have I repented of giving my sanction to his going out to New Zealand; and I fully believe that God will prosper his work. I did not contemplate his becoming a bishop, nor is that the circumstance which gives me the great satisfaction I feel. It is his devotion to so good a work, and that he should have been found adequate to its performance;

whether as bishop or as priest is not of itself of so much importance."

The reference to the bishopric is explained by the fact that gradually, during the last two years, Patteson had been more and more working independently, opening up new paths, and attesting not only a power of marking out available lines of enterprise, but giving ample proof of the desirability of having a fresh sphere of labour, into which he would feel more free to carry his remarkable organising gift. Not that he himself had ever felt in any way hampered by his association with Bishop Selwyn; wholly the reverse. He was rather inclined to regard himself as disqualified to assume a position of authority, as the following quotation from a letter referring to the very first hint of his appointment to a Melanesian bishopric will show :—

"Seriously, I am not at all fitted to do anything but work under a good man. Of course, should I survive the bishop, and no other man come out, why, it is better that the ensign should assume the command than to give up the struggle altogether. But this, of course, is pure speculation. The bishop is hearty, and I pray God may be Bishop of Melanesia for twenty years to come, and by that time there will be many more competent men than I ever shall be to succeed him, to say nothing of possible casualties, climate, &c."

But the counsel of others prevailed in this matter. He was consecrated bishop on the 24th February 1861, and on the 28th was installed at Kohimarama. No sooner was the installation ceremony over than he wrote thus to his father :—

"How can I thank you for giving me up to this work, and for all the wise and loving words with which you constantly cheer and encourage me? Your blessing comes now to cheer and strengthen me, as work and responsibilities are fast accumulating upon me. I thank God that He enables us at the two ends of the world to see this matter in the same way, so that no conflict of duties arises in my mind. . . . I almost fear to write that I am a bishop in the Church of Christ. May God strengthen me for the duties of the office, to which I trust He has indeed called me! . . . What some of you say about self-possession on one's going about among the poor people being marvellous, is just what of course appears to me commonplace. Of course it is wrong to risk one's life, but to carry one's life in one's hand is what other soldiers besides those of the Cross do habitually ; and no one, as I think, would willingly hurt a hair of my head in Melanesia, or that part of it where I am known.

"How I think of those islands! How I see those bright coral and sandy beaches, strips of burning sunshine fringing the masses of forest rising into ridges of hills, covered with a dense mat of vegetation! Hundreds of people are crowding upon them, naked, armed, with wild uncouth cries and gestures ; I cannot talk to them but by signs. But they are my children now! May God enable me to do my duty to them!"

His next seven months' trip among the islands was delayed owing to the difficulty of finding a craft to take the place of the "Southern Cross," which during the former voyage had run on a shoal called the Hen and Chickens, at the head of Ngunguru Bay, and had speedily broken up, after full five years' good service. There was nothing to approach, not to speak of equalling, her. "Vessels built for freight," says the bishop, "are to the 'Southern Cross' as a cart-horse to a thoroughbred steed, and we must have some vessel which can do the work quickly among the multitude of the isles, and many other reasons there are which *we seamen* only perhaps can judge fully, which make it quite essential to the carrying on of this peculiar mission that we should have a vessel of a peculiar kind." The best that could be done meanwhile, however, was to charter the "Dunedin" —a vessel not in the best repair, "the pumps going every two hours," to carry them to Mota, after having undergone some preliminary "caulking."

At Erromango the bishop heard of the mournful deaths of Mr. and Mrs. Gordon, the Scotch missionaries, who had become victims to the wild superstitions of the people. But Bishop Patteson had full faith in his own safety. Indeed, very shortly after this, as we have been informed by one who knows well, he landed on Erromango, and made his way to the graves of Mr. and Mrs.

Gordon, and read over them the funeral service *as a mark of his respect* for these his brave and martyred fellow-workers in the South Pacific.

Reaching Mota, and finding the home that had been erected on a former visit all secure, he soon set out in an open boat to pay a round of visits to the other islands of the Banks group, returning to their homes such of the Banks Islanders as he had had with him. "As we pulled away from Aruas," he tells us, " one elderly man drew his bow, and the women and children ran off into the bush, here, as everywhere almost in these islands, growing quite thickly some twenty yards above watermark. The man did not let fly his arrow. I cannot tell why this small demonstration took place." Probably the reason that the man desisted as he did was simply that the bishop, when an arrow was pointed at him, was wont to look the archer full in the face with his bright smile, and the look of cheery confidence and good-will made the weapon drop. When another time, at Ambrym, an incident of the same sort took place—a man raising his bow and drawing it, then unbending it, and finally bending it again, as others were apparently dissuading him from letting fly the arrow — the bishop simply regards this as a result of not landing oftener, and writes: "We must try and make more frequent landings."

H. M. S. "Cordelia," under Captain Hume, which took him off Mota on this occasion, and carried him to the

Solomon Islands, for his next visitation there, brought him word of the serious illness of his father; so that it was hardly a shock to him when on reaching Norfolk Island, on his return, he learned the first news of the Judge's death from the Sydney papers. He took it as though it had been long prepared for; and the only evidence of change towards those about him was, if possible, a greater sweetness in his manner and ways towards them.

It was during this voyage that Bishop Patteson so engaged the interest of Lieutenant Capel Tilly, R.N., that that officer undertook to return to England with the "Cordelia" to watch over the building of the new "Southern Cross," and return again with her to the South Pacific, to act as her commanding officer.

On his return to Kohimarama in the end of the year the old life was resumed, and Lady Martin thus sketches the settlement at the time :—

"The new settlement was then thought to be healthy, and he and his boys alike rejoiced in the warmth of the sheltered bay after the keenness of the air at St. John's on the higher ground. The place looked very pretty; the green fields, and hawthorn hedges, and the sleek cattle reminded me of England. As a strong contrast, there was the white shelly beach and yellow sands. Here the boys sunned themselves in play-hours, or fished on the rocks, or cooked their fish at driftwood fires. On calm days one or two would skim across the blue water in their tiny canoes. One great charm of the place was the freedom and naturalness of the whole party. There was no attempt to force an overstrained piety on those wild fellows who showed their sincerity by coming with the bishop. By five in the morning all were astir, and jokes and laughter, and shrill, unaccountable cries, would rouse us up, and go on all day, save when school and chapel came to sober them. The bishop had not lost his Eton tastes, and only liked to see them play games, and the little, fat, merry-faced lads were always on the look-out for a bit of fun with him."

Mr. Whytehead has given the following graphic picture of the bishop and his scholars at this period, which may well supplement Lady Martin's description :—

"On proceeding down to Kohimarama to join the vessel, I found her moored off the station, and preparations being made for the voyage. Spars were being sent aloft, gear was being rove, and sails bent. All day the boats, manned by pupils in charge of teachers, were bringing off stores, personal effects, &c. It was then that I first saw some of the natives of the Western Pacific. Very intelligent-looking, bright-eyed little fellows were these boys, and exceedingly nice they looked in their loose shirts, straw hats, and canvas trousers. They worked heartily too, and seemed to enjoy the bustle of preparation, no doubt anticipating the joys of once more seeing their friends and homes, and relating the wonders they had beheld in the white man's country. The first time I saw Bishop Patteson I was struck with the wonderful power of attraction which he seemed to possess. It was not in his face alone, but in his whole manner that this force was to be found. I was walking on the beach one evening after working hours, a day or two after joining, when he came out of his rooms, which formed part of the main building of the school. The boys were all playing on the grass before the doors, but his appearance was the signal for them all to leave off their various little amusements and run clustering round him. Some seized his hands, others the skirts of his coat, and all had a word of happiness at seeing him. The scene reminded me of nothing so much as a hen gathering her chickens under her wings. He passed each arm round the neck of one of the taller boys, and with the rest tripping along like a body-guard on all sides of him he slowly advanced towards the beach. I stood smiling at the spectacle. The group neared me, and the bishop, remarking my expression, said that he supposed I had never seen anything of the kind before. I confessed that I had not, but that it was very delightful to see such intelligent and affectionate-looking boys. He asked me how I liked the place, if things were comfortable on board the vessel, and other questions, showing that he took a kind and lively interest in the comfort and happiness of every one of his party. It was this kindness in little matters of detail which always gained for Bishop Patteson the love of those with whom he came in contact. I do not believe there was a man belonging to the ship's company who would have hesitated at anything to serve the bishop. He was thoroughly respected and looked up to, and yet at the same time he was loved by those around him in such a way as few men ever have the happiness to be."

This was the summer of his year, during which he enjoyed the peaceful sunshine of society with minds, so far, congenial; it was different when he was on his voyages, exposed to all sorts of perils. He thus indicates one class of these in writing to Mrs. Martyn :—

"Those nights when I lie down, in a long hut, among forty or fifty naked men, cannibals—the only Christian on the island—that is the time, Sophy, to pour out the heart in prayer and supplication, that they—those dark wild heathens about me—may be turned from Satan to God."

The year 1862 was remarkable for a voyage in a chartered vessel, the "Sea-breeze," in which various islands of the Solomon and New Hebrides groups were visited, and frequent landings made on the island of Santa Cruz at points where they had not landed before. The natives are very ingenious—carving elaborate arrows, and as elaborately poisoning them; but the bishop met only with kindness and attention.

"Two or three of the men took off little ornaments and gave them to me; one bright pretty boy especially

I remember, who took off his shell necklace and put it round my neck, making me understand, partly by words, but more by signs, that he was afraid to come now, but would do so if I returned, as I said, in eight or ten moons. Large baskets of almonds were given me, and other food also thrown into the boat. I made a poor return by giving some fish-hooks and a tomahawk to the man whom I took to be the person of most consequence. On shore the women came freely up to me among the crowd, but they were afraid to venture down to the beach. Now, this is the island about which we have long felt a great difficulty as to the right way of obtaining any communication with the natives. This year, why and how I cannot tell, the way was opened beyond all expectation."

At Leper's Island and Malanta, at Misial and at Ysabel, such pleasant days were likewise spent; and even at Tikopia, where the people are very powerful in person and unmanageable in spirit, a good impression was made. In November the bishop returned to Kohimarama, and immediately set about the work there. He congratulates himself on the increased openings for mission stations, and though he felt the lack of workers, he was full of hope that the Banks Archipelago would soon supply a working staff. One of his great ideas, indeed, was to form centres for independent native missionary effort— having become more and more convinced that the Melanesians would be the most efficient missionaries to each other. Hence the concern with which he now warned those at home about the "right men" for his staff, knowing that any false ideas imported from home would have a very alien influence on the natives. Here is one passage in which we gather up his oft-repeated convictions on this head :—

"You know I have long felt that there is harm done by trying to make these islanders like English people. All that is needed for decency and propriety in the arrangements of houses, in dress, &c., we must get them to adopt, but they are to be Melanesian, not English, Christians. We are so far removed from them in matters not at all necessarily connected with Christianity, that unless we can denationalise ourselves and eliminate all that belongs to us as English, and not as Christians, we cannot be to them what a well-instructed countryman may be. He is nearer to them. They understand him. He brings the teaching to them in a practical and intelligible form. . . . .

"I solve the difficulty in Melanesian work by saying, 'Use Melanesians.' I tell people plainly I don't want white men. . . . I have no intention of taking any more from England, Australia, or New Zealand. I sum it thus : they cost about ten times as much as the Melanesian (literally), and but a very small proportion do the work as well."

The carrying out of this principle of equality, however, was one so surrounded with difficulties that only a man like Bishop Patteson—patient, trustful, affectionate, and winning men by his affection—could possibly have succeeded in it; and it was above all necessary, in view of this, that he should be supported and assisted not only by men like-minded, but men constitutionally gifted with patience, prudence, and common sense, almost equal to his own. Hence it was that, in writing home, he got into a habit of discouraging the sending out of helpers; but still, at the same time, urging on his friends the peculiar qualities required in any who should come.

In another place he thus signalises other qualities most necessary in the men who should be chosen to join such a work as his. And his words may be held to have a value for all missionaries at work amongst the heathen :—

"Men are needed who have what I may call strong religious common sense to adapt Christianity to the wants of the various nations that live in Melanesia, without compromising any truth of doctrine or principle of conduct; men who can see in the midst of the errors and superstitions of a people whatever fragment of truth or symptom of a yearning after something better may exist among them, and make that the *point d'appui* upon which they may build up the structure of Christian teaching. Men, moreover, of industry, they must be, for it is useless to talk of 'picking up languages.' Of course, in a few days a man may learn to talk superficially and inaccurately on a few subjects; but to teach

Christianity a man must know the language well, and this is learnt only by hard work."

He was harassed with the idea that his perpetual voyaging from place to place was a great cause of loss of influence with his boys; and on this point he thus touchingly expresses himself:—

"The main difficulty remains of retaining our hold upon boys. Oh, that I could live permanently in twenty islands at once! But I can't do so on even one; and all the letter-writing and accounts, and worst of all, the necessity for being trustee for matters not a bit connected with Melanesia, because there is no one else, interferes sadly with my time. I think I could work away with the languages, &c., and really do something with these fellows, but I never get a chance. I never have two days together which I can spend exclusively at Melanesian work. And I ought to have nothing whatever to distract me. Twenty languages calling for arrangement and comparison cause confusion enough."

But in spite of all this, he is able to record as the result of the work of 1862 :—

"We have never had so satisfactory a set of scholars. Out of twenty-eight (exclusive of three native teachers), only one, who has been an invalid almost all the summer, is unable to read and write. The first class (which indeed should, by rights, be subdivided) consists of nine. All may be regarded as catechumens. I should not hesitate to baptize them at once, if attacked with sudden illness, for example."

Another confession of a somewhat singular kind we also came on at this time, of which some record may here be made, for it is exceedingly characteristic of the bishop.

"I am less shy than I was, and with real gentlemen feel no difficulty in discussing points on which we differ. It is the vulgar, uneducated fellow that beats me. The Melanesians, laugh as you may at it, are naturally gentlemanly and courteous and well-bred. I never saw a 'gent' in Melanesia, though not a few downright savages. I vastly prefer the savages."

He found so many demands made on his time by indifferent matters while in New Zealand, that already he felt, as a strong inducement to transfer the school from New Zealand within the tropics, the hope of escaping from some of the unnecessary worry and consultation. What he wrote later, in 1865, would so far express the feeling that very often visited him now.

"Sometimes I do feel tempted to long for Curtis Island, merely to get away from New Zealand. I feel as if I should never do anything here. Everything is in arrears. I turn out of a morning, and really don't know what to take at first. Then just as I am in the middle of a letter, down comes some donkey to take up a quarter of an hour (lucky if not an hour) with idle nonsense; then in the afternoon an invasion of visitors, which is worst of all. That fatal invention of 'calling!'"

Of his manner of life at Kohimarama at this time he thus tells his sisters, with a little of the quiet humour that he was wont to throw across dull and ordinary routine—

"Up at five, when I go round and pull the blankets, not without many a joke, off the sleeping boys; many of the party are already up and washing. Then just before prayers I go to the kitchen and see that all is ready for breakfast. Prayers at 5.45 in English, Mota, Bauro, &c., beginning with a Mota hymn, and ending with the Lord's Prayer in English. Breakfast immediately after: at our table, Mr. Pritt, Mr. Kerr, and young Atkin, who has just joined us. At the teachers' table, five Norfolk Islanders, Edward (a Maori), five girls, and two of their husbands, and the three girls being placed at the table because they *are* girls; Melanesians at the other three tables indiscriminately."

The new "Southern Cross," procured mainly by the efforts of Mr. Keble and Dr. Moberly, arrived on the 28th of February 1863, and was found every way well suited for her purpose. He thus announced her arrival to Miss Yonge:—

"'The 'Southern Cross' arrived safely this morning, thanks to God! What it is to us even you can hardly tell; I know not how to pour out my thankfulness. She seems admirably adapted for the work. Mr. Tilly's report of her performance is most satisfactory: safe, fast, steers well, and very manageable. Internal arrangements very good; after-cabin too luxurious; but then that may be wanted for sick folk; and as it *is* luxurious, why I shall get a soft bed, and take to it very kindly."

It must have been a proud moment to the bishop when he set out in his first trial voyage in the new ship, bearing his own flag—the mitre and Southern Cross constellation in gold on a blue field—an ensign the natives soon began to know and welcome and look for.

But the joy that was felt over this event was soon dashed by a distressing visitation which carried off several of the native lads. Miss Yonge thus indicates its nature :—

"Whether it was from the large numbers, or the effect of the colder climate, or from what cause could not be told, but a frightful attack of dysentery fell upon the Melanesians, and for several weeks suffering prevailed among them. How Bishop Patteson tended them during this time can be better guessed than described. Archdeacon Lloyd, who came to assist in the cares of the small party of clergy, can find no words to express the devotion with which the bishop nursed them, comforting and supporting them, never shrinking from the most repulsive offices, even bearing out the dead silently at night, lest the others should see and be alarmed. Still no mail, except during the voyages, had ever left New Zealand without a despatch for home; and time was snatched in the midst of all this distress for greetings in the same beautiful, minute, clear hand as usual."

In a letter home, at this trying time, he says: "Since this day fortnight I have scarce slept night or day, but by snatching an hour here and there; others are working quite as hard, and all the good points of our Melanesian staff are brought out, as you may suppose."

Six of the children were taken thus—the last one Sosaman, "a dear lad, one of the Banks Islanders, about ten or twelve years old." By him, at the last, Bishop Patteson knelt, closing the eyes in death. "I can see his mother's face now," he writes. "What will she say to me, she who knows not the Christian's life in death? . . . I washed him, and laid him out as usual in a linen sheet. How white it looked! So much more simple and touching than the coffin—the form just discernible as it lay where five had lain before."

It can easily be imagined how severe would be the trial of visiting the relatives of the deceased islanders on the next voyage; but that was got over with less pain than might have been expected; for in the hearts of most of them the seed of Christian faith had struck root and grown—one father at Mota saying to him, "It is all well, bishop; he died well. I know you did all you could; it is all well." And fresh scholars came from these islands in plenty.

"At Aruas, the small island close to Valua, from which dear Sosaman came, it was just the same," he tells us; "rather different at the west side of Vanua Lava, where they did not behave so well, and where (as I heard afterwards) there had been some talk of shooting me; but nothing occurred while I was on shore with them to alarm me."

Their landings, never wholly without risk, now became at some points so dangerous that many men would have altogether desisted from going ashore.

The death of Sosaman and the other scholars practically re-opened the question whether New Zealand would be a safe residence for the great body of Melanesian youth, and it was decided in the negative. A visit to Melbourne, Sydney, and other places, enabled the bishop to make appeal for aid towards establishing another station, which did not pass without response; and plans were formed to transfer the school to a healthy and well-watered part of Curtis Island, east of Queensland. This was mainly fixed on with the idea of native Australians also being taken to the mission station. But though Curtis Island was visited, it was not found possible to leave a party there then to try the experiment; and the "Southern Cross" sailed to Santa Cruz, to meet that fatal attack in Graciosa Bay, which in its results stands out a mournful episode in the life of Bishop Patteson. The party were shot at, and three of them severely wounded with arrows.

Mr. Whytehead thus describes the appearance of the boat when it reached the vessel:—

"Stretched beneath the thwarts, his face looking deathly white, and with the broken end of a large arrow protruding from his bare breast, lay poor Pearce, groaning heavily. On one thwart sat Edwin Nobbs with another broken arrow sticking in his cheek; whilst Fisher Young tried to smile, in spite of the agony of an arrow which had transfixed his wrist. Atkin and Christian, the uninjured ones of the crew, were working the boat, whilst Bishop Patteson, a look of inexpressible grief upon his beautiful features, was directing the proceedings."

Tetanus or lock-jaw supervened, and Fisher Young and Edwin Nobbs died in great agony; whilst Pearce, whose wound had been the worst, completely recovered. Young and Nobbs were Norfolk Islanders, "two of the most beautiful characters," says Mr. Whytehead, "I ever met; and were to the bishop as the apple of his eye." For the former, indeed, the bishop had all the affection of a father; he loved all the scholars, but he loved Fisher Young in quite a peculiar way, as he thus indicates in a touching note to his sister:—

" But, my dear Fan, Fisher most of all supplied to me the absence of earthly relations and friends. He was my boy; I loved him as, I think, I never loved any one else. I don't mean *more* than you all, but in a different way; not as one loves another of equal age, but as a parent loves a child. I can hardly think of my little room at Kohimarama without him. I long for the sight of his dear face, the sound of his voice. It was my delight to teach him."

And shortly afterwards he wrote in this strain :—

"Oh, how I think with such ever-increasing love of dear Fisher and Edwin! How I praised God for them on All Saints' day! But I don't expect to recover spring and elasticity yet awhile. I don't think I ever shall feel so young again."

It was a relief to the bishop on this occasion to reach home, to find some rest and recruitment; for the unusual strain and incessant tax on his energies had tried him greatly. And well pleased he must have been to find that his helpers were always so assiduous in his absences. During the year 1865 a great advance was made in the industrial department of the mission work. About seventeen acres of land were taken in hand and worked by Mr. Pritt, with the Melanesian lads. "We have our own dairy of thirteen cows," he says, "and, besides supplying the whole mission party, numbering in all seventy-seven persons, with abundance of milk, we sell considerable quantities of butter. We grow, of course, our own potatoes and vegetables and maize, &c., for our cows. The farm and dairy work affords another opportunity for teaching our young people to acquire habits of industry."

In the end of 1865 an official offer of a station on Norfolk Island was made; and though Curtis Island had not ceased to be thought of, the offer was all the more readily embraced in that the bishop's mind had for some time been made up on the expediency of a change to a place which was likely to suit both English and tropical constitutions alike, and he hoped to make the experiment the ensuing winter with Mr. Palmer and a small body of scholars; Norfolk Island being not only six hundred miles nearer to the Melanesian Islands than Auckland, but these the six hundred cold and boisterous miles that must be weathered at the end of each return voyage.

This change to Norfolk Island was charged with great issues for the mission; and on going back there the bishop must have been delighted to see the progress that had been made in the way of clearing and preparing by the party who had been left under Mr. Palmer: and, the time being come, he proceeded on to the Mota settlement, full of hope. Here he was absorbed in the scheming out of a Christian village—a long-cherished idea of his own, which had been happily met by a suggestion of George Sarawia, one of the earliest and best of the Banks pupils who had been ordained; and this was varied by quiet work of several kinds. "How he read, wrote, or did anything, is the marvel, with the hut constantly crowded by men who had nothing to do but gather round, in suffocating numbers, to stare at his pen travelling over the paper. . . . It is useless," he says, "to talk about it, and one must humour them, or they will think I am vexed with them. The scholars, neatly clothed, with orderly and industrious habits, were no small contrast, but I miss as yet the link between them and the resident heathen people."

He has, however, one cause for gladness that might well surprise students and dignitaries at home. He can congratulate himself that now he does not need to take any trouble about cooking, having got from England a supply of preserved meats, which leaves him freer for the pleasant occupation, for an hour or so each day, in clearing away the bush, that in one year grows up surprisingly here. But he adds quaintly, "I can make myself all sorts of good things, if I choose to take the trouble, and some days I do so. I bake a little bread now and then, and flatter myself it is uncommonly good." A beautiful property, between Veverao and Maligo, of some ten acres, was chosen for the site of the village; and the intricate affair of settling with some sixteen different owners having been got over, the business of clearing and building was set about energetically. Then, having seen a start made, with George Sarawia established as head of the village, he departs on his voyage among the islands; and now we first get definitive hints of the evils being done by that semi-legalised slave-trade between the South-Sea Islands and New Caledonia and the white settlers in Fiji. The bishop writes :—

" I have made a little move in the matter. I wrote to a Wesleyan missionary in Fiji (Ovalau) who sent us some books. I am told that Government sanctions natives being brought upon agreement to work for pay, &c., and passage home in two years. We know the impossibility of making contracts with New Hebrides or Solomon natives. It is a mere sham, an evasion of some law—passed, I dare say, without any dishonourable intention—to procure colonial labour. If necessary, I will go to Fiji or anywhere to procure information. But I saw a letter in a Sydney paper which spoke strongly and properly of the necessity of the most stringent rules to prevent the white settlers from injuring the coloured men."

Though Bishop Patteson had followed his own judgment on two decided points — the removal to Norfolk Island, and the use of the Mota language instead of English, and did not repent having done so —yet still the being left with none to whom to look up to as an authority was a heavy trial and strain on mind and body, and brought on another stage in that premature age that the climate and constant toil were bringing upon him when most men are still in the fulness of their strength; and this notwithstanding that the party were in excellent health, and the land found to be so productive that it was hoped they would very soon have an export; whilst as to the adoption of the language of Mota, he could say that it was beginning to be a very fair channel for communicating accurate theological teaching, they having to a large extent made it so by assigning deeper meanings to existing words.

Other departments of mission work did not pause. In July 1868—though an outbreak of typhus in several of the islands had given great concern, carried off some of the scholars, and tried the bishop much—he tells us "they have now in Mota, in print, St. Luke and the Acts, and soon will have St. John, which is all ready; the Prayer-Book, save some of the Psalms, and a few other small portions; and in manuscript they have a kind of manual of the Catechism, abstracts of the books of the Old Testament, papers on prophecy, &c. All this work, once done in Mota, is, without very much labour, to be transferred into Bauro, Mahaga, Mara, &c., as I hope, but that is in the future."

The stations on Norfolk Island and at Mota formed excellent resting-points for the bishop, and lightened his labours materially, so far as the sea-voyaging was concerned. But he knew no real rest. Wherever he was, there were others to be cared for, and he was instant in season and out of season. What ominously varies the record of his work during the last two years, is that running protest against the nefarious kidnapping which went on more and more as the demand for labour increased in Fiji and Queensland, and towards which Government seemed to be supine, or indeed wholly indifferent. In November 1869, the bishop writes:—

"I know of no case of actual violence in the Banks Islands, but in every case they took people away under false pretences, asserting that the 'bishop is ill and can't come, and he has sent us to bring you to him;' or 'the bishop is in Sydney ; he broke his leg getting into his boat, and has sent us to take you to him,' &c. In most places, where any of our young people happened to be on the shore, they warned their companions against these men, but not always with success."

The knowledge of this must have added considerably to the bishop's sense of danger ; but he had self-control enough to exhibit no trace of fear, and went from island to island with the same frank, trustful bearing as before. Some time before this he had written these words, which now required strictest practical illustration, though it was wonderful how he still managed to restrain all show of suspicion or timidity :—

" I must not forget that I have some islands to visit in the next month or two where the people are very wild, so that I, of all people, have least reason to speculate about what I may hope to do a year hence. The real anxiety is in the making up my own mind whether or not I ought to lower the boat in such a sea-way ; whether or not I ought to swim ashore among these fellows crowded there on the narrow beach."

There can be no doubt whatever that the additional anxiety which these circumstances caused him did much to bring on such depression and ill-health as led his friends, who deemed that his case was worse than he had represented it, to urge him to come home to England for a short furlough, that he might procure proper medical advice. But to this he would not listen, and replies :—

"I should gain nothing by having medical advice there. I am quite satisfied that I know what is the matter with me, and the way to treat my malady; and the voyages and the life in England, and the climate, would be all much against my health. And I get on very well again now. Humanly speaking, I may do a good deal of work yet, rather in a quieter way perhaps than of old; but then I need not have any more adventures, except in one or two places, perhaps, like Santa Cruz. That stage of the mission is past in a good many islands, and I can devolve some part of it on my really excellent and very dear friends and helpers in the other islands. Brooke and Atkin (both in priests' orders) spend three months in their respective fields of work on the Solomon Islands, among wild fellows (still practising, at times, cannibalism); and when you can get fellows to do this cheerily and making nothing of it, doing it as a matter of course, you may feel pretty sure you have fellows of the right stuff."

So he went on, pursuing his regular round of work, now at Norfolk Island, teaching theology and aiding in the various crafts there practised; again at Mota, and helping in farm work, and once more moving from island to island and reef to reef, bringing off his boys, and later in the year landing them again; whilst his helpers were finding access to Tikopian giants, who had visited them at Mota, and otherwise forwarding the work. Santa Cruz caused him much concern; but at

Nukapu, in 1870, he is well received, the women dancing in his honour and giving small presents. The people, when they came on board, asked, "Where is Bisambe?" He replies, "Here I am." "No, no," say they; "the Bisambe *tuai* (of old): your *matua* (father). Is he below? Why doesn't he come up with some hatchets?"—showing that they well remembered Bishop Selwyn and the former visit.

On October 11th he makes this record:—

"A topsail schooner in sight between Ambrym and Paama—one of those kidnapping vessels. I have any amount of (to me) conclusive evidence of downright kidnapping. But I don't think I could prove any case in a Sydney court. They have no names painted on some of their vessels, and the natives can't catch nor pronounce the names of the white men on board."

On April 27th, 1871, he started on his last voyage. Mota was visited; then came a cruise among the islands of the New Hebrides group; after that a few weeks back at Mota, baptizing children, &c.; and then on to the Santa Cruz group. Almost everywhere were tokens of the kidnapper—some of the islands were half depopulated; and now the bishop began to realise the necessity and the prudence of "not going near the islands, unless we have a good breeze, and can get away from the fleets of canoes, if we see reason for so doing." As they approached Nukapu, that "lay with the blue waves breaking over the circling reef, the white line of coral sand and the trees coming down to it," the bishop had spoken to them on the death of St. Stephen. He had collected many presents to take ashore, and, going into the boat, pulled towards the canoes. The men in them seemed undecided what to do. When, however, he offered to go ashore they assented, and the boat having gone on to a part of the reef, some of the men proposed to take the bishop into their canoe. As he found the entering of their canoes a good means of disarming suspicion, he complied; but soon after he heard the ominous word *tabu*, or warning, and yams and fruits were presented to him, no doubt in the hope that he would, according to their superstition, touch something *tabu*, and thus justify their striking him. The bishop, having waded through the surf, landed on the beach, and he was lost to the sight of the crew of the boat, which was now drifting about among the canoes. But suddenly a man in one of the canoes stood up and shot one of their yard-long arrows toward the boat, and his companions in other two canoes immediately did the same, calling out as they aimed, "This for New Zealand man! This for Bauro man! This for Mota man!" Before the boat could be pulled back all were wounded, and with difficulty they made their way to the ship. No sooner, however, had an arrow-head been extracted from Mr. Atkin's shoulder, giving him intense pain, than he, as being the only one who knew the way by which the reef could be crossed in the rising tide, went with some others in search of the bishop. As they were trying to cross the reef a canoe came towards them, "with a heap in the middle," and when they met it the two words "the body" passed, and it was lifted into the boat, rolled in the native mat. "The placid smile was still on the face; there was a palm-leaf fastened over the breast, and when the mat was opened there were five wounds—no more,"—these having been given by clubs.

Joseph Atkin, the son of a settler, who was only twenty-nine, but had already done great service, and Stephen Taroniara, a native of Tanna, who was twenty-five, followed their master; but it was their lot, unlike his, to pass through prolonged tortures before death delivered them.

So passed Bishop Patteson and his followers, martyrs to the woful cupidity of civilised men! From the wounds and other indications on the bishop's body, it was clear that his death was the vengeance for five of the natives carried away. But it may be that his mournful death will further the Gospel in Melanesia more than his life would have done. Year by year, the scholars he taught will return to tell what his objects were; what he wrought and prayed and died for; and his story, in not far-distant days, when communication between the islands shall have become easier, will work as with a charmed power upon the hearts of the people. "Poor Santa Cruz people!" said Fisher Young when dying; and may we not say of the bishop what he then said to his disciple, " My dear boy, you will do more for their conversion by your death than ever we shall by our lives"? And yet how can we but mourn the close? He seemed as if born for the work he had undertaken. He was so patient, so humble, with such power to elicit the best in those he came in contact with, and, above all, so full of faith and hope. In him what is best in the English gentleman had received consecration : he was manly, catholic-minded, and with that pre-eminent care and consideration for others, which, apart from Christian influence, is so apt to degenerate into sentimental weakness. He was at once tender and self-reliant, scorning all noise and pretence so sincerely that, though " they bothered him to put anecdotes of adventures into his Reports, he could not do it;" yet so appreciative was he of good intentions in those by whom he was surrounded, that soon in his honest conception they came to surpass him. Any little narrowness that may be detected in him, he may be said to have inherited, and, with genuine Christian manliness, he rose above most of these, realising an ideal of priestly service such as has been exhibited by only a few men in any generation.

His character is not of the kind that tempts to analysis. His greatness lay in a few very simple elements. He was above all sincere, and whilst he held the faith fast, he never subsided into the mere dogmatist. His humanity was too broad, and his heart too tender for that. His respect and love for the missionaries—Presbyterian and other—who had found a sphere in the islands of the South Pacific, and his brotherly conduct towards them, will mark him out with the greater honour the more that his contact with them is made known. Besides his kind attentions to Mr. Paton at Tanna, to Mr. Geddie at Anaiteum, and to the poor bereaved women at Fate, which Miss Yonge has recorded, there is that striking incident at Api which surpasses them all. Two Raratongan teachers and their wives had been settled on that island, and had fallen under the anger of the fierce shore tribes. The men died or were put to death, and the women escaped to the hills. Bishop Patteson, touching at the island and hearing of their fate, made his way to the hills, and, in face of risk and danger, found them out, offering them a passage in his vessel. This they unwisely declined, fearing that the crew of the *John Williams*, when she came, would be disappointed at not finding them. They had suffered much already; the bishop urged that they might suffer more and worse trials: but they would not go with him. And they did suffer. They lived as they could for a while on yams and taro or such fare as they could find, and then they sold garment after garment to the natives for food, till only one was left, and with that they would not part, to go dressed in the mat of the native women—they said they would die rather. They were reduced almost to skeletons before they were relieved by their own mission-ship.

This incident brings out Bishop Patteson's rare sympathy and fearlessness in the strongest light. To do such a thing was with him a matter of every day, was felt by him to be no more than duty, and it has found no record in his life; but it was a piece of heroism such as has made many men famous, and such as there is but occasional room for even in a soldier's life.

In thinking over the main details of such a life, filled with constant effort and self-denial, one is apt enough unconsciously to fall into the idea that much must have been owing to mere strength of constitution—to good spirits springing from abounding health and muscular strength. But it may surprise some to know that in spite of fine physical development, Bishop Patteson was never what could be called strong. He often suffered; and was very sensitive to colds, as Miss Yonge incidentally tells us in her very striking portrait of him :—

"He was tall and powerful of frame, broad in the chest and shoulders, and with small neat hands and feet, with more of sheer muscular strength and power of endurance than of healthiness; so that, though seldom breaking down, and capable of undergoing a great deal of fatigue and exertion, he was often slightly ailing, and was very sensitive to cold. His complexion was very dark, and there was a strongly marked line between the cheeks and mouth, the corners of which drooped when at rest, so that it was a countenance peculiarly difficult to photograph successfully. The most striking feature was his eyes, which were of a very dark, clear blue, full of unusually deep, earnest, and, so to speak, inward yet far-away expression. His smile was remarkably bright, sweet, and affectionate, like a gleam of sunshine, and was one element of his great attractiveness. So was his voice, which had the rich, full sweetness inherited from his mother's family, and which always exerted a winning influence over the hearers."

The following sonnet from the pen of one of our truest poets and most philanthropic women (now, alas! gone from us), may not unfitly close our sketch of this great and earnest missionary:—

BISHOP PATTESON.

An angel came and cried to him by night,
 "God needs a martyr from thy little band ;
Name me the purest soul, that, closely scanned,
 Still overflows with sweetness and with light,
That finds no limit till they reach the Land
 Where their spring rose!" Weeping for what must be,
He named them all, with love adorning each ;
 And still that angel smiled upon his speech,
And, smiling still, went upward silently,
 Not marking any name. Amazed he knelt,
Discerning not the truth. But when the stroke
 Fell, not an angel, but the Master spoke
With words so strong that nothing else was felt,
 "Thou art the man! Belovèd, come to Me!"

M. B. S.

JOHN G. FEE AND THE FREEDMEN OF AMERICA.

IN the year 1843 a young man, the son of a Kentuckian slaveholder, ventured to question the right of a Christian to hold slaves. He had been educated for the Church, and a distinguished career seemed to await him. Nothing but obloquy and loss was likely to result to him from the adoption of such views. Nevertheless he persisted in the course he had marked out for himself. His father at first refused him the house, and finally disinherited him. The public influence in Kentucky was against him, and when, coincidently with his father's alienation from him, his consequent sorrow, and yet more sacred devotion of himself to the cause of the slave, he heard of the efforts that the Tappans and their friends were making in the North to found a missionary society chiefly to aid and to teach the bondmen, he gladly cast in his lot with theirs. The American Missionary Society, whose remarkable progress we now mean to trace, was the result of the association. It was founded in 1846, and shortly after its foundation John G. Fee, the disinherited, became its leading agent. He travelled from end to end of the country, ceaselessly active in his endeavours to stir up others to an interest in the good cause. He wisely adopted the colportage plan, and found proper agents; and was certainly one of the main instruments in making this society the great influence it has become. That we are right in naming it "a great influence" will be manifest by a very brief glance at the facts.

When the American Missionary Society was founded, the slaveholding interests were powerful enough to modify political action in all directions. The slaveholders seemed to have agents everywhere, and to exercise a sort of ubiquitous revenge. It was no pleasant matter to be an anti-slavery man in the United States then: life itself was sometimes endangered. The stores of the Tappans were several times mobbed, and the men themselves assaulted. Daniel Worth and Gerrit Smith fared hardly better, and John Brown, an early friend of the society, became a martyr to the cause. And when at length, after great struggles, apparently resultless, public opinion had ripened to such a degree that it seemed as if the federal Government was about to curtail the slaveholding power, the slaveholders themselves arose, as if by an irony of Providence, only to precipitate the downfall of their system amidst unprecedented bloodshed. Two millions of men fell in that grievous war : by it four and a half millions of men and women who had been doomed to a worse than Egyptian bondage—bought and sold like cattle in the market-place —were set free.

"They came up poor, homeless, naked, and in want of all things. It was a touching sight to see them coming, in motley crowds, around the military camp, mothers carrying a child, and not unfrequently two children, in their arms; strong men bearing the decrepid and aged on their shoulders, believing that, as Israel of old, they were to be led by the Lord through the wilderness—to the promised land—to a higher and better life." And then it was seen by what providential discipline of patient waiting and working the American societies, but more especially the American Missionary Society, had been educated and prepared to cope with a result so radical—as unprecedented, as but a short time before it had been unexpected. There were not wanting at this time (at what time have they been wanting since Nehemiah had to deal with them when he returned to build up the walls of Jerusalem?) good people to predict dark things. They prophesied that the latter state of the poor negroes would be worse than the first, that in their freedom they would simply sink in grovelling idleness and bestiality, and that the country would have cause to regret their enfranchisement more than the most foolish political measures any legislature had ever passed. They had no power to govern themselves, it was urged;

motives of self respect were lacking to them. And it needs to be frankly acknowledged that from an *a priori* point of view their opinion seemed not far wrong. Dark races have so often succumbed under the freedom of civilisation's blessings and vices. Race after race has died out. The Indians of the Far West and the Maoris of New Zealand are being decimated. The Tasmanians have totally disappeared. But the Negro, if he has his peculiar weaknesses, has also his peculiar strength, both physical and moral, and this the prophets of evil did not fully realise. That their direful prophecies have not been fulfilled, but wholly falsified by the event, is owing in great measure to the society best known in England as the "Freedman's Aid Society," that being the name given to its branch or auxiliary in our country, under the presidency of Lord Shaftesbury. From the first, attempts had been made by the Society to teach the negroes, and to establish schools for them and their children amidst unnameable difficulties. Regular day-schools for freedmen had been started at several points, the first being that at Hampton in Virginia, by the Rev. L. C. Lockwood, in 1861. Its first mistress was a coloured woman, the daughter of a white father by a mulatto mother; and though she herself had scarcely a trace of colour, and was free-born, she had experienced to the full the fatal prejudice which had excluded such even as she was from the white schools. For never was a cruel prejudice more cruelly enforced than this. No ex-slave or child of a slave-mother was allowed to enter any school where white children were taught. Dr. White, the secretary of the Freedman's Aid Society in this country, tells us that he has seen the children of slave-mothers with fair skin, light hair, and blue eyes, yet these were hopelessly shut out from the white schools, and doomed to the degradation of an alien race. And so this first coloured school is historical. Almost on the very spot where it stood, two hundred and forty years before, the first slave-ship entered, and planted the seed of that baleful harvest; and that woman, the representative of both races, "though by the bitter logic of slavery classed with the oppressed, will be remembered as the teacher of the first coloured school in the slave States that had legal authority and the protection of the national guns." She died within a year after the school was opened, but not before many other schools had sprung up over the land.

The moment emancipation was decreed, a new era began. Soon the capacities of the negroes for education were triumphantly demonstrated. The patient Christian character which in slavery had been formed in many of them presented a favourable soil on which to work. They were eager to learn to read, chiefly in order that the Scriptures might be opened to them, and soon the more favoured intellectually began to be exercised by thought of efforts for the more ignorant of their brethren. The business of the society since then has rather been to direct and to utilise a great enthusiasm than to stir it. Schools and colleges have arisen over the land, and the details of their work are not more interesting than some of the characteristic stories told of those who by reason of age cannot hope to be personally much benefited by these institutions. Dr. White tells that one will often see aged men and women bending over the Primer with young children, studying till late at night by the light of the pine-knots of the country, because they are too poor to have any other light. One woman, eighty years of age, worked for her board and went to school. When she had mastered the alphabet, she said, in the peculiar dialect of her people, "Now let me spell de name of Jesus, for it 'pears like all will be easier when I learn to spell de blessed name." And it seems quite true, as Dr. White says, that in the educated negro we have promise of a new type of Christian character—strong in intuition, simple, and full of a large-hearted practicality and hopeful faith. One anecdote that he tells will illustrate the promise of this :—

In one of their churches, the poor old minister, who had been a slave, and could not read, wanted some deacons to aid him in his work. Two were found. Then this man said, "If any one knows de reason why dese bredderen may not be consecrated to dis office, he shall tell of dat, and now object." An old slave man rose to say, "I has to object." "What for dus you object?" says the minister. "Dem can't read," was the reply. "Well," the minister continued, "can you read?" "No; but I wants to be led by dem dat knows more dan I." The minister replied, "None of de members knows to read; dese is de best wes got, and we must ask de Lord to bless dem, dat dey may help to lead de people to a higher and better life." So the two knelt before him, and this old sable servant of God laid a hand on the head of each, kneeled down, and lifted his eyes to heaven, while the tears were on his cheeks, and said, "Massa Jesus, you knows wes just come out of de house of bondage, dat wes a poor, ignorant, feeble portion of de children of Adam, dat wes got no edication, but we wants to do what we can for de people, and for de glory of de Lord. O dear King of de kings, now help dese wes chosen for de office of deacons in dis church. You knows dat dey can't read de blessed book, but, Massa, *deys de best wes got*, and, derefore, we *consecrates dem* to dis office, and to de God ob de people." What an appeal is in this for sympathy and aid from those to whom God has given so many gifts richly to enjoy! There are thousands of these people, we hear of, who are equally anxious to be prepared to do all in their power for their own race, and for the cause of the Master. Some of the pupils in the schools of the society have reached the place of study, coming thinly clad and barefooted across the frozen ground, day after day, in the bleak season of the year. Often the tears will be on their cheeks from actual suffering. Another anecdote bearing this out is so touching that we must quote it :—

Three young men, anxious to be prepared for their great life-work among their own people, walked four hundred miles in the heat of the summer to one of the colleges for coloured students, and asked to be permitted to enter for a course of study. The president had to tell them, with tears in his eyes, that he could not receive them, as there were more already in the college than could be supported on the money given for that purpose. They went away and consulted together, and after a little came back. Then one of them said, "Take *this one in*, and let him be educated, for he has the gifts, and we will go out and work on the plantations to raise the money to pay for it." But three gentlemen, having heard of the case, asked what would be needed for them, and when told, they furnished the money.

The manner in which the Fisk University has been built and endowed, and the noble efforts of the Jubilee Singers generally, are evidences known to the whole world of the desire of the educated negroes to benefit their race. Schools and colleges of the highest class are now springing up throughout the length and breadth of the States, and the influence of this education is already evident, socially, in the many men of colour who now fill situations of trust and honour in America. The society recently had at work over 60 missionaries, 200 teachers, and 24 matrons; there were 56 churches in the South, 2 among the Indians, and 7 in the foreign field; it had 3601 church-members in the South, and about 600 elsewhere; it had 32 schools in the South, 7 chartered institutions, and 17 other institutions; and it had altogether nearly 10,000 pupils, while of pupils in the South now taught by former pupils, there were 64,000. There were nearly 5000 in the upper grades, from what is designated normal, up through collegiate preparatory, collegiate and law, to theological. And it is quite possible that the few years which have elapsed since these figures were taken have seen a considerable increase.

It is clear that to carry on such a work as this a very perfect machinery is required. We read in a recent report, "It is estimated that from Great Britain more than £200,000 has been contributed, in money and clothing, through various channels for the freedmen. The American Missionary Society has shared largely in the kind words that have come across the water. Its representatives have been welcomed by the Congregational Union of England and Wales, the General Assemblies of Scotland, and also by the British and Foreign Anti-Slavery Society." It is pleasant to read such words; and we hope that this country will not cool in its enthusiasm in the cause, or reduce the amount of aid that it has given. Still more will be needed, and we know it will be well applied in carrying forward yet wider enterprises of a truly cosmopolitan character. The movement in America for the education of the negro is seen day by day to have a more direct bearing on the great question of the evangelisation of Africa. This is the way in which God in His Providence works. He prepares a field; far distant from it He prepares also suitable workers, and they come forward at the right moment. The American Missionary Society, with the distinct purpose of making the African a means to raise his race, has in view an extension of its field by settlements at places where it would be most hazardous for white men to attempt it. At various points of entrance to the great African field, the white missionary within a few years seems almost inevitably to succumb to the climate. The experience at Sierra Leone, for one place, attests this. There the Church Missionary Society lost thirty missionaries in twelve years; the Wesleyan Society buried forty in the same period; and ten out of seventeen missionaries of the Basle Society died within two years of entering on their work. The American Board, the Presbyterian and Baptist Societies, have all suffered severely in Africa. Hence the value of the work which the American Missionary Society has done, and is doing. Its aim is to send Africans to Africans—to train them to true knowledge, aptness in handicrafts as well as in learning, and to make them *the* missionaries to their own race. Dr. Moffat, than whom it would be hard to find a better authority, said some time ago at a public meeting in London, "It is utterly useless, humanly speaking, for us alone to attempt to evangelise Africa; but in the trained members of the African race we may look for glorious results." To this conviction the missionary mind seems to have conclusively come, and the character of such missions as those at Lovedale and at Livingstonia sufficiently attests it. A native ministry is the best, the cheapest, and the only efficient one in such a climate. And it is due to the American Missionary Society to acknowledge that it was amongst the first to give practical application to this idea. Every school and mission sustained in the South not only attests the capacity of the freedmen for fair intellectual acquirements, but is prophetic of the importance that this people may become to Africa as teachers and missionaries. The coloured man of the South will do his part to carry the knowledge of Christ across the sea. "The Little done, the Much remains to do." Results so far are encouraging, and show more and more clearly the best methods for the future. Yet, when contrasted with the vast extent of the field, but the outer borders seem to have been touched. Only a few millions out of upwards of two hundred millions have as yet been reached with the influences of Christianity. It is estimated that 75,000,000 in Central Africa alone have never yet heard of the Saviour. Surely then, every Christian will heartily wish success to the American Missionary Society, and its branch best known to us, "The Freedman's Aid Society."

By way of a closing word, we may cite from a disinterested authority, who some time ago wrote in the *New*

York Nation, "I write from the feeling that, like myself, the majority of the Republican rank and file at the North have been taking too hopeless a view of Southern problems. I write from that portion of South Carolina which has the largest preponderance of negroes. The extent to which these negroes, of all ages, have learned to read and write, and their eagerness to acquire the rudiments of knowledge, together with their industry, docility, and their political sagacity, are no less gratifying than surprising. . . . . Under the patronage of the American Missionary Association, normal schools of a high grade, and largely attended, are maintained at numerous centres. There is great progress in the coloured churches, and they are founding theological schools of their own."

APPENDIX.

I.

MORAVIAN MISSIONARY FACTS.

OUR readers who have followed us with any interest through our sketches of Oglethorpe and Zeisberger, may be interested in learning some further facts about the Moravian missionaries who have done such wonderful work with such limited means. As we have said, the Moravians have established missions in the West Indies, the Moskito coast, Australia (among the natives), South Africa, Central Asia, and Surinam, besides Labrador and Greenland, with which they have been in a special sense associated. The following general summary from the Year-book may here be given by way of introduction to what is to follow :—

"Our Church maintained, in June 1878, ninety-six mission-stations in various parts of the earth, which were served by 327 missionaries (of whom 34 were native) and 1504 native assistants. There were under our care 23,843 communicants, 49,327 baptized adults, candidates for baptism, &c., making a total of 73,170. There were 222 Day Schools, with 16,461 scholars, and 86 Sunday Schools, with 11,492 scholars. The income of our missions, for which we are mainly dependent on the contributions of members and friends, amounted in 1878 to £16,909, and the expenditure to be met by this sum to £20,298, leaving a deficiency on the year's account of £3388. The special appeal for the deficiency in 1879 (£4959) having produced £3623, there remained in December 31, 1878, a net deficiency of £4734.

"The sums raised annually at the various stations towards the support of the work (by contributions of the members or by trade, as well as special donations for school purposes) are estimated at about £25,000, including the interest of capitals left for the support of specific missions, Government aid, &c.; the actual expenditure of our whole Mission work in the year 1879 reached a total of about £48,000. The number of brethren and sis:ers employed in this service from its commencement 147 years ago, is about 4000."

Over and above this the congregations at various places devote themselves to special branches of Home-Mission work, and the figures regarding these objects do not appear in this summary. For example, we read—

"The German province carries on a work of its own, in addition to undertaking a share in the general liability. This consists in maintaining an evangelising agency, and in supporting to a great extent an orphanage at Rothwasser, containing 120 children, begun by Dr. Hattwiz, in 1869, on his own responsibility. The liberal help given by members and friends in all the provinces towards the rebuilding of this orphanage, which was nearly destroyed by fire on September 17, 1873, has been most gratefully acknowledged by the committee. The total contributed from one province for this purpose was £240, and the entire sum expended on the new building, £600."

With regard to the individual fields our space will allow us to give but the briefest report. First, of Greenland. It is somewhat saddening to read that, in spite of the devotion which the Moravian Brethren have shown towards Greenland, and the sacrifices they have undergone for it, the work does not meet with the reward that might have been expected for it. Of course, the field is a very backward one—the people are so poor that it would almost be too much to expect they should do much towards the support of pastors, &c., but we were sorry to read the following :—

"Externally the condition of the Greenlanders has not improved, as was hoped. Hard times have been of frequent occurrence, ep:demics carried off great numbers in the years

1871-2 and 1856-7, especially in the three southern stations. Multiplied facilities for procuring European articles of food and clothing have fostered a taste for these things, which is most prejudicial to the well-being of the natives. The diminished number of able-bodied men, whose labour provides food for the community, partly owing to accidents at sea, partly to epidemics, is a very serious drawback to the general prosperity.

"Spiritually the Greenlanders show no decided improvement, in the opinion of the missionaries, and the number of exclusions for gross immorality has rather increased. Whether our Greenland congregations will ever attain to a capacity for self-government and self-support, the future must decide: progress in that direction is exceedingly slow. The native ministers employed by the Danish mission are all half-Europeans, in no case pure Greenlanders.

"In 1868 there were in this field 1734 souls in charge of 24 brethren and sisters; in 1878 there were 1526, and the number of missionaries was 22."*

A later report in so far explains the position and accounts for it:—

"The efforts to lead the congregations to a position of greater independence have met with very slight success during the last ten years. In spite of the training-schools at New Herrnhut and Lichtenau with a curriculum extending through six winter terms, it has not yet been possible to obtain a supply of natives able to take the place of the missionaries in the direction and service of the congregations. With regard to self-support, although some voluntary contributions towards the extension of the kingdom of God have been received, yet poverty prevails so generally among the natives, and no less the custom of living from hand to mouth, without a notion of providing against bad times, that there is little prospect of ever bringing them so far as to support the mission themselves. Entirely dependent on sealing and fishing for their means of subsistence, they used to find in the former an ample provision for food and clothing. The facilities of trading have led them to

* From Report of the Directing Board to the General Synod of 1879.

exchange the necessaries of life for such articles of food as are not adapted to their circumstances, and to abandon the old fur clothing, which enabled them to brave the rigours of their Arctic climate. In former times there was no lack of kayaks and women's boats, for the produce of the chase remained in the country. The sad result of this change of circumstances is the frequent appearance of severe epidemic diseases among them. Thus in 1871-2 and 1875-6, in the congregations of Lichtenau, Igdlorpait, and Fredericksthal, one-tenth of the small population died. Frequent disasters at sea also carried off useful men almost every year. This is especially the case at Lichtenfels, and is the more to be deplored, as it is entirely the labour of the men that provides for the wants of the family."

In Australia, on the contrary, much fruit is ultimately promised from the seed sown.

"It is a peculiar feature that our stations here are not on land belonging to the mission, but on the native reserves, the control of which is in the hands of the Government. Here rations are supplied through the missionaries to those natives who are unable to earn their own living. At Ramahyuck promising arrowroot and hop-grounds have been successfully worked by the blacks for the benefit of the station, while for the same object at Ebenezer some sheep-farming has been carried on. A Royal Commission, recently appointed to inspect the aboriginal stations, and ascertain whether their results justified their continuation or enlargement, expressed the opinion that a distribution of the native population among the whites was preferable to their collection in separate villages or settlements. A continuance of our work in Australia in the same manner as hitherto is, therefore, by no means assured.

"During the last ten years the number of converts has almost doubled, and many a sheaf of ripe corn has been gathered into the garden of the Lord from seed sown in faith by our brethren in this trying but interesting field of missionary labour. Looking at the blessing alone which God has graciously bestowed here, we were strongly desirous of accepting the repeated invitations, which we have received of late years, to extend our operations in Australia ; but the difficulties connected with the direction of a work at so great a distance, and the heavy expense, far exceeding our means, induced us to decline the various invitations of our Christian friends in Australia." *

A few months later we read :—

"This field has not been extended since the last Synod ; the same two stations, namely, *Ebenezer* in the Wimmera district, and *Ramahyuck* in Gippsland, are still our sole centres of activity. They have become neat little villages, with pretty churches and clean and tidy dwellings ; a cursory glance at the natives here shows that 'godliness is profitable unto all things.' Many of the blacks, who used to lead licentious lives in their camps, have by degrees gathered at our station ; and while in earlier decades mortality had greatly increased, this rapid dying out of the race has of late been checked, if not stopped. Children of Christian parents, born at our stations, are healthier than others, and the number of births has exceeded the deaths. But the nation as a whole is gradually dwindling away, and all friends of missions are putting forth every effort in order to bring all the remaining blacks under the influence of the Gospel. Consumption, resulting in a great measure from their former licentious life, is the disease which carries off the natives. At present it is estimated that the whole black population in the colony of Victoria scarcely numbers one thousand persons. Many children have been entrusted to the missionaries at both stations to be educated by them, and suitable buildings have been erected for their accommodation."

It would, we think, be a great pity were the work of the Moravians to be curtailed, or altogether stopped, through the action of Government, lack of funds, or the difficulties arising from the great distance from headquarters.

From the South African stations there are cheering news :—

"Towards self-support progress has been made, the annual contributions from the district being about £428.

* From Report of the Directing Board to the General Synod of 1879.

By utilising local resources, carrying on various businesses, &c., this portion of the South African province is able to meet all its expenses, except the charges for journeys to and from Europe. The schools are much improved, and many of the teachers have received a recognition of faithful and efficient service in the shape of a pecuniary gratuity. The work of building up the churches here has continued in a satisfactory manner, in spite of the serious drawback lying in the circumstance that many have to earn their living by labour, which takes them out of the reach of the missionaries and Christian instruction for several months of the year."

The work on the Moskito coast, in spite of the greatest obstacles, is encouraging :—

"Here our brethren minister in the Gospel to 1031 persons belonging to our Church, of whom 528 are Indians, and the rest mostly Creoles. At Blewfields some 300 persons in addition attend regularly, but do not join our Church. Schools have made progress in the last decade. There has been no marked pressing forward towards the fold of the true Shepherd on the part of the Indians; but at some places a powerful interest in the Gospel has been manifested, and has lasted for some time; this was especially the case among the Tungla tribe on the Prince Apolca River, and at Ephrata with its adjacent station, at Kukalaya and Karata. Both of these have been commenced within the last few years, the latter in consequence of the generous gift of £1000 of our friend, Mrs. Hall, of Bristol, who had previously devoted some years of her life to missionary work in the Moskito territory in connection with our brethren.

"Political disquietude, in consequence of Nicaragua's attempts to obtain possession of the Moskito country, since Great Britain withdrew from the protectorate, has marked this decade, but the Lord has graciously warded off any act of violence. A constitutional government has been introduced, at the head of which was a young king or chief, whose early education was received in the house of one of our missionaries. The good promise, which there was good reason for entertaining at his accession, has not been fulfilled, as he has fallen a victim to habits of intoxication. Another serious hindrance in the progress of the work has been the continued evil influence of traders, who frequent the country in considerable numbers to procure india-rubber, tortoise-shell, deer-skins, &c.

"In spite of these drawbacks, the brethren report that the number of the real living Church members is on the increase, and that the young people are showing more longing for the salvation that is in Christ Jesus, and more growth in divine knowledge."*

It will be inferred from what has been said that the Moravians aim, not only at planting churches amongst the native peoples, but at forming them into Christian communities, directed according to strict rules and principles by which good order and habits of industry are formed and fostered. This kind of work, at centres from which no great *éclat* can be expected, is precisely of the character that should not only draw out the practical sympathy of other Christian denominations, but the active and substantial aid of governments in a far greater degree than it has hitherto done.

Nor should we, in any account however summary, omit mention of the Lepers' Hospital at Jerusalem, in which an heroic work has been done. The annual cost amounts only to about £300. Of this sum we learn two-thirds have been raised by English friends and one-third by friends in Germany and Switzerland. In thirteen years the brethren and sisters there have continued at their repulsive "labour of love" unremittingly, till the health of Brother and Sister Tappe broke down under the strain —and little wonder.

We have been particularly depressed at the struggles which the Brethren have had financially with an increasing deficit for the past few years—a mere trifle of £4000— which, however, is enough to hamper them and greatly to paralyse their activity. We gladly note a paragraph to the following effect in one of the last reports :—

* From Report of the Directing Board to the General Synod of 1879.

"Very truly FINANCIAL RELIEF for our burdened Treasury has recently been afforded us, for which we desire to ask our friends to unite with us in praising God. Some years ago a Christian nobleman in Germany, with princely liberality, handed over a large sum of money for our missions, in which he took great interest. A portion of this amount was destined for the pensions of retired missionaries, but conditions were attached to this gift which prohibited its being made use of until the present year. The interest on the capital, which has been accumulated by the will of the donor, now amounts to more than £1000, and will appear for the first time in the financial statement for the current year (1879)."

But abundant room will still remain for members of other Christian Churches to extend some aid and sympathy to this oldest of Missionary Churches, which, on the testimony of impartial witnesses, including Mr. Andrew Wilson, author of the "Abode of Snow" (and not even excluding Dr. Rinek!) does so well deserve it.

APPENDIX II.

SOME FURTHER FACTS ABOUT ZEISBERGER.

ZEISBERGER'S method of dealing with the Indians, as we have seen, involved two distinct ends: first, conversion to the Christian religion, and next the establishment of settled communities, separated as far as could be from heathen influence. It has recently been urged against many species of missionary work that baits of self-interest and ease are held out to the heathen to be baptized, in order to swell the agent's returns. It is evident that Zeisberger scorned any such devices as these. A mere glance at the rules he drew up for the government of Indian Christian communities will show that there was little temptation put forward by him to the Indian in the direction of self-interest or ease. Let our readers cast such a glance as we have suggested over these Rules—

1. We will know of no other God, nor worship any other, but Him who has created us, and redeemed us with His most precious blood.
2. We will rest from all labour on Sundays, and attend the usual meetings on that day for divine service.
3. We will honour father and mother, and support them in age and distress.
4. No one shall be permitted to dwell with us without the consent of our teachers.
5. No thieves, murderers, drunkards, adulterers, and whoremongers shall be suffered among us.
6. No one that attendeth dances, sacrifices, or heathenish festivals can live among us.
7. No one using *Tschappich* (or witchcraft) in hunting shall be suffered among us.
8. We will renounce all juggles, lies, and deceits of Satan.
9. We will be obedient to our teachers, and to the helpers (national assistants), who are appointed to see that good order be kept both in and out of the town.
10. We will not be idle and lazy, nor tell lies of one another, nor strike each other; we will live peaceably together.
11. Whosoever does any harm to another's cattle, goods, or effects, &c., shall pay the damage.
12. A man shall have only one wife, love her and provide for her and the children. Likewise a woman shall have but one husband, and be obedient unto him; she shall also take care of the children, and be cleanly in all things.
13. We will not permit any rum or spirituous liquor to be brought into our towns. If strangers or traders happen to bring any, the helpers (national assistants) are to take it into their possession, and to take care not to deliver it to them until they set off again.
14. None of the inhabitants shall run in debt with

traders, nor receive goods on commission for traders, without the consent of the national assistants.

15. No one is to go on a journey, or long hunt, without informing the minister or stewards of it.

16. Young people are not to marry without the consent of their parents and taking their advice.

17. If the stewards or helpers apply to the inhabitants for assistance in doing work for the benefit of the place, such as building meeting and school-houses, cleaning and fencing lands, &c., they are to be obedient.

18. All necessary contributions for the public ought cheerfully to be attended to.

19. No man inclining to go to war, which is the shedding of blood, can remain among us.

20. Whosoever purchases goods or articles of warriors, *knowing* at the time that such have been stolen or plundered, must leave us. We look upon this as giving encouragement to murder and theft.

Many very striking anecdotes of rescue from danger might have been added to those given in the text, room must here be found for the following :—

"On one of his journeys Zeisberger and his companions experienced a remarkable preservation. They were kindly entertained by a white trader who spread a quantity of straw on the floor of an apartment for them to sleep upon. He warned them that several barrels of gunpowder were in this room, one or two of which were open ; and they retired to rest, leaving the candle on the outside. A traveller, however, who accompanied them prevailed on their host to allow him the candle to examine and dress a wound in his foot, promising to put it out as soon as he had finished his operation. The missionaries reminded him to beware of the danger, but, being much fatigued, lay down and fell asleep. The traveller also, being weary, fell asleep and left the light burning. In the morning Zeisberger called his brother missionary out of the house into the wood, and showed him the candle. 'My brother,' said he, 'had we not had on us the eye of Him who never slumbereth nor sleepeth, we should all have this night been blown into the air, and no one would have known how it happened. I slept soundly, being extremely fatigued, and was in my first sleep, when I felt as if some one raised me with a violent shake. I sat up, and saw the wick of the candle hanging down on one side in a flame, and the burning candle on the point of falling into the straw, which I was just in time to prevent. After that I could not fall asleep again, but lay silently thanking the Lord for the extraordinary preservation we had experienced, one fit of shuddering after another seizing my whole frame when I reflected on our danger."

In Heckewelder's "Narrative of the Mission of the United Brethren among the Delaware and Mohegan Indians" we find the following sketch of Zeisberger, which we here present chiefly for the portrait, and the record of personal traits :—

"Having once devoted himself to this service, from the most voluntary choice and the purest motives, he steadily pursued his object—the glory of God and the good of his fellow-men. Never was he so happy as when he had ground for believing that his endeavours had been the means of converting one sinner from the error of his ways, and leading him to the knowledge of Jesus Christ our Lord. This, in his estimation, was of far higher value than if he had acquired possession of the whole world. It may be said with truth that he watched over his Indian flock with the solicitude of a parent and cherished them as a nurse doth her children. He followed them in all their wanderings, cheerfully bearing with them the heat and burden of the day, and during the last forty years of his life he was never, at any one time, six months absent from his charge.

"He was blessed with a cool, active, and intrepid spirit, unappalled by danger, and with a sound judgment and clear discernment. He was therefore very seldom taken by surprise, and was generally prepared to meet and to overcome difficulties. If once convinced that he was in the path of duty, he patiently submitted to every hardship, and with firm fortitude endured the severest sufferings. In the course of a long life spent among savages he was exposed to many privations, and at times suffered persecution from the enemies of divine truth, who more than once sought his life. But none of these things dismayed him ; they rather increased his zeal in the Lord's cause, and in more instances than one has he had the pleasure of baptizing Indians who not long before had lifted up the hatchet to murder him. At the same time he was of a humble and meek spirit, and always thought lowly of himself. He was a most affectionate husband ; a faithful and never-failing friend ; and every lineament of his character showed a sincere, upright, benevolent, and generous soul, with perhaps as few blemishes as can be expected in the best men on this side the grave.

"In the evening of his days, when his faculties began to fail him, his desire to depart and to be with Christ increased. At the same time he awaited his dissolution with uniform, calm, and dignified resignation to the will of his Maker, and in the sure and certain hope of exchanging this world for a better. His last words were, 'Lord Jesus, I pray Thee come and take my spirit to Thyself!' And again, 'Thou hast never yet forsaken me in any trial, Thou wilt not forsake me now.' A very respectable company attended his funeral. The solemn service was performed in the English, the Delaware, and German languages, to suit the different auditors. Two sermons were preached from Rev. xii. 11, and Prov. x. 7.

"Zeisberger was a man of low stature, yet well-proportioned, of a cheerful countenance, and endowed with a good understanding. He was a friend and benefactor to mankind, and justly beloved by all who knew him, and who could appreciate genuine worth. His words were few, and never known to be wasted at random or used in an unprofitable manner. Plain in his habits, temperate in all things, he generally enjoyed good health, and lived to an advanced age.

"He made himself complete master of two of the Indian languages, the Onondago and the Delaware, and acquired some knowledge of several others. Of the Onondago he composed two grammars, one written in English, the other in German. He likewise compiled a dictionary of the Delaware language, which in the manuscript contained seventeen hundred pages. Nearly the whole of the manuscript was lost at the burning of the settlements on the Muskingum. A spelling-book in the same ianguage has passed through several editions. A volume of sermons to children, and a hymn-book containing upwards of five hundred hymns, chiefly translations from the English and German hymn-books in use in the Brethren's Church, have also been published in the Delaware (or Lenape) language. He left behind him, in manuscript, a grammar of the Delaware language, written in German, and a translation into the same language of Lieberkuehn's 'Harmony of the Four Gospels.' The former of these works has since been translated into English for the American Philosophical Society, by P. S. Du Ponceau of Philadelphia; and the Female Auxiliary Missionary Society of Bethlehem undertook the publication of the 'Harmony.'"

As a curiosity in its own way, we may add here Zeisberger's translation of the Lord's Prayer into the Delaware language:—Ki Wetochemelenk, talli epian Awossagame. Machelendasutsch Ktellewunsowoagan Ksakimawoagan pejewigetsch. Ktelite hewoagan legetsch talli Achquidhackamike, elgiqui leek talli Awossagame. Milineen elgischquik gunigischuk Achpoan. Woak miwelendammauwineen 'n Tschannauchsowoagannene eliqui niluna miwelendammauwenk nik Tschetschanilawequengik. Woak katschi 'npawuneen li Achquetschiechtowoaganüng, tschukund Ktennieen untschi Medhicküng. Aloa Knihillatamen Ksakimawoagan, woak Ktallewussowoagan, woak Ktallowilüssowoagan, ne wuntschi hallemiwi li hallamagamik. Amen !

APPENDIX III.

THE BECHUANAS.

SINCE our sketch of Dr. Moffat and his work was written, the venerable missionary has given the following sketch of the labours of himself and his fellow-missionaries among the Bechuanas. We have much pleasure in reproducing it here in a slightly condensed form:—

IN BECHUANA LAND.—BY THE REV. ROBERT MOFFAT, D.D.

THE name Bechuana or Bachuana, or, as latterly written, Bechwana or Bachwana, includes all the tribes speaking the Sechuana language. There have been various opinions as to its origin. Ba or Be is a personal pronoun, when the adverb *chwana* is applied to persons, and thus, according to some, *they are alike* or *the same* kind of people. Others have supposed that the name is derived from *nchu*, black, the diminutive of which would be *chwana*, meaning a little black, and applied to a person, Mochwana, one dark-coloured—not black. *Mo* is the prefix to the singular number, and *Ba* to the plural, when persons are spoken of. All the tribes have the prefix *Ba*, whatever be the name by which they are distinguished. Some are named after certain animals, from which it has been supposed that at some distant period they were addicted to the worship of animals, like the ancient Egyptians. For example, we have the *Batlhapi*, the tribe to which the Gospel was first sent ; *Ba-tlhapi*, they fish, or, of the fish ; *Ba-khatla*, they of the monkey ; *Bakuena*, they of the crocodile ; *Batau*, they of the lion. When an individual is asked to what tribe he belongs, sometimes the question will be, What do you dance ? The reply will be, *Kea bina kwena*, or whatever the tribe may be. It is said they hate these animals by which they are named, and dread killing them.

The Bechuana tribes were first visited by missionaries at the beginning of the present century. Many long years, however, passed over before any important result was attained. They did not want the Gospel—they hardly wanted the missionaries, and sometimes wished to drive them away. The customs and superstitions in which they and their forefathers had been brought up, they did not wish to abandon, for they considered them to be altogether good. Their character, though bad, was no worse than that of other tribes in South Africa. They were brave and proud, displayed a great love of independence, and with all their barbarousness were not without some noble sentiments. But their minds were very dark and their hearts very cruel and wicked.

The Bechuanas had no idols, no temples, no altars, and had no symbols or signs of any form of heathen worship. No fragments existed among them of former days, as mementoes to succeeding generations, that their ancestors ever loved, served, or reverenced a being greater than man. A profound silence reigned on this subject. It is wonderful, as showing to what depths the human spirit may be degraded, that Bechuanas, Hottentots, and Bushmen seem to have had every vestige of religious impression erased from their minds, leaving them without a single ray to guide them in the dark and dismal future, or a single link to unite them with the skies. Thus the missionary could make no appeals to them respecting God and immortality, and to other religious ideas which mankind generally in some form entertain. If they had ever had a religion, it had entirely disappeared, like those streams in the wilderness which lose themselves in the sand. To tell even the gravest of them that there was a Creator, the Governor of the heavens and the earth, that man had fallen and had been redeemed by the sacrifice of Christ; to speak to them of the resurrection of the dead, of immortality and eternal life, was to address them on matters which appeared more fabulous and extraordinary than many of their own extravagant stories about lions, hyenas, and jackals. The influence of "the rain-maker" over the people was exceedingly great; but although they recognised in his agency what they supposed to be a mysterious power, yet this in no sense could be regarded as of the nature of religion.

In their intercourse with other tribes the Bechuanas were vindictive and treacherous. Their expeditions against the Bushmen especially were characterised by intense ferocity and cruelty. They seemed to take a pleasure in slaughter. Many of their wars were mere predatory expeditions, undertaken for the purpose of destroying the villages of their neighbours, of butchering their inhabitants, and of carrying off their cattle. In their persons they were very filthy, and lubricated their bodies with grease and red ochre. Indeed, they could not understand our habits of cleanliness, and were much amused at our putting our legs, feet, and arms into bags, and using buttons for the purpose of fastening bandages around our bodies, instead of suspending them as ornaments from the neck or hair of the head.

A great obstacle to our work was polygamy. Any innovation on this ancient custom was looked upon with extreme suspicion. While war, hunting, watching the cattle, milking the cows, and preparing furs and skins for mantles, were the work of the men, the women had by far the heavier task of agriculture, building houses, fencing, bringing firewood, and the like. They were, therefore, the drudges of their haughty and lazy husbands, who found them too useful to part with any of their number. During the greater part of the year they were constantly employed in laborious work of many kinds, living on a coarse and scanty fare, and having a baby frequently fastened to their backs while they tilled the soil or performed other heavy manual duties.

After remaining among the Bechuanas for more than six years, we seemed to have made no progress at all. They had by this time become perfectly callous and indifferent to all instruction, except it were followed by some temporal benefit. Moreover, they seemed to regard us as lawful prizes, to be used and plundered at pleasure. They would rob our houses, our smith's shop and garden, and would carry off our cattle from the field, or through love of mischief would drive them into a bog, and leave them to perish there or to be eaten by wild beasts. Because of the scarcity of grain and vegetables, we lived for the most part on animal food. Our sheep were procured from a distance, but before they reached us we generally lost a considerable number which had been stolen from the flock on the way. They would break their legs, cut off their tails, and frequently carry them entirely off. Our saws, axes, knives, spoons, they especially coveted; and very often, if we went away from the spot where we were engaged at work, even though not many yards distant, we had to take all our tools with us.

Our duties at this time were exceedingly heavy, for we had to do nearly everything with our own hands. We built our houses and planted our gardens. But our labours were constantly thwarted, for, when we had dug a trench of several miles for irrigating our land, the water which ran into it from the Kuruman river would be diverted from its channel by the natives for their own fields, leaving us without a drop either for garden or household purposes. Mr. Hamilton and myself have had to watch in turn the whole night in order to save the few vegetables growing in our gardens; and when, after all our vigilance and labour, we had saved what was so necessary to our health, the natives would steal them by day as well as by night, and, after a year's toil and care, we scarcely reaped anything to reward us.

During these earlier years the few people who attended public worship did so from purely interested motives, either to receive from us tobacco, or a tool, or our personal help, or some other favour. They very often manifested the greatest indecorum. Some would snore, others would laugh, while others would work or amuse themselves in a manner very distressing to us to witness. Never having been accustomed to chairs or stools, some, by way of imitation, would sit with their feet on the benches, having their knees, according to their usual mode of sitting, drawn up to their chins. In this posture one would fall asleep and tumble over, to the great merriment of his fellows. Sometimes, when the missionaries were absent from their homes at public worship, the opportunity would be embraced to pilfer their property. Mr. Hamilton and myself, when we met in the evening, had almost always some tale to tell of our losses, but never of our gains, except those of resignation and peace, the results of prayer, patience, and faith in the unchangeable purposes of God.

The prospects of the mission at this time were of the

gloomiest character, and, as we proceeded in our work, appeared to become darker than ever. We were suspected of befriending the Bushmen, who annoyed the Bechuanas incessantly by capturing their cattle and killing the men who watched over them. The ground of the charge was, that when we sent our men to assist in retaking the cattle driven away, we enjoined upon them not to kill the Bushmen. They acknowledged that we wronged no man, but at the same time regarded us as the authors of many of their troubles, and as the causes of the drought which afflicted the land. Everything wrong done by a Griqua, while hunting in the country, was thrown in our teeth; and if any one of the natives felt himself aggrieved during a visit to that people or to the South, we were told that we ought to have prevented it. To reason with them only tended to arouse their passions.

But now heavy judgments came upon the land, which were to be the prelude of brighter days. War and bloodshed, drought and locusts, devastated the country and tamed the people, making them more inclined than they had hitherto been to listen to the preaching of the Gospel. This was at first manifest by an increasing number of natives coming to the mission chapel, and by the greater attention which was paid to the words of the preacher, as well as by the readiness with which many answered the questions on the Bible which were put to them. Towards the end of 1828, on the return of Mr. Hamilton, who had visited the colony for a season, we were favoured with the manifest outpouring of the Spirit from on high. The moral wilderness was now about to blossom. Cheeks bedewed with tears attracted our observation. To see females weep was nothing extraordinary. According to Bechuana notions, it was their province, and theirs alone. In family or national afflictions, it was the women's work to weep and wail. But men would not weep. They would sit in sullen silence brooding over deeds of revenge and death. The simple Gospel now melted their flinty hearts; and eyes wept which never before shed the tear of hallowed sorrow. Our temporary little chapel became a place of weeping; and the sympathy of feeling spread from heart to heart. The chapel became crowded with anxious inquirers, and for some time it was impossible to maintain order or even decorum among them. Those under concern for their souls held prayer-meetings from house to house; so that the sounds predominant throughout the village, instead of rioting and folly, as in former times, were those of singing and prayer. When there were none able to engage in prayer, they sang till a late hour, and before morning dawned assembled again at some house for worship, and then went forth to their daily labour.

The first converts were baptized in the month of June 1829. They had given very satisfactory proofs of a change of heart. After full examination separately, they were found to possess a much larger knowledge of the Scriptures than had been anticipated. Although they had long listened with unbelieving hearts, and often with disgust, their memories were retentive—a general characteristic of such as never use memoranda. They exhibited great simplicity of faith, and an implicit reliance on the atonement of Christ, of which they appeared to have a remarkably clear conception, especially when we remembered the darkness of their minds previously. The new chapel and schoolhouse was crowded to excess on the occasion, and the greatest interest was excited by the ceremony. A sermon was preached on John i. 29, and a suitable address was delivered to the candidates. In the evening we united with them in celebrating the sacrament of the Lord's Supper. It is impossible to describe our feelings at that time.

Our joy was great. But we rejoiced with trembling, for we knew that the heathen party was still very powerful, and would probably soon display a violent opposition to the spread of the Gospel among the Bechuanas. Being satisfied, however, that the work was of God, we knew that it was under His guidance, and that He would not suffer it to be impeded. There were many prejudices yet to be overcome. The relation in which the young converts stood to their heathen neighbours would expose their faith to trial. The excitement in the village would gradually pass away, and might be followed by a reaction.

Christianity brought with it civilisation—for those who embraced the new religion were at once seized with the desire to reform their personal habits and social usages. Cleanliness began to be practised, and instead of besmearing themselves with grease they washed themselves with water. Ornaments which were formerly in high repute as adorning, but more frequently disfiguring, their persons, were now turned into bullion to purchase skins of animals, which, being prepared almost as soft as cloth, were made into jackets, trousers, and gowns. For a long period, when a man was seen to make a pair of trousers for himself, or a woman a gown, it was a sure intimation that we might expect additions to our inquirers. Abandoning the custom of painting the body, and beginning to wash with water, was with them what cutting off the hair was among the South Sea Islanders, a public renunciation of heathenism. Thus, by the slow but certain progress of Gospel principles, whole families became clothed and in their right mind. In their eagerness for improvement the people sometimes arrayed themselves in grotesque garbs. One would have on a coat of many colours; another would wear a jacket with only one sleeve, because the other was not finished, or cloth was wanting to complete it. The people were now anxious to learn how to use the needle, and to make garments; and at first it was no easy matter for them to do this, as the hands of many were hard and horny from field-work, and the tiny needle was scarcely perceptible to their touch. Our congregations became a variegated mass of people of all descriptions, from the lubricated wild man of the desert, to the clean, comfortable, and well-dressed believer. It was the work of the men to sew and prepare garments. I never saw a woman with a needle, or rather bodkin, with which the men sew with great neatness and skill.

Then came the desire for improvement in their households. Formerly they had been contented with sitting on the floors of their huts, eating their food by the light of flickering wood embers, and lying down to sleep wrapped in their mantles which they had worn during the day. But now they wished to have, like ourselves, chairs, tables, chests, candles, and other articles contributing to the comfort of a house. These they came to make under our direction, though of course very clumsily at first. It is singular, however, what rapid progress in the arts of civilised life a people will make when once the desire for reformation has taken thorough possession of them. The Bechuanas were like men waking up from a long sleep, and anxious to redeem the time they had lost. They began to take great interest in field and garden labour. In place of restricting themselves to their native grain and a few vegetables, such as pumpkins, kidney-beans, and water-melons, they thankfully accepted the seeds and plants of grain and vegetables we had introduced, namely, of maize, wheat, barley, pease, potatoes, carrots, and onions, and planted fruit-trees wherever they could irrigate. There was also a demand for ploughs and spades for the proper tilling of the soil, and also for bullock-waggons. The men were no longer too proud to put their hands to the cultivation of the ground, but set to work with a will; and in a few years the country all around was smiling with fertility.

The most pressing want of these awakened Bechuanas was now the Bible in their own tongue. Having finished a translation of the Gospel of St. Luke, in Sechuana, I went all the way to Cape Town for the purpose of having it printed. The Governor kindly allowed it to be printed at the Government press. The paper was supplied by the British and Foreign Bible Society. A small hymn-book was also printed in the same language. While at the Cape I learnt the art of printing; and, returning to Kuruman, brought with me not only an edition of the Gospel and of the hymn-book, but also a printing-press, and a supply of types, paper, and ink. Soon the press was put into operation, and catechisms, spelling-books, lesson-books, and other works, were printed for the schools. This was a new era in the mission, for the people were now being taught to read, and were becoming thereby more enlightened. The work of translation was a slow process, being able to attend to it only at intervals; and it was not until about the year 1840 that I had completed the entire New Testament in Sechuana. Then followed the Psalms; and afterwards, at intervals, the books of Proverbs, Ecclesiastes, and Isaiah. In 1849 the "Pilgrim's Progress" was in circulation among the Bechuanas in their own language, and was read with wonderful avidity. Many years elapsed before the entire Bible was completed. I felt it to be an awful work to translate the Book of God; and, perhaps, this has given to my heart the habit of sometimes beating like the strokes of a hammer. When I had finished the last verse I could hardly believe that I was in the world, so difficult was it for me to realise the fact that my work of so many years was completed. Whether it was from weakness or overstrained mental exertion, I cannot tell; but a feeling came over me as if I should die, and I felt perfectly resigned. To overcome this, I went back again to my manuscript, still to be printed, read it over and re-examined it, till at length I got back again to my right mind. This was the most remarkable time of my life, a period which I shall never forget. My feelings found vent by my falling upon my knees, and thanking God for His grace and goodness in giving me strength to accomplish my task.

Meanwhile the people of Kuruman and the neighbourhood made rapid progress in Christian knowledge as well as in civilisation. My colleague, Mr. Edwards, who had come up with me from the Cape, and his excellent wife, had classes for instruction in reading. Out-stations were established, and a rich blessing from above attended all our labours at every place where the Gospel was read and preached. The natives purchased waggons, and clothed themselves decently. They also broke in oxen for labour in the fields formerly performed by their wives. A new and spacious chapel was erected, and when it was opened in 1838 between eight and nine hundred Bechuanas assembled together for the worship of Jehovah. In the afternoon of the following Sabbath one hundred and fifty persons united in commemorating the dying love of Him who had redeemed them by His blood, and brought them by His providence to participate in this heavenly banquet. I was afterwards joined by Mr. Ashton, who rendered valuable service to the mission in many ways; but he, after long service, was removed to the station at Lekatlong. His place, however, was filled at Kuruman by my son, John Moffat, who entered on his work there in the year 1866, and who in turn has been removed to the station once occupied by Dr. Livingstone, and latterly by Mr. Price, now of the Ujiji or Tanganyika mission.

Formerly, travellers among the Bechuanas were exposed to great danger. Now they may go for many miles in all directions without fear of molestation. A considerable trade has sprung up between these tribes and Europeans from the Cape colony; and foreign manufactured goods of the value of two hundred and fifty thousand pounds are annually imported into the country, and exchanged for native produce. There was no commerce or barter carried on between Europeans and the Bechuana tribes at the commencement of missions among them, nor could they be induced to trade, till through the Divine blessing converts were made. These were the first to adopt a European dress. During the previous years traders came as far as the Kuruman mission station, bringing all kinds of tempting articles which they displayed before the natives, who could not be made to see either comfort or beauty in them. These men, who had hoped to realise a profit by ostrich feathers, ivory, cattle, &c., &c., could only dispose of a few pounds of beads, and returned some hundreds of miles sadly mortified. The example set by our first converts approved itself to others, and it being entirely out of our power to supply them with what was required, having but a scanty supply for our own wants, they were instructed to make dresses from skins prepared for the purpose, and in which they made a very respectable appearance. They had an example in Mrs. Hamilton and myself, who generally wore parts of our dress of the same material. It was soon found necessary to apply for a merchant to come and settle on the station.

The Gospel has thus changed the moral aspect of a large portion of the Bechuana tribes, and its gracious influence has been felt among the Bakwaries, Bamanguatos, as far even as the distant Matabeles; and many true believers in Christ are to be found not merely in Kuruman, but also in many other parts of the country. Heathenism still exists in some places, but it is gradually dying out, and giving place to Christianity. Education is spreading, and young men are being trained as preachers and teachers. The people are very fond of their Bibles, which they study most diligently, and also take great delight in the singing of hymns. And they have never lost the pleasure of attending the public services in the mission chapels, where they assemble together with singular regularity. But they need more depth of knowledge, which I trust they are gradually receiving.

530 BROADWAY, NEW YORK,
OCTOBER, 1880.

NEW BOOKS

AND NEW EDITIONS OF IMPORTANT BOOKS,

PUBLISHED BY

ROBERT CARTER & BROTHERS.

⁎ *Any Book in this Catalogue, not too large to go by mail, will be sent postage prepaid, on receipt of the price.*

The End of a Coil. A Story. By the author of the "Wide Wide World." 717 pp. $1.75.

My Desire. A Tale. By the author of the "Wide Wide World." $1.75.

Christie's Old Organ, Saved at Sea, and Little Faith. In one volume. $1.00.

Christ and His Religion. By Rev. John Reid, author of "Voices of the Soul," &c. $1.50.

The Sun, Moon, and Stars. By Agnes Gilberne. Illustrated. 12mo. $1.50.

The Gentle Heart. By Rev. Alex. Macleod, D.D., author of "Wonderful Lamp," &c. $1.25.

The Cup of Consolation; or, Bright Messages for the Sick-Bed. $1.25.

In Christo. By J. R. Macduff, D.D.

Family Prayers. By J. Oswald Dykes, D.D.

Voices of Hope and Gladness. By Ray Palmer, D.D $1.50.

Modern Scottish Pulpit. Sermons by Scottish Ministers. 8vo. $1.50.

*****Murdock's Mosheim's Ecclesiastical History.** A cheap edition. Three volumes in one. 1,461 pp. $3.00.

BOOKS PUBLISHED BY

Nora Crena. By L. T. Meade. $1.25.

Andrew Harvey's Wife. By L. T. Meade. $1.25.

* **Pool's Annotations.** 3 vols. Royal 8vo. 8,077 pages. In cloth. Price, $7.50. (Half the former price.)

"Pool's Annotations are sound, clear, and sensible; and, taking for all in all, I place him at the head of English commentators on the whole Bible." — *Rev. J. C. Ryle.*

* **Matthew Henry's Commentary on the Bible.** 5 vols., quarto. (Sheep, $20.00.) Cloth, $15.00. Another edition in 9 vols., octavo. Cloth, $20.00.

Rev. C. H. Spurgeon says: "First among the mighty for general usefulness we are bound to mention the man whose name is a household word, — Matthew Henry. He is most pious and pithy, sound and sensible, suggestive and sober, terse and trustworthy. . . . I venture to say that no better investment can be made by a minister than that peerless exposition."

* **Dr. McCosh's Works.** New and neat edition (reduced from $15.00). 5 vols., 8vo., uniform, $10.00. Comprising: —

1. DIVINE GOVERNMENT. 3. THE INTUITIONS OF THE MIND.
2. TYPICAL FORMS.   4. DEFENCE OF FUNDAMENTAL TRUTH.
5. THE SCOTTISH PHILOSOPHY.

Any volume sold separately at $2.00.

"Thousands of earnest, thoughtful men have found treasures of argument, illustration, and learning in these pages, with which their minds and hearts have been enriched and fortified for better work and wider influences." — *N. Y. Observer.*

DR. McCOSH'S LOGIC. 12mo $1.50

CHRISTIANITY AND POSITIVISM. 12mo . . 1.75

* **Dr. Merle D'Aubigne's History.** 13 vols., uniform, $12.50, viz.: —

* HISTORY OF THE REFORMATION IN THE SIXTEENTH CENTURY. 5 vols. Brown cloth. In a box. $4.50.

* HISTORY OF THE REFORMATION IN THE TIME OF CALVIN. 8 vols. Brown cloth. In a box. Reduced from $16.00 to $8.00.

"The work is now complete; and these later volumes, together with the original five, form a library relating to the Reformation of incalculable value and of intense interest. The pen of this master of history gave a charm to every thing that he touched." — *N. Y. Observer.*

Guide to Family Devotion. By the Rev. Alexander Fletcher, D.D. Royal quarto, with 10 steel plates (half morocco, $7.50; Turkey morocco, $12.00), cloth, gilt, and gilt edges, $5.00.

"The more we look over the volume the more we admire it, and the more heartily feel to commend it to families and devout Christians. It is emphatically a book of devotion, from the standpoint of an intelligent, broad-minded Christian minister, who has here expressed many of the deepest emotions and wants of the soul. The selections of Scripture and the hymns are all admirably adapted to increase devotion; and the prayers are such as can but aid the suppliant, even when not uttered from his precise standpoint, and are especially valuable to many heads of families who find it difficult to frame words for themselves in conducting family worship." — *Journal and Messenger.*

The A. L. O. E. Library. In 55 vols., 18mo, in a neat wooden case, $40.00.

"All these stories have the charm and pure Christian character which have made the name of A. L. O. E. dear to thousands of homes." — *Lutheran.*

"The writings of this author have become a standard, and the mystic imprint, A. L. O. E., is ample assurance that the truth of the Gospel is beneath." — *Episcopalian.*

Bickersteth (Rev. E. H.). Yesterday, To-day, and Forever. A Poem. Pocket edition, .50; 16mo, $1.00; 12mo, $1.50.

"If any poem is destined to endure in the companionship of Milton's hitherto matchless epic, we believe it will be 'Yesterday, To-day, and Forever.'" — *London Globe.*

Butler (Rev. William Archer). Sermons. 2 vols., $2.50. Lectures on Ancient Philosophy. 2 vols., $2.50.

"A few weeks ago we spoke of the reprinting, by Carter & Brothers, of the Sermons of Archer Butler, a body of preaching so strong and massive as to be really wonderful. The 'Lectures on Ancient Philosophy' that are now added, were delivered at the University of Dublin, about the year 1840, when the author was scarcely thirty years old." — *Watchman.*

The Book and Its Story. 12mo. $1.50.

Fresh Leaves from the Book and Its Story. 12mo. $1.50.

"Let any one who is inclined to think the bare Scriptures 'dry' reading, peruse them in connection with a volume like this, and they will be clothed to him with a new life. He will learn how the separate books of the Bible were, as it were, built into one another, and made to form a glorious whole; he will read intelligently and with deep interest." — *Keystone.*

Bonar (Horatius, D.D.). Hymns of Faith and Hope. 3 vols., 18mo. $2.25.

Bible Thoughts and Themes. 6 vols. 12mo, viz.: —

GENESIS	$2.00	ACTS, &c.	$2.00
OLD TESTAMENT	2.00	LESSER EPISTLES	2.00
GOSPELS	2.00	REVELATION	2.00

"With no attempt at exposition, except what is found in comparing Scripture with Scripture, and drawing illustrations and means of impressing rich gospel truth from almost every source, the author proceeds with theme upon theme, giving floods of edifying and comforting light from beginning to end. It is a good book for the private Christian to have on his table for frequent use, and ministers will often find in it that which will be suggestive and useful." — *Christian Instructor.*

WAY OF PEACE	$0.50	THE RENT VEIL	$1.25
WAY OF HOLINESS	.60	MY OLD LETTERS	2.00
NIGHT OF WEEPING	.50	HYMNS OF THE NATIVITY, gilt,	1.00
MORNING OF JOY	.60	THE CHRIST OF GOD	1.25
FOLLOW THE LAMB	.40	TRUTH AND ERROR	.60
THE EVERLASTING RIGHTEOUSNESS			$0.60

Chalmers (Thomas, D.D.). Sermons. 2 vols. in one. $3.00.

Cowper (Wm.). The Task. Illustrated by Birket Foster. $3.50.

Cuyler (Rev. T. L.).

POINTED PAPERS	$1.50
THOUGHT HIVES	1.50
EMPTY CRIB	1.00

"Dr. Cuyler holds steadily the position which he reached years ago, as the best writer of pointed, racy, religious articles in our country." — *Presbyterian.*

Dick (John, D.D.). Lectures on Theology. 8vo. $3.00.

"It is, as a whole, superior to any other system of theology in our language." — *Christian Journal.*

Dickson (Rev. Alexander, D.D.).

ALL ABOUT JESUS	$2.00
BEAUTY FOR ASHES	2.00

"His book is a 'bundle of myrrh,' and will be specially enjoyed by those who are in trouble." — *Rev. Dr. W. M. Taylor.*

"Luscious as a honeycomb with sweetness drawn from God's word." — *Rev. Dr. Cuyler.*

Dykes (Oswald, D.D.), on the Sermon on the Mount.
3 vols., $3.00.
    ABRAHAM, THE FRIEND OF GOD $1.50

"We are ever and anon surprised by some new view or fresh thought that never had occurred to us in this connection. The book (Abraham) is a thoughtful, scholarly production, in vigorous English." — *N. Christian Advocate.*

* Edwards (Jonathan). Works. In 4 vols., octavo. $6.00.

"I consider Jonathan Edwards the greatest of the sons of men." — *Robert Hall.*

Fraser (Rev. Donald). Synoptical Lectures on the Books of the Bible. 3 vols., $6.00.

"Dr. Fraser has observed, like many others of us, the mischief which results from cutting the Bible into fragments, and using it piecemeal. In these volumes he discourses of the Bible at large, indicates the scope of each book, and furnishes a brief digest of its contents. The design was in itself most laudable, and it has been well carried out." — *Spurgeon.*

Green (Prof. Wm. Henry, D.D.). The Argument of the Book of Job Unfolded. 12mo. $1.75.

"That ancient composition so marvellous in beauty, and so rich in philosophy, is here treated in a thoroughly analytical manner, and new depths and grander proportions of the divine original portrayed. It is a book to stimulate research." — *Methodist Recorder.*

Guthrie (Thomas, D.D.). Life and Works. 11 vols. $15.00.

"His pages glow with the deep piety, the Scriptural beauty, the rich imagery, and the tender pathos which breathed from his lips." — *N. Y. Observer.*

Hamilton (James, D.D.). Select Works. 4 vols. $5.00. Containing The Royal Preacher; Mount of Olives; Pearl of Parables; Lamp and Lantern; Great Biography; Harp on the Willows; Lake of Galilee; Emblems from Eden; Life in Earnest.

"Those familiar with the works of Dr. Hamilton will perceive that this set of volumes contains the choice gold from the author's mine. They are put up in a neat box, and sold at the low price of $5 for the set." — *Interior.*

Hamlin (Cyrus). Among the Turks. 12mo. $1.50.

Hanna (Rev. William, D.D.). Life of Christ. 3 vols. 12mo. $4.50.

"We can heartily commend the 'Life of our Lord,' by Dr. Hanna." — *Congregational Quarterly.*

"Besides the beauty of the style and the careful scholarship which mark these volumes, we cannot too warmly commend them for their deep piety and hearty enforcement of the doctrines of Christianity." — *N. Y. Observer.*

Hill (George). Lectures on Divinity. 8vo. $2.50.

"The candor and fairness of this author are remarkable, an unfailing indication of real greatness." — *Christian Mirror.*

Hodge (Charles, D.D.). Commentaries.

On Romans. 12mo	$1.75
On Ephesians. 12mo	1.75
On Corinthians. 2 vols. 12mo	3.50

Rev. C. H. Spurgeon says: "Most valuable. With no writer do we more fully agree. The more we use Hodge, the more we value him. This applies to all his Commentaries."

Hodge (Rev. A. A., D.D.). Outlines of Theology. Revised and Enlarged Edition. 8vo. $3.00.

"At its first publication in 1860, this work attracted much attention, and ever since it has had a large sale, and been carefully studied both in this country and in Great Britain. It has been translated into Welsh and modern Greek, and has been used as a text-book in several theological schools. Prepared originally in good part from notes taken by the author from his distinguished father's lectures, with the assistance of standard theological writers, after fourteen years of service as a theological instructor, he has, with increased knowledge and experience as a teacher, embodied in this new and enlarged edition not only the treasures of the volume as it first appeared, but the rich results of his additional studies and investigations. This new edition contains fifty per cent more of matter than the former one. Two chapters have been dropped, and five new ones have been added." — *Presbyterian Banner.*

Holt (Emily Sarah). Historical Tales.

Isoult Barry. 12mo	$1.50
Robin Tremayne. 12mo	1.50
The Well in the Desert. 16mo	1.25
Ashcliffe Hall. 16mo	1.25
Verena; A Tale. 12mo	1.50
The White Rose of Langley. 12mo	1.50
Imogen. 12mo	1.50
Clare Avery. 12mo	1.50
Lettice Eden. 12mo	1.50
For the Master's Sake. 16mo	1.00
Margery's Son. 12mo	1.50
Lady Sybil's Choice. 12mo	1.50
The Maiden's Lodge. 12mo	1.25

"Whether it is regarded in its historical or its religious aspect, 'Isoult Barry of Wynscote' is the finest contribution to English literature, of its peculiar class, which has been made in the present century." — *American Baptist.*

www.ingramcontent.com/pod-product-compliance
Lightning Source LLC
Chambersburg PA
CBHW022118290426
44112CB00008B/722